Cinema and Sensation

Cinema and Sensation
French Film and the
Art of Transgression

Martine Beugnet

Edinburgh University Press

© Martine Beugnet, 2007, 2012

First published in hardback by Edinburgh University Press 2007

Edinburgh University Press Ltd
22 George Square, Edinburgh EH8 9LF

www.euppublishing.com

Typeset in 11/13pt Ehrhardt MT
by Servis Filmsetting Ltd, Manchester, and
printed and bound in Great Britain by
Printondemand-worldwide.com

A CIP record for this book is available from the British Library

ISBN 978 0 7486 2042 5 (hardback)
ISBN 978 0 7486 4936 5 (paperback)

The right of Martine Beugnet
to be identified as author of this work
has been asserted in accordance with
the Copyright, Designs and Patents Act 1988.

Contents

Acknowledgements

I am grateful to the Arts and Humanities Research Board for the Research Leave Award, and to Edinburgh University's Research Fund for the grants that enabled me to carry out this work. Thanks to Sarah Edwards at Edinburgh University Press. Thanks also to Phil Powrie and Susan Hayward, editors of *Studies in French Cinema*, as well as to Carrie Tarr, commissioning editor of *Nottingham French Studies* and of *Modern and Contemporary France* for granting me permission to use material published in these journals. Thanks to Vincent Dieutre and to Pierre Grise Distribution for their help. Thanks to Marie Campbell and to Éliane and Jacques Beugnet. And special thanks to Erja and Alex Zoré for making this project possible.

To E, S and T.

Beginnings

Sombre

A group of children at a puppet show. Engrossed in the spectacle, they are shouting, cowering and crying out. The alternation of medium and close-up shots, the humming of the sound-track that mingles with the thrilled exclamations and screaming, and the throb of the speeded-up images convey the sheer excitement of the audience, seized with delightful terror, yet eyes riveted on the spectacle that fascinates and terrifies them. Oddly reminiscent of a similar episode in *Les Quatre cents coups*, like Truffaut's, Grandrieux's images refer to the lost pleasure of the complete rapture often experienced in childhood. There is a sinister undercurrent to the sequence in *Sombre*, however, an ominous sense of threat, carried by the vibrations, that appears to permeate the frame from the outer field. In effect, the main character of this enigmatic crime film, the puppet master Jean, is a murderer whose journeys are punctuated by brutal and apparently random killings of women. We do not know this at this stage – indeed, kept off frame, both the puppeteer and his show remain invisible for the duration of these early scenes. The sequence could offer a familiar, endearing sight; yet it creates an unsettling feeling, as if something vampiric was at work in these shots drained of light and images,[1] the distortion of the picture and sound emphasising the ambiguous mix of pleasure and abysmal fear of the children's reactions.

Leçons de ténèbres

In contrast with *Sombre*'s beginning, the opening sequence of Vincent Dieutre's *Leçons de ténèbres* takes place in a space normally associated with silence and composure – an art museum. However, its picture gallery

---

[1] The number of images recorded per second diminishes as the sequence progresses – 8 to 6 images per second instead of 24 – to create a trembled effect. A similar technique is at work at the beginning of *La Vie nouvelle*. I will come back to both the question of vampirism, and to Grandrieux's use of light and speeded-up movement at a later stage.

provides the setting for an unusual visit. The film's first frames are filled
with elements of a painting: fragments of bodies emerging through striking chiaroscuro effects, and set on an as yet inchoate sound-track (a mix of
noises including footsteps, keys and chains, the sound of a heavy door being
unlocked and pushed open). Following a first cut, a man (Vincent Dieutre
himself) appears, shot from behind while climbing a narrow, under-lit
flight of stairs; it is by the back door that visitor and camera finally enter a
museum gallery. The hand-held camera follows Dieutre closely till he
stops in front of a painting by Caravaggio, *Christ at the Pillar*.[2] The initial
dismal effect of overcrowded walls vanishes as the camera zooms in on the
picture till it fills the screen; the camera then closes in to let the gaze be
immersed in the sumptuously textured plane and explore the strange luminosity of the livid flesh that appears sculpted out of the dark background.
In the corner of the frame, Dieutre shakes his head in awe; soon, his silhouette is but a blurred mass that occasionally interposes itself between
camera and painting, while details of the painting contemplated in close-
up come into focus: the corner of a mouth, an ear, shadowy zones where
the flesh is absorbed into its surroundings, wrinkles lining the skin under
the fine cracks that layer the surface of the painting itself. Next, Dieutre's
hand moves into view and, as if irrepressibly drawn by the paint volumes
and textures, travels very close to the surface; tracked by the camera, it
follows the shapes and folds of the figures in a slow stroking movement.
Suddenly, as the camera focuses again on a specific fragment – the faces of
secondary characters this time – we hear, off frame, the sound of a fall. The
camera points towards the floor where Dieutre lies unconscious, the
worried soundman swearing as he kneels next to him. There is a brutal cut,
then the title credit: *Leçons de ténèbres*.

Cinema and Sensation

The deeply sensual, synaesthetic effect of the film image and sound-track
reverberates through the eloquent *mise en scène* of the spectator's experience presented in these sequences. Characteristic of Grandrieux's film
work, the images and sounds create an impression of volume and density
and appear to mutate, as if they were being sculpted within the space of the
take itself. Similarly, in the mix of art forms, the choice of motifs as well as
the formulation, Dieutre's introductory shots are an invitation to experience film with all our senses, stressing, in particular, cinema's intensely
tactile quality.

---

[2] The work dates from circa 1607.

Hence, it is the materiality of the medium of the moving image that first comes to the fore here, even if, as we will see, the repercussions are suggested reflexively through the *mise en scène* of other art forms. Rather than establish an informative context and give viewers the elements necessary to orientate themselves and piece together the beginnings of a story, these early sequences focus on those fundamental qualities of the cinema that come before, yet tend to be overruled by its representative and narrative functions: those variations in movement and in light, in colour and sound tonalities that make up film's endlessly shifting compositions. Moreover, as will be exemplified and explored further in subsequent chapters, both these sequences play on vision and sound's capacity to evoke the other senses and seem to invite a *'haptic'* gaze.[3] In these cases, the distancing effect of perspective is defeated: in *Leçons*, by the tension between the flatness of the Digital Video image and the tactile, engulfing darkness which forms the background of the Caravaggio painting; in *Sombre*, by the sense of free-floating, 'gaseous' perception[4] created by the throbbing, under-lit images; and in both extracts, by the amorphous nature of the sound-track. Though she is discussing an entirely different set of films, the following comment by Laura U. Marks seems equally relevant in the context of the opening sequences of *Sombre* and *Leçons de ténèbres*:

> Haptic images can give the impression of seeing for the first time, gradually discovering what is in the image rather than coming to the image already knowing what it is. Several such works represent the point of view of a disoriented traveler unsure how to read the world in which he finds himself. (Marks 2000: 178)

There is an inherently transgressive element to this kind of filmmaking; as we are reminded by Dieutre and Grandrieux's images, to open oneself to sensory awareness and let oneself be physically affected by an art work or a spectacle is to relinquish the will to gain full mastery over it, choosing intensity and chaos over rational detachment.

In his reflections on art and perception, Maurice Merleau-Ponty remarked that in Cartesian thinking, as in classical, perspective-based art, where our representation of space is reduced to that of a 'pure',

[3] The term, borrowed from Alöis Riegl, is used by Gilles Deleuze in his seminal work on Francis Bacon in particular. The 'haptic gaze' or 'haptic visuality' will be discussed more fully in the following chapters (Riegl [1902] 1999; Deleuze [1981] 2002). See also Laura U. Marks 2000: 162–7.

[4] Deleuze uses the term in the context of experimental films, where perception seems detached from any sense of purposeful subjectivity, and akin to the kind of perception experienced in hallucinatory state, for instance (Deleuze 1986: 84).

'disembodied intellect',[5] the only vision and understanding of the world considered worth while is that of the rational adult (Merleau-Ponty [1962] 2002: 376–7; [1948] 2004: 70–3). There is no place for 'aberrant forms of life and consciousness'; the scientific approach is impervious to the experience of the world as it is expressed through the voices of 'children and madmen', for instance.[6] Yet, he adds: 'one of the great achievements of modern art and philosophy has been to allow us to rediscover the world in which we live' (2004: 39).

> the transition from classical to modern was marked by what might be thought of as a reawakening of the world of perception . . . So the way we relate to the things of the world is no longer as a pure intellect trying to master an object or space that stands before it. Rather, this relationship is an ambiguous one, between beings who are both embodied and limited and an enigmatic world. (2004: 69–70)

Merleau-Ponty's description of the way our contact with art in particular can enhance and enrich our apprehension of the world is echoed in the *mise en abyme* of the spectatorial experience found at the beginning of *Leçons de ténèbres* and *Sombre*. However, there is an undercurrent of nostalgia in the way both films bring forth the yearning for a relationship to exist between art work and audience that would still allow for the magic and power of art to operate. It is through the unselfconscious, expressive freedom of childhood on the one hand, and the 'excess' or 'inadequacy' of the response of the museum visitor on the other, that the overpowering, equivocal mix of frightening abandon and extreme pleasure of this experience is evoked. The particular relation of subject and object that is posited here from the outset, and refracted from the diegetic viewers to the filmmakers, and to us, the potential spectators, thus reflexively questions the way cinema could or should affect us.

---

[5] Merleau-Ponty starts from the connection between the emergence of classical rationalism's scientific thinking, the denial of embodied knowledge and the establishment of perspective as a mode of representation. In particular, he compares classical painting, where visual impressions are represented through a perspective-based framework that 'controls the movement of their unfolding', yet also 'kills their trembling life' ([1948] 2004: 52), to impressionism, where space is no longer 'the medium of pure intellect', 'apprehended by an absolute observer' ([1948] 2004: 54). In the first instance, 'the art work remains at a distance and does not involve the viewer.' Yet, the synaesthetic and tactile dimensions of perception deny a relationship of mastery between subject and object and infer, instead, 'the appropriation of the possessor by the possessed' ([1948] 2004: 61).

[6] One should say the white, male rational adult. In remarks first published in 1948, Merleau-Ponty himself unwittingly concurs with the narrowness of the kind of Cartesian thinking he criticises when, in addition to the unheard voices of children, madmen and animals, he speaks of that of the non-westernised cultures whom he calls 'primitive people'.

In the conventional conception of the observer/observed relation, the (observer's) self theoretically stands as a separate entity. In the extracts discussed here, however, the effect of looking and listening takes on a mimetic quality indicative of an involvement with the object of the gaze that pre-empts or supersedes this state of detached self-awareness. In the case of the puppet show, the spectacle remains out of frame, but we see the children move as they follow the puppets through chases and fights; in the museum scene, Dieutre's body movements initially follow the outlines of the painted figures and his collapsing recalls the reclining figures of female mourners in Renaissance painting's crucifixion scenes. Based on Walter Benjamin's writings, Marks encapsulates mimesis as 'an immanent way of being in the world, whereby the subject comes into being not through abstraction from the world, but compassionate involvement in it'. She further comments on how Benjamin 'valued children's ability to relate to things mimetically . . . and suspected that the mimetic relationship need not be superseded by an "adult" way of relating to things as merely objects' (Marks 2000: 139–40).

The intensity and physicality of the reactions shown on screen are echoed in the deep involvement, conveyed by the sensuous and tactile quality of the shots, of the filmmakers with the scenes they have composed and captured. (Tellingly, Dieutre chooses to act out the episode himself.) Put into words, in his typically expressive style, Grandrieux's description of his work as a filmmaker evokes a sensual and mimetic connection, where the border between subject and object collapses:

> to be able to behold the power of the real, its outpouring, its hallucinatory vibration; to be able to convey this, and for the duration of a shot, to become the sky or a moun-tain, a river, or the tumultuous mass of the ocean. That's when cinema is great. The rhythm, the way bodies are framed and lit, that's when we start to lose ourselves, and cinema comes closest to what it essentially is: a sensual experience of the world. (Grandrieux 2000: 88)

The approach to cinema that Grandrieux puts forth, and the kind of filmmaking and film viewing that it implies, depart in fundamental ways from the models that dominate feature-film production today. Familiar with mainstream cinema's standardised formats, we have become used to thinking of and enjoying feature films first and foremost in terms of plot and characters, identification and narrative logic. A sensual apprehension of film works affords different, yet equally potent gratifications. Indeed, most students and film lovers would agree that, once they become attuned to or regain their sense of film as a material entity (that is, when they start to engage with images and sounds as moving compositions and experience a film in itself rather than solely as the by-product of a pre-existing story), their experience of cinema and the pleasures they draw from it are continuously enriched. In her book on horror cinema, Anne Powell relates such a shift to the growing importance of Deleuzean approaches in film studies, and, borrowing Deleuze's terminology, describes it as a change of focus, 'from the "molar" politics of representation to the "molecular" materiality of film',[7] which offers a 'concrete, and medium-specific, way into extending our awareness' of the cinema (Powell 2005: 208).

However, to make films that wilfully engage with the medium not merely as story or discourse, but as an object of perception, and to view them as such, is to run against the long-held belief that valuable experience and knowledge must necessarily come as a process of 'enlightenment' that distances us from the unreliable input of sensual perception. (How many times have we dismissed a film because it had 'no story', 'no characters' with whom to identify, or was not 'clear' or 'logical' enough?) The title of Dieutre's film, *Leçons de ténèbres*, refers to seventeenth-century musical compositions played at mass to accompany the text of Jeremiah's *Lamentations*. As the recitation unravelled, the candles would be blown out one by one till obscurity and silence prevailed. If such a ritual initially represents a compelling allegory for the experience of a godless world, in the context of Dieutre's film it is also a lesson in humility: the recognition, through a powerful sensory experience, that we have to unlearn before we can learn to see and feel again.

Sombre, *Leçons de ténèbres*: both titles speak of darkness and, in effect, both works, by foregrounding the sensual affect of film over representational and narrative functions, deviate from the custom of constructing a feature film as a process of progressive clarification. Like the other fiction films cited in this book, *Sombre* and *Leçons de ténèbres* develop a story line, albeit an elliptical one. The films are extremely different in their premise and treatment, yet both Dieutre's fictional diary and Grandrieux's experimental portrait of a killer adopt a loose road-movie format and include characters or figures with which identification is at least partially possible. A spectator's involvement with the film, however, is likely to take place predominantly at a 'primary' level of identification – identification with the

---

[7] I will refer to this distinction throughout the subsequent chapters, as I explore how cinema as cinema of sensation creates bridges between sensory perception and interpretation; the terms, coined by Deleuze and Guattari, distinguish between the 'molecular', micro level of perception – that is, a film's material components (visual and sound matter in movement) and the way they interact and change – and the macro or 'molar' level of organisation concerned with ideological, social and psychological frameworks (Deleuze and Guattari 1984–8).

material aspect and transformations of the film body itself above identification with its figurative and narrative content.[8] Indeed, conventional, scenario-based schemas would have been ill suited to the directors' projects and, in turn, as with the majority of works discussed in the following chapters, the customary tools of film studies (narrative and genre studies, semiology or even psychoanalysis) would yield few clues or openings in the case of these two works. Whether it takes the form of a personal trajectory (*Leçons de ténèbres*) or that of an archetypal figure (*Sombre*), what is at stake is the evocation, irretrievably enmeshed in the very texture of the images and sound, of those borderline states that reveal the inherent vulnerability of the self. By grounding their exploration of the shadowy recesses of the human psyche in the material dimension of their medium, Grandrieux and Dieutre can exploit cinema's specific faculty to generate contradictory effects: merge the fearful and the pleasurable, the abject and the sublime, and affect us viscerally as well as intellectually.

The opening sequences are exemplary, however, playing fully on their impact as prologues to eschew conventional identification with, or appropriation of, the object of the gaze and encouraging a sensual engagement with the work instead. Denied the distancing effect of explanatory introductions and establishing shots, the viewer is left to experience the powerful, perplexing affect of the imagery. Grandrieux emphasised that his foremost wish was for 'the spectator to be stunned, in front of something that keeps him or her spell-bound' (Grandrieux 1999c: 40). For critic Antoine de Baecque, the spectator of *Sombre* is immediately wrapped up in the images, his or her senses 'summoned, as if saturated by the effect of the under-exposure, of the sonorities, the feeling of suffocation, the violence that inhabit the film' (de Baecque 1999: 37). Similarly, Vincent Dieutre talks about the opening of *Leçons de ténèbres* in terms of the 'physical emotion' provoked by a work of art, and his attempt to show 'the physical consequences that it has on the body'. In the director's words, the sight of the painting dazzles the viewer – he talks of an 'éblouissement premier'. What Dieutre experiences initially blinds him; he is moved and feels the impact of viewing the art work through his body as a whole because he does not attempt to distance himself – because, as he himself admits in interview, he accepts that he is unable actually to comprehend the painting (Dieutre interview, supplement to French DVD release). Evidently, these

---

[8] Hence, by primary identification I do not mean merely or chiefly identification with the gaze or point of view relayed by the camera (as proposed in the chapter dedicated to the issue of identification in Aumont, Jacques, Alain Bergala, Michel Marie, Marc Vernet (1997), *Aesthetics of Film*, trans. Richard Neupert, Austin: University of Texas), but identification with the film's variations in rhythms, tonal intensities, framing and so on.

comments do not imply that when we look at an art work and go to the cinema we should abdicate our capacity to analyse and assess critically what is presented to us. What is suggested, rather, is that there are alternative ways of approaching and thinking through such an experience. Here, the initial sensory shock is not dismissed but welcomed as the first step of a process of sensual awareness which will shape our response and our reflections. By the same token, it is through the 'molecular' dimension, at the level of material appearance and formal variations, that the thought process emerges; film itself, as the medium of moving images and sounds, is a form of embodied thinking. As Powell puts it, 'Film, like literature, painting and philosophy, is a distinctively embodied thought process' and 'rather than mapping pre-existing thought onto film as text allegory', we should seek to gain 'an understanding of medium-specific operations of lighting, sound, framing and montage' through which this process takes place (Powell 2005: 2). Hence, Dieutre's attempt at capturing something of the significance of art as affect depends on the ability, specific to his own medium, to capture a Caravaggio painting in close-up and through the mobile gaze of the camera, and to further relate it, through editing, to the vulnerability of the living flesh exposed, as he does with the sequence that directly follows the opening credits. More than the content of the scenes, it is thus their concrete and aesthetic qualities as film matter – the choice of framing and camera movements; the variations in light and sound; the rhythm of the editing – that shape the conception of art and spectatorship suggested in the extracts discussed here. Modernist in the way it foregrounds its own materiality, this kind of cinema does not, however, subordinate formal experimentation to the denunciation of set forms of discourse (although such critique takes place by inference); rather, it reassesses the significance of sensual perception as that which pre-empts the ('molar') discursive level.

Is it still possible to make art cinema, feature films, primarily as an exploration of film's material dimension; to develop filmmaking practices that bring forth the medium's specific formal and affective potential, as indeed was the project of the early avant-garde filmmakers when cinema was still in its infancy? Interestingly, in *Leçons de ténèbres* and *Sombre*, it is through the *mise en scène* of different artistic practices – theatre and painting – that the question initially arises. The *mise en abyme* thus stresses the desire to return to, but also the difficulty to reclaim territories that are still occupied by other art forms, but to which feature film, in its rapid absorption by the commercial sector, seems to have largely lost access. Set apart from experimental cinema on the one hand, and from pornography's and gore's cinema of 'excess' on the other, the bulk of feature-film production appears to fall almost entirely into the province of narrative forms and photographic realism. Yet, in their practice, directors like Grandrieux, Dieutre and the other filmmakers cited in this book demonstrate that crucial links circulate through the whole corpus, blurring the borders that theoretically separate these categories. Indeed, I would argue that in contemporary feature cinema, it is precisely here, this in-between zone of hybrid cinema (Noguez 1999: 186), where (as in a Deleuzean process of 'becoming') the more sensual and experimental facets of the medium permeate and work to destabilise the primarily narrative and representational models, that the most exciting forms of filmmaking are currently offered.

In effect, it is those territories and practices of contemporary cinema that also seem to develop in correspondence with, if not to inspire, the recent renewal in theoretical approaches. Gathering impetus in the late 1990s, new theoretical proposals have thankfully started to offset the process whereby an audio-visual form of expression like film came to be studied primarily as an intellectual object separate from its existence as a sensual entity. Relayed by the publications of journals, editors and websites such as *Rouge profound*, *Trafic* and *Simulacres*, the work of French theorists like Raymond Bellour, Nicole Brenez and Vincent Amiel, amongst others, resolutely advocates a return to fine textual analysis. In Anglo-Saxon film studies, new approaches, strongly indebted to the writings of Deleuze, have developed simultaneously, with a tendency to focus more on phenomenological aspects and spectatorial response, however. The writings of Laura U. Marks, Steven Shaviro and Vivian Sobchack, not to mention Linda Williams' important study of the so-called genres of 'excess', have stressed the value of the contribution that the study of film as sensual experience has to offer. More specialised, both Barbara Kennedy and Anne Powell's books apply an alternative, Deleuzean framework to a corpus of films that are usually discussed in representational or genre terms. In the new thinking environment that is thus created, the prescriptive debate on realism and representation is sidelined in favour of close encounters with film matter.[9]

---

[9] In effect, in the process of reappraisal that took place, film theory's established methodologies have been systematically stigmatised for their universalist, transcendental ambitions. Deleuze's whole project is based on the critique of existing linguistic, ideological and psychoanalytical models. Similarly, in his introduction, Shaviro dismisses the psychoanalytical approach in characteristically definitive accents, describing its methods as entirely irrelevant: 'the psychoanalytic model for film theory is at this point utterly bankrupt; it needs not to be refined, but to be discarded altogether' (Shaviro 2004: ix). In film theory in particular, the psychoanalytical model is generally seen to subordinate the object of its studies

As Jérôme Game points out, the 'synchronicity' between theory and practice in the current shift towards a cinema of the senses is particularly manifest in French cinema. Game links this specificity of the French scene to the richness and multiplicity of French theoretical sources that fed into the elaboration of these new approaches – sources that reflect the importance of the renewed interface between contemporary philosophy, film, and film theory in particular. These references are not necessarily acknowledged as such, however; Game talks of the 'uneasiness of the contemporary French critical discourse on the cinematic body with respect to its own philosophical presuppositions'.

> Such uneasiness is symptomatic of contemporary criticism (be it literary or art criticism) in defining its own epistemological position, intervening as it does after a series of philosophical discourses which have ventured into aesthetics as never before, so constituting the postmodern paradigm: namely the work of Barthes, Foucault, Deleuze, Lyotard and several others. (Game 2001: 47)

Where film-as-thinking-body is concerned, it seems artificial, however, to draw a line between the work of postmodern thinkers and that of the theorists of the early avant-gardes mentioned in the previous pages, or with the writings of a phenomenologist like Merleau-Ponty which appear to fall somewhere in between. Indeed, the latter's attempt to rethink the relationship between cinema and philosophy remains key, even if his reflection appears, in the end, partly based on a reductive description of what film can be.[10] The philosopher's approach to cinema as a material phenomenon, an 'object to be perceived', which, in turn, can tell us something of our 'presence to the world' (Merleau-Ponty [1948] (1964): 96, 103) certainly prefigures the path revisited and reinvented by today's theories on film's corporeity.

Footnote 9 (*cont.*)
   to that of a system of representation governed by a set of pre-established rules (determined, in turn, by the overarching norm of male, heterosexual desire). However, even if it was regarded as a conditioned trend of thought linked to a specific period of film theory, the complete denial of the psychoanalytical line of investigation would need to be queried not only in terms of its historical significance (in particular where feminist and gender studies are concerned), but also because elements of it have necessarily permeated other branches of film studies and, indeed, inspired filmmaking techniques. Yet, Shaviro is right in pointing to its limitations. Not only, in order to function fully, does the psychoanalytical model need to be considered as transcendental to its object of study and too often relies on the assumption that its models are universal, but it also generally fails to take into account the specificity of film's corporeality.
[10] In his insistence on the importance of dialogues and the issue of film as illusion in particular, the question of the moving image's own material presence is thrown back into the background (Merleau-Ponty [1948] (1964), pp. 85–105).

Doing away with the Context?

The reticence to take on board a legacy of theoretical precedents is mirrored by the denial of historical contexts where the films themselves are concerned. The theorists who have, in recent years, become interested in cinema as a perceptual object have claimed the freedom to base their observations on apparently arbitrary samples of films, chosen irrespective of date and place of release, as well as genre and other categories. As Nicole Brenez puts it, to pursue the exploration of film as a material phenomenon has permitted that 'temporarily at least, the film itself takes precedence over the context' (Brenez 1998: 10). At the same time, transnational studies and the questioning of national labelling have gained more prominence in the field of film studies as a whole.

Within this context, to choose to concentrate on French cinema could be construed as limitative and rather old-fashioned. I am highly aware that in focusing on a corpus that is defined in geographical and national–cultural terms as well as time of production, I appear to start from a framework of a-priorities that might weaken the appraisal of the films as primarily material, sensory phenomena. My aim, however, is to open an array of historical and cultural resonances that will feed into the description and discussion of the films which form the basis of this book. Indeed, I would argue that the relevance of a combined approach becomes evident through the exploration of the films themselves. Moreover, to embed the aesthetic study of the works in a historical and cultural context and draw attention to potential intertextual connections is to respond to some of the shortcomings, briefly highlighted in the following paragraphs, necessarily bred by purely ahistorical approaches.

In a number of recent studies, a degree of acknowledged personal input, reflecting the subjective element inherent in the exploration of a work based on its sensory apprehension, has been put forward in denial of conventional methods based on categorising (national, generic, popular-versus-auteur cinemas and so on; Shaviro 2004: vii) and as a response to the limitative would-be objectivity of the dominant academic theories. Shaviro, thus, describes his book, *The Cinematic Body*, as:

> 'personal' first of all on account of its idiosyncratic choice of works to discuss; I'm aware of the incongruity of setting George Romero next to Robert Bresson, or Jerry Lewis beside Andy Warhol. By foregrounding my own 'taste' in this manner I seek to emphasize the roles of singularity and chance, against the objectifying scholarly tendency, which seeks to reduce particulars to generals, bizarre exceptions to representative patterns, specific practices to the predictable regularities of genre. In the second place, this book is 'personal' in the sense that it foregrounds visceral,

affective responses to film, in sharp contrast to most critics' exclusive concern with issues of form, meaning and ideology. (Shaviro 2004: viii)

In turn, Shaviro initially portrays his experience of film as detached from any historical or cultural framework:

> I am violently, viscerally affected by *this* image and *this* sound, without being able to have recourse to any frame of reference, and form of transcendental reflection, or any Symbolic order.' (2004: 32)

However, as Brenez acknowledges (1998: 10), the insistence on the primacy of the work over its context of production and on the option of extreme eclecticism in the choice of a corpus is not without problems. On the one hand, there is the temptation of the purely speculative path, ultimately as vacant as the claim for scientific objectivity professed in the most knowingly obscure of academic analysis. On the other hand, the risk is to develop a way of describing and extrapolating from the films that can be applied to all films irrespective of their genesis and end up constructing yet another ahistorical or universalising method of appraisal.[11] In the end, though it is to established methodologies that Shaviro applies the term 'exclusive', it is equally important not to treat the 'visceral, affective responses' themselves as exclusive and exhaustive – they are necessarily coextensive (as indeed Shaviro's own film analysis demonstrates) with the formal choices that help produce them and the references and ideology that underpin the film. In effect, in her critique of the kind of 'primitivist understanding of the senses' that underpins, in her opinion, the writings of Shaviro, Laura U. Marks reminds us that the senses are 'cultivated':

> By paying attention to bodily and sensuous experience, we will find that it is to a large degree informed by culture. Perception is already informed by culture, and so even illegible images are (cultural) perceptions, not raw sensations. (2000: 145)

The way film operates as an interface between sensual experience and embedded memory[12] is one of the central arguments of Marks' book, *The*

---

[11] Steven Shaviro's eclectic corpus does in fact create interesting resonances. Yet, to me, his most persuasive chapters are the ones devoted to American cinema, where the author provides convincing historical and political frameworks as a background to his close analysis of the films.

[12] As Marks stresses, even our most immediate response to films is dependent on the way our senses are trained, as well as the viewing habits and the cinematic knowledge and memory that are ingrained in us; our reaction to violent, obscene images, our ability or incapacity to engage with the physical qualities and rhythm of a non-narrative film, or with images presented in styles of filmmaking developed outside of the Western models, have been shaped by our viewings, readings, and understanding of a film's context.

Skin of the Film (2000). Hers is an exploration of forms of haptic visuality grounded in the examination of a defined corpus with a specific geo-political and cultural context. (Marks looks at works made by contemporary filmmakers and video artists who live in exile or have integrated a culture which is not that of their native country.) Her book demonstrates that there are crucial advantages in following the inkling one might have that a group of works, highly diverse yet bound by a related historical background and parallel aesthetic quests, have a comparable effect on us and raise similar questions of film form.

Ultimately, in phenomenological and aesthetic terms, just as in issues of representation or genre, a cultural/historical backdrop is necessary to apprehend the mutations undergone by the cinema (and the implied changes in the spectatorial experience and perception). This work of con-textualisation does not necessarily entail the verification of a historical logic built on 'progressive' models; as we will see, in the context of a cinema of the senses in particular, mutations in filmmaking and viewing practices can usually be appraised simultaneously in modern or postmodern terms, as backward-looking or as innovative.[13]

To outline the wider circuit of historical, cultural and artistic currents in which a film appears and circulates does not replace a proper formal exploration of the way a film's singular power of evocation might operate – that which, in Brenez's words, 'gives back to the work its depth, its richness, its fragility, the density or opacity that is unique to it, in other words, its problematic virtues' (Brenez 1998: 11). What it can do, however, is accompany and enhance the aesthetic analysis of the film image and help us grasp more than one facet of the significance of its material presence.[14]

The simultaneity of the current shift towards a cinema of the senses in practice and in theory suggests a blurring between borders where cinema's input as a thinking process can indeed be explored anew, including in reflexive terms. If the relation between theory and practice functions like an exchange, then theory develops most fruitfully where it is initially found already present, elaborated in and by the films themselves. As 'thinking machines',[15] films generate their own meaning and questions; in turn,

---

[13] The introduction of the digital camera and the changes in the figuration of the body in space, for example, is construed by many as a departure from cinema-making proper – a denial of cinematic pleasures. Yet as we will see in subsequent chapters, it has opened fertile territories and played a crucial role in the development of film forms based on the renewed exploration of the material dimension of the cinema in particular.

[14] 'Material' in the sense of the practical conditions of film production (its funding, for instance), however, will only be indirectly mentioned in the book.

[15] For Deleuze, film's mechanical grounding does not deny but, on the contrary, forms the basis for cinema's creative potential as a thought process. It is precisely because it is not dependent

however, the traces of various ways of thinking about cinema will also be found woven into the texture of the works. Therefore, in the end, even when aesthetic analysis initially imposes itself as the most relevant for a specific film, it does not rule out the need to resort to other ways of making sense of the experience of watching it.

This book's focus, then, is on an aesthetic of sensation, where the material dimension of a cinematic work is initially given precedence over its expository and mimetic/realistic functions. These functions, however, are not discounted; they are, rather, addressed through the prism of the medium's material qualities. As Anne Powell points out, the advantage of such an 'interstitial, transverse connection across existing approaches' (Powell 2005: 208) lies with the possibility of exploring not only how the two planes (the 'molecular' and the 'molar') coexist, but also how film's material make-up pre-empts and determines its construct as narrative process, system of representation, or articulation of an ideological discourse.

French Cinema and Transgression

The strongest argument in favour of defining a corpus here comes, of course, from the films themselves; if the emergence of a contemporary cinema of sensation clearly concerns a diverse collection of filmmakers across the world,[16] France nevertheless offers an intriguing case in point. A specific sense of momentum emanates from the work of a number of contemporary French filmmakers, evidenced by the release, in close succession, of a batch of films which betray a characteristic sensibility to and awareness of cinema's sensuous impact and transgressive nature. *Adieu*; *À ma sœur*; *Baise-moi*; *Beau Travail*; *La Blessure*; *La Captive*; *Dans ma peau*;

Footnote 15 (*cont.*)
on the movement and rhythm of external realities, because it is an event in itself, that film invites us to move into alternative forms of thinking: 'the cinematographic image is the movement-image, that is to say that it does not represent something or someone who is moving, but that it moves by itself and in itself, that it is au-to-ma-tic. And it is as an automatic image that the cinematographic image can elicit an image of thought' (Deleuze 2001, translation mine).

[16] It is an expanding, international range of film works – some of which were long deemed unworthy of academic interest – that has been attracting the attention of contemporary critics and theorists. Extremely diverse, they are nevertheless connected as examples of filmmaking practices based on an aesthetic of sensation. Prominent instances include, amongst others, the films of David Lynch and David Cronenberg (see, for example, Astic 2004), Abel Ferrara (whose flamboyant productions are currently the subject of Nicole Brenez's writing), Alexander Sokurov, Wong Kar-Wai (see, for example, Jousse 2006), Hou Hsiao-Hsien, Takeshi Kitano, and horror specialists like Mario Bava and Dario Argento.

Demonlover; Flandres; L'Humanité; L'Intrus; Les Invisibles; Lady Chatterley; Leçons de ténèbres; Romance; Sombre; Tiresia; Trouble Every Day; Twentynine Palms; Vendredi soir; La Vie nouvelle; Wild Side; Zidane, un portrait du XXIème siècle, all released between 1998 and 2006, are amongst a longer list of works that are referred to in this book – some mentioned in passing, some more fully explored.

There is something particularly engaging in finding this kind of cinematic practice, with its emphasis on the corporeality of film, so much in evidence in contemporary French cinema. In the first instance, it goes against the traditions of scenario and/or dialogue-based cinema that dominate French production, not only in its mainstream forms, but also as far as the auteur strand is concerned. Though recent trends have included realistic dramas with a strong sociological element, the prevailing stereotype of a French auteur film remains that of the *drame intimiste* – the intimate, character-and-dialogue-based psychological investigation. Secondly, and in more general terms, the return of a cinema as an art of the senses also goes against the ingrained, Cartesian bent towards the abstract that forms the basis of modern French culture.[17] Amongst others, Deleuze, in his reflections on 'the image of thought', forgoes the tendency, characteristic of French thought, to project a 'scientific image of itself', and singles out cinema's potential as a source of renewal of conventional ways of thinking (Deleuze 2001).

However, even if 'the French cast of mind' has by now been questioned and challenged long enough for its denunciation to become a cliché in itself, the objections typically directed at filmmakers who approach their medium as a corporeal object confirm that it still holds its ground. As will be discussed in the following chapters, in feature filmmaking, works that foreground the concrete, sensual dimension of cinema are often dismissed as examples of mere formalism or, worse, as sheer sensationalism by critics who also tend to address this kind of practice as a separate category of French cinema. Yet, the sample of filmmakers cited in this book does not correspond to a 'movement' (indeed, some of the directors would voice, I suspect, a strong dislike for each others' work) and, accordingly, this book is not intended to be an exhaustive survey of a particular class of French film. If anything, these films tend to be best defined as 'unclassifiable', and, as we will see, the disregard for genre boundaries is as much a feature of

---

[17] As Merleau-Ponty reminds us, since Descartes, Western thought has been dominated by the belief that 'It befits our human dignity to entrust ourselves to the intellect, which alone can reveal to us the reality of the world,' a 'cast of mind' that is 'particularly strong in France' ([1948] 2004: 42, 40).

the cinema of the senses as the blurring of the border between figurative and abstract. There is a temptation to single out the element of transgression found in many of the films so as to justify the creation of yet another genre or grouping. 'Extreme cinema', 'cinema of evil', 'cinema of the abject':[18] these are some of the expressions that crop up in articles on contemporary French cinema. In effect, some of the recent French film production seemingly brings art cinema to new heights of horror or graphic description. I will argue, however, that to focus on the 'sensationalist' facet to the detriment of the films' other achievements is to ignore some of the most fertile dimensions of a phenomenon that concerns a much broader spectrum of films, for the sake of creating one more category or genre. On the contrary, to approach these films as perceptual objects rather than as illustrations of specific generic conventions allows us to identify the stylistic figures and motifs that connect them, not only with film forms usually found outside of feature-film cinema, but also with traditionally realistic trends in French production. In the majority of feature films, even critical approaches operate primarily as mirrors of reality's appearance, captured from an 'objective', detached stand-point. The films concerned here offer an alternative vision, an affecting and thought-provoking way of questioning our status as observers and 'consumers' of the pro-filmic reality.

Ultimately, however, if the cinematographic corpus as a whole is envisaged as a plane, differentiation becomes a question of variation in intensity rather than a work of classification into a series of separate types or genres of film. As if 'probing a wound',[19] the cinema of sensation tends to move us closer, dig deeper into our perception of things, show that which escapes the naked eye and ear and, ultimately, immerse us in the pleasure and terror of the 'formless'. Claude Chabrol's masterful *La Cérémonie* concludes on a striking image. Caught in close-up is the face of the murderess who has just assassinated all the members of the family that employed her as a servant; around the young woman's face, the background has suddenly vanished and she is surrounded by the deepest shade of black. Grandrieux's *Sombre* could be said to start here, in the fissure opened by the darkness of the images' background, just as Assayas' *Demonlover* or de Van's *Dans ma peau* unravel like the absent counter-shot to the terrified, oblique glance on which Laurent Cantet's *L'Emploi du temps* concludes.

Loosely calling it 'cinema of the senses' or 'of sensation' (terms which I use interchangeably) does not designate it as a distinct category of work but,

---

[18] See, for instance, McKibbin 1999; Quandt 2004.

[19] To paraphrase the expression used by Hal Foster in his study of contemporary art forms (Foster 1996).

rather, refers to the way certain films capture and reshape the pro-filmic reality. As I hope to suggest by bringing together contrasting examples, these works appear in a continuum with the rest of the production; if the works may seem to operate on a heightened level of visual or sound waves, it does not mean their filmmakers are less preoccupied with the issues that inform our daily lives, but, rather, the contrary. It is not, then, about mere 'sensationalism'. The cinema of sensation starts where other films draw to a close and resonates with the myriad of untold stories and sensations that the self-contained world of conventional filmmaking fails to convey (Bellour 2005: 16–17). Such a cinema bears the mark of its unfinishedness in the openness of its narrative structure and through the audio–visual fluctuations that animate its surface; several of the films cited in the following chapters contain sequences where the image and the sound-track, as if caught into a wider field of different speeds, seem literally to vibrate with intensity waves coming from the outer field.

As Aumont, paying tribute to Jean Epstein, summarises it: 'images think – they are not merely a means of expression for a thought process' (Aumont 2005: 10). Films do not just provide life-like testimonies on their contemporary world; as flowing, embodied forms of thought, they can help us imagine ways out of the dead ends down which dual thinking leads us. I hope to show how French cinema, emerging against the backdrop of modernity's contradictions, offers valuable, thought-provoking variations and lines of flight on those issues that have been at the core of contemporary debates on culture, identity and change.

Obviously, this book can in no way claim to have the kind of scope demonstrated by the works mentioned in this introduction – some of which do, as in Jérôme Game's comment about Brenez's study of figure (Brenez 1998), provide a 'substantial and quite ambitious conceptual production which aims to offer a coherent method for interpreting films' (Game 2001: 48). With the present study, I am content to offer an illustration of how the reinstatement of aesthetic analysis as core approach can open up the study of a corpus on to less chartered territories. In effect, in the way it diverts from the expected frame of references as well as pure aesthetic analysis, this exploration of a particular trend of French filmmaking will appear rather flawed to the purists.

Firstly, I will not attempt to apply a single framework or particular terminology (even if it is an alternative one), as some of the elegant Deleuzean studies cited before. A looser frame of reference leads me to superimpose concepts, as when I relate Deleuze's (positive) notion of immanence with Bataille's (angst-ridden) evocation of the 'formless'. Secondly, since I do not do away with the context, neither do I exclude completely conventional methods of addressing the works. The aim here is not, as Powell puts it, 'to replace more traditional methods of analysis by a new orthodoxy' but to use film aesthetics to 'both extend and critique extant ways of reading' (Powell 2005: 208).

In Chapters 1 and 2, some of the points outlined in the introduction will be considered in more depth. In Chapter 1, I will take Artaud's call for a 'third path' in cinema as a cue to discuss the convergence of filmmaking practices and film theory generated by the emergence of a cinema of the senses. I will look at cinema's specific history with regard to art and materiality, before going back to the issue of transgression and sensationalism. Based on recent Deleuzean-orientated writings in particular, I will argue the need for an alternative approach in addressing the films that constitute my corpus.

In Chapter 2, I will look further at how the work of some contemporary filmmakers elaborates processes of synaesthesia and correspondences: that is, the evocation, through sound and images, of other sensory effects as well as concepts and embodied thoughts and memories. I will explore the ways by which these films construct haptic modes of vision that destabilise our common apprehension of the relationship between subjective body and objective world.

Chapter 3 explores forms of cinematic 'becomings' and cinematic embodiment. As embodied thought process, the cinema of the senses suggests alternative ways of approaching those questions at work in the persistence of the French *malaise*. The growing supremacy of technology permeating all areas of human existence, globalisation, exclusion, ethnic diversity and national identities and the blurring of gender and genre definitions – such are the issues that, rather than being addressed in the representational or metaphorical mode, appear literally embedded in the 'flesh' of the film-text, imprinted in the texture and combination of its images and sound. Hence, the films not only set out to evoke the uncertainties of modern man's identity through the vulnerability of his/her body, they are themselves constructed primarily like sensory entities that, as Barbara Kennedy puts it, 'perform as a body'. Ultimately, as in Artaud and Deleuze's words, some of the films work like 'bodies without organs' – limb-like sequences or blocks of sensations pieced together to form monstrous constructs caught in a constant process of metamorphosis.

Summarised in this fashion, the content of this book may sound rather abstract. Thus, it is worth insisting on the fact that the arguments presented in the following pages develop from the films themselves. As Stanley Cavell, drawing a parallel between philosophy and film studies, once underlined, description should take place first and form the source of further interpretation or analysis (Cavell 2005: 169). Accordingly, in this book, the comprehensive description of specific sequences and motifs, which allows us to engage with the films as thinking processes, is the basis and determines the structure of the text. In other words, the point here is not merely to think about film, but to think with and through film.

Some of the films discussed in this book have attracted attention mainly because of the controversial nature of their subject matter. However, few have reached a very large audience at the time of their release, and no matter how outstanding their achievement, some have been very little seen. I purposely concentrate on films that have been, or will soon be, released on DVD and/or VHS. There is no need to insist, particularly in the case of the cinema concerned here, that the films should be seen in a cinema, in good audio-visual conditions. The DVD format, however, with its possibility of close and repeated viewings, provides an intermediary solution that can help this book meet its main purpose: to spur the curiosity of some of the readers and prompt them to discover or rediscover the films for themselves.

CHAPTER 1

A 'Third Path'

> I started to dream about a film through which I could elaborate new forms of dramaturgy, make an incursion in the world of dreams, follow a logic that would be that of dreams; a film that would give me a new freedom in relation to the tools now available in cinematographic image-making. (Olivier Assayas, in Guilloux 2002)

> You don't get anything by handling the spectator with care. (Guy Debord)[1]

The opening shots of *Tiresia* (2003) transform the screen into a live mass of magma; scale and perspective dissolve into an assemblage of visions of utter chaos, dark matter in fusion filling the frame, heaving and exploding to let flows of combusting molten rocks pour out, while in a strange yet fitting juxtaposition of sensations, the expansive sound-track resounds with the classical composition of Beethoven's seventh symphony.

Working close to a much humbler furnace, Pizzaïolo Boni (*Nénette et Boni*, 1997) kneads a ball of pizza dough while fantasising aloud about the woman he desires. In one long single take, and in extreme close-up, the soft pasty mass is shaped, flattened, smoothed and roughed between Boni's impatient hands. Feverishly punctured by his fingers, the malleable surface metamorphoses from desert-like expanse to a moon-like, crater-filled landscape. Eventually, Boni's face bursts into the frame and sinks into the formless heap.

Both works, in their own way, celebrate the materiality of the medium of the moving image, film's inherent processes of endless becoming. As Michel Guilloux, comparing filmmaking with the kneading of the pizza dough, eloquently puts it: 'Cinema's raw matter is the world in which it is filmed . . . it was necessary to work on this matter to shape the body of the film (*pour que le film prenne corps*), to create a new way of making film' (Guilloux 1997: 12). Such comments remain an exception; in feature-filmmaking, directors are still more likely to be praised for their achievements as story-tellers than for their ability to engage with film as a physical entity. Predisposed as we are to devote our attention to plot and character development and the

---

[1] Guy Debord (1978), *In girum imus nocte et consumimur igni*, Paris (Simar Films), black and white, 35mm, 105 min.

'realism' of special effects, it seems we have become largely desensitised to those qualities that initially define the specificity of the cinematic experience, and which early theorists hailed as the source of cinema's affective and evocative power: its changing audio-visual compositions of movement, light, contrasts, grain and volume, and the fluctuating relations of ground and foreground, form and figure that shape its figural space.

Writing in 1928, Antonin Artaud underlined the need for a 'third' kind of film form, one that would develop between the abstract formalism of the 'pure' cinema and the derivative commercialism of narrative 'psychological' cinema:

> At present, two courses seem to be open to the cinema, of which neither is the right one. The pure and absolute cinema on the one hand, and, on the other, this sort of venial hybrid art. The latter persists in expressing, in more or less successful images, psychological situations which are perfectly suitable for the stage or the pages of a book, but not for the screen, and which only really exist as the reflection of a world which seeks its matter and its meaning elsewhere. . . . Between purely linear abstraction (and a play of shadows and lights is like a play of lines) and the film with psychological undertones which might tell a dramatic story, there is room for an attempt at true cinema, of which neither the matter nor the meaning is indicated by any film so far produced. ([1928] 1972: 19)

Artaud thus shared with the theorists and filmmakers of the early avant-gardes (and in particular, even if they differed where the actual filmmaking practice was concerned, the protagonists of the French avant-gardes – Germaine Dulac, Jean Epstein and the Luis Buñuel who created the (in)famous opening sequence of *Un Chien andalou* amongst others) the belief that the impact and magic of the picture in movement, its capacity to affect, to shock and to make sense, was intrinsic to film itself. If the affective and creative force of the cinema, its capacity to trigger our senses, imagination and thought, derived partly from the effect of verisimilitude of its animated photographic recording, it would only be fully realised when the *effet de réel* was put into the service of defamiliarisation rather than harnessed to narrative requirements. In their eyes, there was precious little scope in subjecting the medium of the moving image to the function of merely documenting an external reality or illustrating a pre-existing story-line; it was the ability of the cinema to create specific sensory universes that needed to be explored. Only if spectators were immersed in the world created by the film itself would their senses and mind be challenged (and, by extension, their understanding and experience of reality – visible and invisible – questioned and enriched). The power of the cinema thus rested with 'purely visual sensations' (Artaud's writings correspond, of course, to the end of the era of the silent movie), 'the dramatic force of which springs from a shock on the eyes, drawn, one might say, from the very substance of the eye, and not from psychological circumlocutions of a discursive nature which are nothing but visual interpretations of a text' (Artaud [1928] 1972: 20). On the one hand, Artaud's claim with regard to the vocation of the medium of the moving image stresses the need for a cinema that would draw its raw material from the recording of a pro-filmic reality rather than resort to the purely conceptual constructs of the proponents of the abstract film avant-garde.[2] Crucially, if he rejects it as a formal a priori, Artaud does not rule out abstraction as part of the actual imaging process; the following description of the movement and mutations in/of the images suggests that the frontier between the figurative and the abstract remains fluid. Artaud thus calls for an initially figurative cinema, but one where film forms should nevertheless be allowed to develop independently from 'realistic' narrative adaptations and 'play with matter itself, [to create] situations that emerge from the simple collision of objects, forms, repulsions and attractions' (Artaud [1928] 1972: 21).

Artaud's approach to filmmaking was too defiant of rational thought and ideological frameworks to correlate with the didactic project that underpins the montage technique developed and theorised by the proponents of the Soviet avant-garde. Yet, he shared with them a belief in film as a signifying process in itself. This had radical implications for their understanding of cinema as a sensory and also an intellectual experience and for their appraisal of the relation between practice and theory. As Gilles Deleuze recalls it, to the creators of 'intellectual montage', the circuit that cinema creates between the sensorial and thought process is an inherent part of the workings of the moving image: 'This is why Eisenstein continually reminds us that "intellectual cinema" has as correlate "sensory thought" or "emotional intelligence" and is worthless without it' (Deleuze 1989: 159). In the following comments, Deleuze recognises that in practice, however, precious little space has been devoted to the exploration of cinema as the medium of 'emotional intelligence'.

> Everyone knows that if an art necessarily imposed the shock or vibration, the world would have changed long ago, and men would have been thinking for a long time. So this pretension of the cinema, at least among the greatest pioneers, raises a smile today. They believed that cinema was capable of imposing the shock, and imposing it on the masses, the people (Vertov, Eisenstein, Gance, Elie Faure . . .). However, they foresaw that cinema would encounter and was already encountering all the ambiguities of the other arts; that it would be overlaid with experimental abstractions,

---

[2] Exemplified by the work of Viking Eggeling, Hans Richter, Walter Ruttman and Oskar Fischinger amongst others.

'formalist antics' and commercial configurations of sex and blood. The shock would be confused, in bad cinema, with the figurative violence of the represented instead of achieving that other violence of a movement-image developing its vibrations in a moving sequence which embeds itself within us. (Deleuze 1989: 157)

A combination of shock as an aim and end in itself and the voyeuristic harnessing of the effect of verisimilitude towards the pornographic accumulation of 'realist' images: Deleuze's scathing assessment of the kind of cinema that came to dominate our screens closely echoes Artaud's own disenchanted proclamation of the 'precocious old age of the cinema' (Artaud [1933] 1972: 76).

The 'precocious old age of the cinema'

Artaud quickly became disillusioned with the medium of the moving image whose 'precocious old age' he foresaw even before the era of the talkies was fully established. In many ways, his prophetic announcement appears to hold true. If the creative, independent exploration of cinematic forms and of the medium's primarily material, sensual and affective manifestations were pursued, it was first and foremost as one facet of experimental cinema and, later, through creations in installation art. These artistic domains prove to be extremely buoyant areas of today's French art and, as some of the works discussed in the following chapters demonstrate, the contemporary French cinema that concerns us offers exciting examples of overlaps and hybridisations between experimental and feature film. Yet, as far as the widely distributed scenario-based commercial cinema is concerned, in France as elsewhere, these alternative practices have had little more than a merely superficial impact.[3] Overall, the establishment of the sets of conventions determined by the requirements of narrative logic and sound synchronicity has lastingly turned the bulk of cinematic production into the kind of 'venial art' decried by Artaud (Ray 1985). While a certain amount of experimentation always remained a necessary condition to ensure the renewal of spectatorial interest, effects and stylistic choice have developed first and foremost in accordance with the needs for narrative and expository clarity. On the big screens, only advertisements and specific commercial genres – the aptly named 'weepies' and spectacular American musicals of the 1950s, for instance, as well as horror, pornography and certain action films with special effects – give pre-eminence to the bodily affective viewing experience in

---

[3] 'Commercial film and television share some interest in the sensuous qualities that experimental works evoke. However, given their constraints (to put it kindly), commercial media are less likely to dedicate themselves to such exploration' (Marks 2000: xii).

'excess' of the needs of a narrative process proper (Williams 1991). However, in those instances, experimentation with cinematic effects is, on the whole, limited or standardised. Controlled and rendered functional, the initial element of excess loses its power of disruption. Generally confined to precise techniques and conventions, and the showcasing of technological novelties which serve specific strategies of 'realism' (Turnock 2001), the intended bodily effects are predominantly designed for and targeted at specific audiences, and serve consumerist tactics that pre-exist and condition the filmmaking choices. Indeed, the effectiveness of the appropriation and channelling of its sensory effects seems particular to the technology-cum-art form that cinema is. Asked to comment on the rarity of directors 'working on sensation', filmmaker Philippe Grandrieux bemoans contemporary cinema's lack of vitality in comparison with other artistic domains:

> Question: *Very few filmmakers today work with sensation, presence.* Philippe Grandrieux: In experimental cinema, as well as in video, there is quite a lot of stuff . . . There are extremely powerful fictional worlds being created in this field [music], as well as in photography, in dance – whereas film does not create anything anymore; most of the time, it bores me terribly. Film is elsewhere, outside of the cinemas. (Béghin et al. 2001, translation mine)

There is little need to recall that, more than any other artistic activity, cinema always was awkwardly set on an edge, at the frontier between art and industry; the sheer mass of the mainstream film production and distribution can make the situation of film as a creative art form look particularly hopeless. Yet, as Deleuze himself underlines in one of his lectures, the mediocrity and predictability of the majority of cinematic production is by no means specific to film: 'the worthlessness of the current production is a law of all so-called "artistic" activities' (Deleuze 2001, translation mine).[4] Even as it appeared that less and less space was left for film forms not strictly structured around scenario-based action and psychological logic to develop, alternative approaches have in fact never stopped flourishing in the margins of prevailing systems of production.[5] Furthermore, there appear to be interesting changes taking place in contemporary cinema's landscape. As

---

[4] The time factor is also key here, and for many of the films included in my corpus, it will probably play a significant role; whereas many 'blockbusters' have resounding but short-lived box-office success, a larger proportion of the films of the independent sector that are, in relative terms, little distributed and little seen at the time of their initial release continue to be watched (in art-house theatres or in VHS or DVD formats) and discussed long afterwards. A variety of alternative film forms thus retains a much greater part of the overall cinematic landscape than the space they initially appear destined to occupy.

[5] See Beugnet (2007).

Stéphane Bouquet remarks: 'If, for a long time, experimentations were kept in the margins of cinema, they now invest its field fully, and come right to its center' (Bouquet 2001: 200, translation mine). Since the 1990s, a different impetus seems to have breathed life into part of French cinema, and several factors suggest that this shift is of particular significance. Firstly, as mentioned in the introduction, it simultaneously affects cinematographic practice and French film theory. In addition, and most uncharacteristically, as Bouquet underlines it, it is the feature film that is primarily at stake here. In other words, the re-endorsement of, and experimentation with, film's physical qualities has started again to exceed the field of experimental cinema proper, to affect, in varying degrees (in some rare cases, it appears to define the work of a director as a whole; in most, it emerges in the punctual description of specific films or specific extracts), the work of a growing number of filmmakers whose films cannot be described as experimental in the more specialised sense of the term (Noguez 1999: 185).[6] Moreover, the willingness of a number of contemporary filmmakers not only to engage with speculative discussions about their films, but also to reflect on the state of cinema in general demonstrates an awareness and a belief that now is a time to consider cinematic practices anew.[7] Again, this is not about the emergence of a 'movement', but about alternative ways of approaching film in terms of practice and also in terms of theory and criticism.

The 'precocious old age' of Film Theory and Criticism

In many ways, the particular slant followed by much of film theory and criticism mirrors the evolution of the dominant cinematic practices. It does in fact provide yet another forceful illustration of what has by now become a truism of contemporary critical thinking: the dominance of Cartesian models of thought. The fact that, in spite of the immediacy of its perceptual impact, the appraisal of film as a material, sensual entity has found significantly little resonance in film theory seems more comprehensible when considered in the wider context of a long-standing Western tradition of rational thinking and categorising. Arguably a perversion of the methodologies first developed during the enlightenment (Brenez 1998: 10), not

---

[6] Again, the question is one of degree rather than strict categorisation here. Dominique Noguez thus stresses how the overall primacy given to formal issues is what determines the development of experimental film forms more or less distinct from art and auteur cinema in particular (Noguez 1999: 185).

[7] Grandrieux is a case in point. His tendency to philosophise about film has exposed him to frequent accusations of intellectual affectation (Quandt 2004); his comments nevertheless offer opinionated and topical views on filmmaking and spectatorship.

only does Western thought's tendency to promote a scientific image of itself extend to the study and appraisal of the creative and artistic domains, but where film theory is concerned, the inclination towards would-be scientific procedures also appears to gain renewed vigour from the 1970s onwards. As Vivian Sobchack underlines, this dominant approach was established not merely in opposition to the kind of epistemological path opened by sensory perception, but also through the actual denial of any valuable knowledge attached to perceptual experience, and, by extension, became embedded in the indifference to the exploration of its objects (Sobchack 2000: 1–3).

> Thus, the language used in the press to describe the sensuous and affective dimensions of the film experience has been written off as a popular version of that imprecise humanist criticism drummed out of film studies in the early 1970s with the advent of the more 'rigorous' and 'objective' modes of description. Thus, sensual reference in descriptions of cinema has been generally regarded as rhetorical or poetic excess – sensuality located, then, always less on the side of the body than on the side of language. (Sobchack 2004: 58)

Similarly, Shaviro denounces the restrictive outlook offered by the effacement of the physical and phenomenological in favour of interpretative methodologies bent on reducing perception to a reflexive discourse of knowledge:

> The Hegelian and structuralist equation suppresses the body. It ignores or abstracts away from the primordial forms of raw sensation: affect, excitation, stimulation and repression, pleasure and pain, shock and habit. It posits instead a disincarnate eye and ear whose data are immediately objectified in the form of self-conscious awareness or positive knowledge. (Shaviro 2004: 26–7)

Furthermore, where cinema – that is, the audio-visual art form of *movement* – is concerned, to explore sound and images in their materiality is not merely to call for a consideration of the necessarily subjective nature of sensory effects (sound and vision as well as, through correspondences, the other senses), but also, as the film unravels, to draw attention to the constant mutations that affect the physical appearance of audio-visual matter. To downplay the normalising process and technical competency of the continuity system and, instead, celebrate cinema as the art of metamorphosis, of 'becoming', is to go against a well-established process of historicising and categorising that encompasses film studies. What is more, as a form of thinking, film epitomises the kind of fluidity that Rosi Braidotti sees as lacking in today's Western thought – so much so that the first sentence of the following remark could well describe the operations of film-as-thought:

Thinking through flows and interconnections remains a difficult challenge. The fact
that theoretical reason is concept-bound and fastened upon essential notions makes
it difficult to find adequate representations for processes, fluid in-between flows of
data, experience and information. They tend to become frozen in spatial, metaphorical modes of representation . . . (Braidotti 2005: 2)

Following the general predilection for 'scientific' rigour, the field of film
studies has become largely divided up between three or four main 'schools'
or methodologies that apply to film's pre-existing models of analysis:[8] the
study of narrative and genre systems; semiotics and the study of cinema
according to the linguistic paradigm or as ideological system of representation and enunciation; and, since the 1970s, psychoanalysis. Finally, soci-
ologically oriented methods have grown in connection with cultural and
reception studies which concentrate on the economic and cultural context
in general. Indeed, the analysis of the films proper (all questions pertaining to the materiality and the aesthetic dimension of the works), left out of
the main agenda, often appears as a mere by-product and process of verification of these chief methodologies. Hence, as Brenez points out, in the
attempt to define, as methodically and objectively as possible, categories,
historical trends and structures that would serve as a reference system
for the study of cinema as a whole, the films themselves become the
insubstantial, interchangeable pieces of a pre-existing framework.

Recognized, defined by its historical, spatial and subjective demarcations, inscribed
within patterns of style and taste, envisaged as the reciprocal source of other stories,
the story of its reception included, the work is, in effect, visited, rendered transparent,

---

[8] At the same time, film theory has become increasingly reticent in engaging with those issues
pertaining to film as a physical entity and sensorial experience. As pointed out by Linda
Williams and Vivian Sobchack, until recently, popular film forms that privilege the sensual or
affective facet of cinematic expression, for instance, have been regarded as reducing cinema
to an apparatus for the manipulation of the viewer and have expectedly been considered, in
Sobchack's words, 'too crude to invite further elaboration' (Sobchack 2004: 3). Likewise,
where cinema and sensation are concerned, overlaps between what is usually defined as
popular and art cinema practices are generally met with suspicion. In the 1980s, France's so-
called *cinéma du look* was a point in case. With the exception of a few notable critics such as
Raphaël Bassan (Bassan 1989), the work of the directors in question (Jean-Jacques Beineix,
Jean-Luc Besson, Leos Carax, and Jeunet and Caro were generally grouped together as the
directors of the *cinéma du look* or as the *néobaroques*) was usually condemned as, at worst,
manipulative and, at best, examples of empty formalism or flashy pastiche. Those techniques
shared by the small, heterogeneous group of directors concerned undoubtedly resulted in a
highly unequal batch of films. In some instances, however, the filmmaking manifested an
unusual sense of space, textures and colours, that was, at first, too readily dismissed as a mere
by-product of the degrading influence of advertisement on artistic practices (Austin 1996:
119–35; Silverman 1999: 118; Hayward 1991: 253).

traversed by that which sanctioned it and by the responses it elicited, reduced at the same time as it becomes absent to itself through the procedures that take it as object. Indispensable and often fruitful, this work of investigation, which in fact occupies today's hermeneutic scene almost entirely, does not, however, appear sufficient. (Brenez 1998: 11, translation mine)

Steven Shaviro, whose wilfully polemical book remains a key text as far as the questioning of the perception/interpretation divide in film theory is concerned, points to another consequence of contemporary film theory's restrictive bent. The gap has grown wider between the material manifestations and the experience of viewing film, and the leading theoretical approaches to film, coached in an idealist, Cartesian distrust for the phenomenological and subjective.

In film viewing, there is pleasure and more than pleasure: a rising scale of seduction, delirium, fascination, and utter absorption in the image. [But] theory derives its particular form from its endeavour to separate itself from these founding impulses. . . . What disturbs me in the founding texts of psychoanalytic and poststructuralist film theory is an almost reflex movement of suspicion, disavowal, and phobic rejection. It seems as if theorists of the past twenty years can scarcely begin their discussions without ritualistically promising to resist the insidious seductions of film. (Shaviro 2004: 11)

Even when confronted with the incredibly fertile field of non-narrative, experimental cinema, the tendency for film theory has been to focus on experimental practices as processes of 'deconstruction' (of the classical techniques and apparatus) rather than as independently and specifically affective modes of artistic expression.[9] In effect, to those proponents of cinema's 'third path', it is the shortcomings of the reflection on cinema, as much as the factual and economic determinants, that proved damaging to the nurturing of cinema's initial promises.

Cinema, or we, rather than cinema, have renounced the ambitions of the cinema of the beginnings. We recognise the exigency or the ambitions of Gance, Eisenstein, Epstein. But they appear a little derisory to us, if not frankly naïve. What happened, we wonder? Here is an art form which, at the beginning, never stopped situating itself in relation to thought; yet today, if you look at the abundant bibliography on cinema, how many contemporary books are concerned or engage with the problematic of cinema's relation to thought? (Deleuze 2001, translation mine)

---

[9] Notable exceptions include the writings of experimental filmmakers themselves, and of writers-cum-directors like Dominique Noguez, whose *Éloge du cinéma expérimental* was first published in 1979. Framed by an in-depth discussion of experimental cinema's context of production, Noguez's survey also appraises its variety of film forms and aesthetic choices on their own terms, and signals its *parti pris* in its very title.

If the abandonment of the fertile debates initiated in the 1920s by the early theorists seems so deeply unproductive, it is precisely because it confirms a general failure to uphold cinema as the quintessential expression of the reunion between experience and reflection, perception and thought, body and mind. Hence, until recently, even, in spite of the richness and variety of approaches it encompasses, in French film theory, the exploration of the medium in material/aesthetic terms was largely overlooked. Considering Deleuze's seminal work on painting, for instance, and in particular the detailed analysis of Richard Bacon's work which will prove an invaluable source of reference for the discussion of the aesthetics of sensation later on (Deleuze 2002), one would expect the discovery of the principles ruling over the affective impact of cinema images as physical entities to come to occupy a large place in his writing. Yet, as Jacques Aumont points out, for all the power and ground-breaking contribution of his reflection on film as a thinking mechanism that operates through the body, in his writing on cinema, the theorist does not engage fully with the evocation of film as a material entity in itself:

> The dominant voice in film criticism, the voice that, from Bazin to Deleuze and Daney, talks of the cinema as a form of representation and as the incarnation of forces through stories and fictional models, has no need for the *matter* of images. It is a burden (Bazin disallows it endlessly; more subtly, but more perversely, the great Deleuze gets rid of it in favor of his vitalist metaphors). (Aumont 2005: 9; italics mine)

Aumont's own book, eloquently entitled *Matière d'images*, is one amongst a number of studies whose publication suggests that film aesthetics is regaining a place alongside contemporary film theory's main methodologies.[10] As mentioned in the introduction, the past twenty years have witnessed a burgeoning of alternative theoretical proposals bent on exploring anew the corporeal and sensuous dimensions of the medium – a

---

[10] The reappraisal of early works also testifies to this shift in analytical approaches. In the latest anniversary events devoted to Étienne-Jules Marey, the inventor of chronophotography, it was the aesthetic value of his work that was hailed, and its sensual resonance, as much as its scientific worth (Colloquium at the Musée d'Orsay, 19–20 November 2004). Similarly, where the films of early directors are reappraised, they tend to be discussed less in terms of representational strategies, than for the *sui generis* affective power of the images created; photography, composition and rhythm are considered in great detail, and for the study of 'characters' proper, a focus on 'figures' has been largely substituted. In an article published during the recent celebrations of Friedrich Wilhelm Murnau's oeuvre, Tag Gallagher underlines the 'emotional intensification' effected by the combination of image and music in Murnau's work. *L'Aurore* is a 'revolution', Gallagher adds, in the way it transforms cinema from mere 'illustration' to 'experience' (Gallagher 2004: 91).

phenomenon characterised, in France, by its remarkable 'synchronicity' (Game 2001: 47) with the development of alternative filmmaking practices.

This synchronicity is not yet the rule, however; in the field of feature-film criticism, unconventional practices have not necessarily been met with enthusiasm. Grandrieux's mix of experimental and feature film aesthetics, for instance, though ground-breaking for some, has been dismissed as mere sensationalism by others.

> To many, the critical reception of *La Vie nouvelle*, which included contempt, sarcasms, insults and even defamatory comments, brought to mind the release of Renoir's film *La Règle du jeu* (1939). . . . . Even for those who had been passionate about Philippe Grandrieux's previous feature, *Sombre*, *La Vie nouvelle* represented an aesthetic shock, a qualitative leap, both deeply affecting and thought-provoking. . . . Only two journals defended the film: *Les Inrockuptibles* and *Trafic*. In France, a land held, since Denis Diderot (not to go further in time), as one of great critical tradition, and a country with a great love of cinema, this phenomenon is becoming ever more conspicuous and worrying: one after the other, important films get crushed against the wall of conventions and neglect. (Brenez 2005: 11)

As Brenez underlines, the reception of Grandrieux's film is symptomatic of a wider issue where the critical appraisal of cinema as an art of sensation is concerned. Because they play on the visceral impact of the medium, destabilising normal patterns of perception and distance, the majority of the films discussed in this book tread close to formal chaos and bodily abjection. This tendency has had one patent consequence in their critical evaluation; in recent French production, it is primarily the potential of certain films to shock that has drawn attention to them. In contrast, and against the lingering temptation to categorise, I would argue with Brenez that, even if part of recent French production does indeed exhibit a tendency towards shock for shock's sake, to focus on the sensationalist aspect, or to build it into the single common characteristic of French film works that foreground film's material dimension and sensuous value, is to miss out on the more significant achievement sought by the cinema of sensation. On the one hand, to insist on creating a separate category is to deny the possibility of looking at the films as being part of a continuum, where transgression operates at the level of the film form and manifests itself in terms of degree of intensity (of vision/affect). On the other hand, to concentrate and generalise on transgression at the representational level can lead to overlooking the transgressive dynamic that takes place at the level of the films' material appearance, permeating the very make-up of images and sound, without which they might indeed appear as meaningless exercises masquerading as subversive expression.

The cinema of sensation is an approach to filmmaking (and, by extension, to the analysis of film) that gives precedence to the corporeal, material dimension of the medium. In contemporary French film, the cinematographic exploration of a sensory, embodied comprehension of reality can take the form of a celebration of the sensual, reflexive bond of subjective body to objective world (*Nénette et Boni*, *Vendredi soir*, *Les Glaneurs et la glaneuse*, *Les Invisibles*, *Lady Chatterley*). It may also lead to the evocation, through graphic violence or sex, of a violently disjointed relationship between subject and object that quickly brings the cinematic experience into the realm of the abject (*Sombre*, *La Vie nouvelle*, *Trouble Every Day*, *Demonlover*, *Dans ma peau*, *Twentynine Palms*, *L'Humanité*). In the work of directors who wilfully engage with cinema as a cinema of the senses, successive films may explore both these dimensions; Denis is a point in case. Furthermore, in many of the films cited in this book, it is the journey from a sense of at-oneness with the world to a feeling of abject terror that comes into play (*La Blessure*, *Tiresia*, *Leçons de ténèbres*, *Flandres*). Indeed, a cinema of the senses always hovers at the edge of pleasure and abjection – between the appeal of a sensuous perception and exploration of the reality portrayed, and the close encounter with the abject, that is, the immersion in the anxiety of the self when individuality dissolves into the undifferentiated and formless. To single out the latter aspect is to give in to a tempting but expedient process of categorisation and deny the existence of a flow or continuum that accounts for our contradictory, fluctuating comprehension of the real. Yet, it is worth while considering and contextualising the arguments developed in the debate on contemporary French cinema and transgression, not only because they raise key ethical issues, but also because they implicitly demonstrate the need for alternative critical and theoretical approaches and, possibly, different viewing habits.

The Trouble with French Cinema: Film and Transgression

The silhouette of a young man leaning towards a young woman appears on the dark screen. They are lying in the back of a car, feebly lit by the blue-tinted glow of a streetlight seeping through the windscreen, and we can barely make out the outline of their faces in the shadowy surroundings. The sound of slow, soft drum beats rises expectantly, as if waiting for the scene to begin in earnest. The lovers' lips touch tentatively, then they start kissing. The music swells into a full melody, the melancholy tune of the piano mixing with the unmistakable moody voice of the *Tindersticks'* singer.

The first images of *Trouble Every Day* have all the ingredients of a romantic scene, the beginning of a love story. Yet, there is something distinctively eerie at work here, a sense of lurking dread that seems to seep from the dark edges of the frame into the picture.

The couple appears in medium close-up, shot through the window of a car, at a slightly raised angle, as if caught by the inquisitive eye of a hidden onlooker. The length of the take enhances the sense of a predatory, voyeuristic presence. As the lovers embrace, the camera gaze moves almost imperceptibly, following the hand of the young man as it covers the exposed flesh of the young woman's neck. Throughout the scene, the spectators finds themselves prying and guessing; more than the human shapes, it is the darkness that imposes its presence – a threatening, textured obscurity that eventually engulfs the lovers, the fade-in dragging the image seamlessly into the void. After a long passage to black, an image of sombre, softly rippling waters, shimmering with the yellowish reflection of streetlights, fills the screen. The following shots are of the bridges over the Seine. Captured in the purple light of dawn, under a dramatically cloudy sky, the views are at once familiar and strange; in *Trouble Every Day*, the 'city of light' is beset by shadows, endowed with an outlandish Gothic feel. The Parisian streets become the wandering grounds of a couple of monstrous lovers whose kisses irremediably turn into deadly bites.

Of the initial young couple, however, we will know nothing; their faces remain obscured and they will not appear again. Like the ghost of all cinematic love scenes, placed as they are at the edge of the film, their frame swallowed by darkness, these opening images function like a gateway between stories, a bridge between film worlds; the horror that lies in wait through Denis' images is the same horror that hides behind the most familiar of settings, in the world of the most innocuous comedy, lurking at the edges of the most reassuring of cinematic clichés. In *Trouble Every Day*, the sense of dread permeates the film, travels between the images and seeps into the frames insinuatingly until it explodes in periods of gore which draw the spectator into a sensation-filled audio-visual chaos.

Like the rest of Denis' fictional feature films, *Trouble Every Day* evokes the ambivalent relationship that modernity has developed with its 'other': the irrational, the disorderly, that which persists in the face of the dominance of the discourses on historical logic and scientific progress. At the same time, venturing as it does into the territories of the genres of excess to experiment with extreme sensory affect, however, the film acquires a particular resonance in the context of the debates on contemporary French cinema and transgression.

There is always something paradoxical and provoking in the return of sensation in art when it is considered in the historical context of a French culture known to be entrenched in Cartesian suspicion. Yet, such a shift arguably conjures up already deeply embedded cultural tensions, patterns of resistance whose resilience was always equal to the force of the rational models of thought. In Silverman's words, 'France epitomizes most clearly modernity's fundamental ambivalence':

> Modernism thrived on the transgression of boundaries – between order and disorder, between uniformity and heterogeneity, between the public and private spheres – and the confusion of distinct realms. Marginality, the transitory, diversity, imagination and desire – indeed, the whole panoply of 'dark' forces and processes which consti-tuted the otherness of rational order – were central to cultural modernism's challenge to the permanence and coherence of rationalized modern society. . . . From Baudelaire to surrealism and beyond, the fleeting and heterogeneous nature of modern everyday life was aestheticised and mythologised . . . inserting it within a different space, in which the boundaries between subjective desire and external 'reality', imagination and rational design, the psyche and the social, the unconscious and conscious are blurred. (Silverman 1999: 4)

Many of the directors whose work is discussed in this book have, at some point, claimed an affiliation with French traditions of counter-culture and described it as crucial to their approach to filmmaking. Olivier Assayas, for instance, playfully describes *Demonlover* as a 'Georges Bataille rewrite of a thriller' (Thompson 2004: 31) and further points out: 'In cinema, as well as artistically and intellectually, I come from a literary tradition in which Sade, Baudelaire, Bataille are essential references' (Guilloux 2002).

By the same token, that the experimentation with the physicality of film drives some of the filmmakers to borrow and subvert elements from genres that rely on sensory shock – namely, pornography and horror – is not new to French cinema. There is a long, established practice of mixing 'high' with 'low' forms of popular expression and, in particular, of bringing ele-ments of cinema's genres of 'excess' into French art film, and it has been considered customary for its directors to venture into such transgressive territories (Austin 1996: 46–7). As such, the late work of Breillat, Denis, Dumont, Grandrieux or de Van – to name but a few of the directors whose filmmaking looks towards pornography, horror or the violent thriller – does not establish a novel pattern but, on the contrary, arguably partakes in a long tradition of French artistic subversion (Powrie, forthcoming).

However, it is precisely the comparison with historical precedents that underpins the suspicion that many critics voice regarding the transgressive value of contemporary art and, more specifically here, of contemporary film works. In the domain of the arts in particular, the debates on the crisis of modernity's values are rendered more complex by the awareness that, within the postmodern reign of appearances and parody, oppositional stances are easily reduced to little more than empty posturing.[11] When they concern the French cultural scene, these questions retain an intensity that is partly rooted in the nostalgia for past and canonised movements of contestation. France is still held up as the cradle of authentic revolutionary spirit, heralded by those major artistic movements that challenged, again and again, well before 1789 and up to May 1968, the social, cultural and artistic establishment. In effect, the beginnings of cinema were contemporary with the activities of the surrealists and major figures of the so-called *Littérature maudite*. The new medium was claimed by the early avant-gardes as a favoured form for the expression of subversion and change. Constantly referred to and compared with these legendary early years, contemporary art cinema that crosses the boundaries of taste and the acceptable in aesthetic and/or thematic terms comes under fierce attack. Thus, for instance, Philippe Muray deplores and denounces what he assesses as a particularly striking display of hypocrisy at the heart of French cinema's recent output:

> Then it is against nothing and nobody that one directs one's attacks, building a rebellious discourse that will seem more infuriated than ever when there is nothing to it save from aping everything that became known as 'rebellious' or 'disturbing' in the previous decades. (Muray 2000: 133)

Characteristically, Muray dismisses present-day cinema's seemingly gratuitous exploitation of formal techniques and shock effects deployed to mask the void left by the disappearance of ideals and ideologies, and compares them to the (retrospectively) legitimated force of past artistic creations motivated by the belief in 'truly' oppositional principles.[12] Many observers similarly dismiss what they see as a contemporary formalist trend merely amounting to a new form of academism: a renunciation to be meaningful hidden behind, in the words of Muray, the 'recourse to the appalling sampling of formal and avant-gardist strategies used as blackmail' (Muray

---

[11] Max Silverman draws on Baudrillard's theorisation of the 'total appropriation of the real by the spectacle and, consequently, the end of all possibility of transgression and subversion', and sums up the issue:

> If this is indeed the case, then we must agree that culture is no longer propelled by a concept of *le beau*, or by a concept of critical engagement with and subversion of the status quo, but simply by the criteria of sensation, pleasure, entertainment and leisure, and driven ultimately by market forces. (Silverman 1999: 121)

[12] See also Berenice Reynaud's comments in connection with *Baise-moi* (Reynaud 2002).

2000: 127). Similarly, art critic James Quandt denounces it as a collective, largely empty gesture, where an array of shock effects and a mannerist tendency for quotation[13] merely disguise an ideological void and a 'failure of both imagination and morality' (Quandt 2004). In effect, Quandt's eloquently entitled article, 'Flesh and blood: sex and violence in recent French cinema', offers a particularly convincing, as well as representative, example of the critical argument bent on dismissing the more 'excessive' aspects of contemporary French cinema as a tactical mistake. In a pervasive and damning appraisal of some of the recent French art-cinema productions, Quandt derides the pursuit of an art cinema unable to emulate the achievements of past, leading counter-culture figures, yet wilfully bent on exploiting those shock tactics traditionally associated with gore, porn and horror productions:

> The critic truffle-snuffling for trends might call it the New French Extremity, this recent tendency to the wilfully transgressive by directors like François Ozon, Gaspar Noé, Catherine Breillat, Philippe Grandrieux – and now, alas, Dumont. Bava as much as Bataille, *Salò* no less than Sade, seem the determinants of a cinema suddenly determined to break every taboo, to wade in rivers of viscera and spumes of sperm, to fill each frame with flesh, nubile or gnarled, and subject it to all manner of penetration, mutilation, and defilement. (Quandt 2004)

While grouping together a number of films[14] on the basis of their emulation of the 'excess' of popular genres like pornography and gore, Quandt also reminds us of the specificity of the national-historical context. Underpinning his argument is the conviction that such cinema amounts to a failure to form an artistic movement proper and to uphold the examples of the past:

> Images and subjects once the provenance of splatter films, exploitation flicks, and porn – gang rapes, bashings and slashings and blindings, hard-ons and vulvas, cannibalism, sadomasochism and incest, fucking and fisting, sluices of cum and gore – proliferate in the high-art environs of a national cinema whose provocations have

[13] As mentioned before, there is no denying that part of French film production seems bent on exploiting shock for shock's sake and formal experimentation as an end in itself. Certain films arguably stand as better examples than others of such a tendency to affectation and self-conscious reflexivity. Though not amongst the works discussed in Quandt's article, for instance, C. S. Leigh's *Process*, released in 2004 and starring Béatrice Dalle and Guillaume Depardieu, seems a point in case. An exercise in visual and thematic citation, it chronicles a woman's journey of self-destruction through a series of mannered *mise en scènes* inspired by performance art. In a radically different style, Gaspar Noé's *Irréversible* arguably harnesses an absence of substance to a display of technical virtuosity.

[14] Although he denounces the opportunistic tendency of the critic to create convenient new categories and designations, the author nevertheless follows suit.

historically been formal, political or philosophical or, at their most immoderate, at least assimilable as emanations of an artistic movement (Surrealism mostly) . . . [Hence] one begins to suspect a deeper impulse at work: a narcissistic response to the collapse of ideology in a society traditionally defined by political polarity and theoretical certitude, perhaps. (Quandt 2004)

As could be expected, *Trouble Every Day*, with its graphic scenes of violence and sex, is amongst the films that Quandt wholeheartedly rejects. He sums up the film as 'a horror show in which Béatrice Dalle is cast for her ravenous mouth as Coré, a cannibal sated only when she consumes the bodies of her hapless lovers', and further remarks 'An enervated Denis barely musters a hint of narrative to contain or explain the orgiastic blood-letting' (Quandt 2004). Beyond the issue of taste and the debate about the film's qualities, these comments are revealing about our general expectations where art cinema and transgression are concerned.

Quandt's brief account of the film is characteristic of the critical reception that met *Trouble Every Day* on its release.[15] Newspaper reviews abounded, gleefully recounting the film's première in Cannes, where members of the public allegedly fainted or, seized by nausea, had to leave the cinema. In the end, however, the descriptions give much prominence to the film's two or three scenes of graphic horror, each lasting a few minutes, within a one-and-a-half-hour feature that is indeed filled with sensation-saturated images and sound-track, but is also characterised by its melancholic tone, slow rhythm and contemplative mood. For all the force of their impact, the scenes of cannibalistic killings that drew so much attention are not meant to emulate the strategies of successful horror or gore features (that rely on the sheer accumulation, variety and flamboyance of gory effects to captivate their amateurs). Like many of the films mentioned before, and in spite of its knowing reworking of the conventions and traditions of specific genres, Denis' is a film of 'terror' rather than a horror or gore feature, a work that elaborates an aesthetic of dread or angst rather than one of systematic, plethoric shock and disgust (Beugnet 2004b: 169). Paradoxically, then, what the responses to a film such as *Trouble Every Day* suggest is that it is less the 'gore' effects in themselves which attract disapproval than the fact that neither the filmmaker, nor the film itself, can be fully assimilated into the generic terms and categories that the film evokes. In other words, the film sits awkwardly at the crossroads between art and popular cinema; there is either too much or not enough gore.

---

[15] As with many features of atypical calibre, *Les Inrockuptibles* was an exception in point and presented a more nuanced and positive appraisal of the feature. See, for instance, Kaganski, Serge, Frédéric Bonnaud (2001), '*Trouble Every Day*', *Les Inrockuptibles*, 3 July, pp. 32–5.

Moreover, not only does the film eschew the self-justifying ironical mode now prevalent in commercial horror and gore; neither do the slow-paced, elusive story-lines that eventually lead to the sudden outburst of horror provide the clear, causal justifications and denials that might be expected to legitimate the intrusion of extreme effects.

> Alone or in combination, heavy doses of sex, violence and emotion are dismissed by one faction or another as having no logic or reason for existence beyond their power to excite. Gratuitous sex, gratuitous violence and terror, gratuitous emotion are frequent epithets hurled at the phenomenon of the 'sensational' in pornography, horror, and melodrama. (Williams 1991: 3)

If such are the accusations generally levelled at the 'lowly' cinematic genres, the expectations we have of art cinema make our acceptance of shock effects even more problematic. Whereas Linda Williams seeks to unearth the 'system and structure' at work in the so-called genres 'of excess', here, as well as more specifically in my exploration of the effect of horror in *Trouble Every Day*, I am interested in the affective and aesthetic force of shock, of which gratuity – that is, the absence of narrative or psychological function proper – is an essential element.

As a rule, then, effects that are anticipated – and as such, even if they are not appreciated or condoned, are at least 'accepted' as generic conventions in a feature marketed as violent thriller, horror or porn film – must be warranted by clear ethical and moral choices in an art film. Furthermore, whereas 'Pornography finds its justification in the authenticity of the filmed performance [and] gore, on the contrary, finds its justification in its artificiality' (Rouyer 1997: 179), art cinema traditionally draws its legitimacy from a recognised ability to balance stylisation with representation mediated by a critical vision.[16] Narrative construct and characterisation, thus, generally become useful crutches, allowing for the integration of unusual formal techniques and sensory effects within a more distanced framework that can be, in turn, more easily identified in terms of underlying message or referred to an underpinning discursive strategy.[17]

---

[16] Where a film establishes itself as a feature-length work of fiction, this also adds to the expectations in terms of narrative and exposition; according to common conventions, only those films which are securely identified as experimental or pornographic (generally, short films or films that are not screened in cinemas) do away completely with the task of constructing a story.

[17] Conversely, Philippe Rouyer draws a parallel between the strategies at work in gore and pornographic genres, and stresses how the systematic focus on the body and the accumulation of shock effects explain the perfunctory role played by the narrative dimension of the films:

> In both genres, this focalisation on the body leads to a de-humanising of the characters that has some narrative implications. The obsession of penetration (with a sex organ or

In art cinema, a relay of discourse and narrative is thus expected to over-rule or at least counterbalance the presence of graphic sex and violence – and all the more so because visceral effects are commonly construed as detrimental to the viewer's interpretative or analytical appraisal of what is being presented to him or her. Hence, in the absence of a clear contextual-isation, ambivalence surfaces, attracting accusations of gratuitous sensa-tionalism and political incorrectness. In this context, Quandt's annoyance at the lack of proper narrative structure in Denis' film is more easily under-stood.[18] Moreover, in Denis' case, previous features had offered subtle and cogent critical visions of the roots of the contemporary French *malaise*, exploring in particular the lingering, alienating effects of the colonial past on contemporary French society (Beugnet 2004b). Thanks to the direc-tor's renewed engagement with formal experimentation, however, the crit-ical element of discourse, already implied rather than exposed in her other works, becomes inseparable from and woven through formal strategies that render the task of deciphering it more complex. The absence of a sub-stantial narrative structure and psychological markers is, then, interpreted as being a step too far towards the popular sub-genre conventions, a sign of an incapacity to rise above mere sensationalism. The suspicion is that, with a film like *Trouble Every Day*, the rich intertextual dimension, the heightened effects produced by the film's distinctive aesthetic vision and the recourse to strong sensory affects are but ways of masking the failure to construct a meaningful commentary about one's world – arguably, a weakness further confirmed by the film's inability to offer more than a shadow of a plot-line.

More sensitive than Quandt to the work's outlandish atmosphere, Prédal suggests it is possible to appreciate as a primarily aesthetic and sensual experience a film that unravels as if 'Claire Denis had decided to leave sense and story line aside in order to stay with the inexplicable horror of purely audio-visual sensations' (Prédal 2002: 155).

Hence, my somewhat trite remarks about shock effects and art cinema lead to an equally evident yet more implied set of assumptions. Implicit in

a weapon) means the creation of an unreal universe where all action leads inexorably to pleasure or to death. The plot, limited to a vague pretext, sometimes merely functions as a transition, to give the spectator a breather in between two scenes with shock effects (pornography or blood bath). (Rouyer 1997: 179)

[18] A similar critique is regularly applied to Denis' subsequent features. A journalist of the *Cahiers du cinéma* thus remarks: 'What is surprising, in *Vendredi soir*, is the great gap between the sumptuousness of the *mise en scène* and the extreme barrenness of the plot' (Blouin et al. 2002: 13).

the comments cited above is the presumption that, whether as affective or aesthetic events, the elements of shock – the blood, the 'rivers of viscera and spumes of sperm' in all their baroque audio-visual excess – can yield little or no subversive and critical value. Yet, I would argue that in *Trouble Every Day*, for instance, it is precisely the breakdown of a linear narrative logic and the impossibility of fully harnessing the shock effects to such a causal chain that give them both affective power and critical edge. I would contend that Denis' film demonstrates how shock and 'excess' – the 'orgiastic bloodletting' – need not be a system and an end in themselves (as in genre movies) nor merely one aspect of a pre-existing discursive strategy (as in traditional art movies). Here, horror operates as a gateway; it grows in the interstices, creating connections between the plane of sensation and that of interpretation. It is in the gratuitous or 'surplus' nature of the vision, in its beholding of the forces of chaos, and in the way it engages us emotionally as well as aesthetically with the irrational and unacceptable, that the critical edge lies (Bataille 1988: 106). In fact, I would suggest that, even in this context of 'extreme' cinema, Deleuze's description of the journey from the action-image regime to that of the time-image has an indisputable resonance:

> In the old realism or on the model of the action-image, objects and settings already had a reality of their own, but it was a functional reality, strictly determined by the demands of the situation, even if these demands were as much poetic as dramatic . . . [on the contrary, when] objects and settings [*milieux*] take on an autonomous material reality . . . the situation is not extended directly into action: it is no longer sensory-motor, as in realism, but primarily optical and of sound, invested by the senses, before action takes shape in it, and uses or confronts its elements . . . between the reality of the setting and that of the action, it is no longer a motor extension which is established, but rather a dreamlike connection through the intermediary of the liberated sense organs. (Deleuze 1989: 4)

However, to allow for what Deleuze calls our 'subjective sympathy for the unbearable' (1989: 18) to come through, a specific type of viewing experience and analytical approach may be required, one that focuses less on the film's representational dimension and narrative structure in order to allow for an empathetic reaction to moods and sensory correspondences and their implications instead. In her study of horror, Anne Powell accordingly draws on Deleuzean aesthetics, and on the concept of affection-image, to approach the issue of shock effects from a non-sensationalist angle:

> Certain films include aesthetic effects divorced from the immediate causal chain. When a pure optical and sound situation occurs, it 'makes us grasp something intolerable and

unbearable'. For Deleuze, the extreme reaction induced by the affection image is more potent than the explicit violence of the action image . . . The affection image 'is a matter of something too powerful, or too unjust, but sometimes also too beautiful, and which outstrips our sensory-motor capacities'. As the sensory-motor function is suspended or breaks down, deeper insight occurs. (Deleuze 1989: 16; cited in Powell 2005: 119)

Horror that Sticks: *Trouble Every Day*

Like most of Denis' films, *Trouble Every Day* (2001) has an elliptical narrative structure which is built around a constellation of characters and the criss-crossing of their trajectories (and, like the other brief synopses given in this book, the summary below, though it provides the analysis that follows with useful short-cuts, inevitably fails to encapsulate the film's enigmatic dimension). American Shane Brown (Vincent Gallo) and Frenchman Léo Semeneau (Alex Descas) are both neuroscientists. Like Semeneau's wife Coré (Béatrice Dalle), Shane is beset by a monstrous illness, consumed by deadly sexual urges which turn him, like her, into a blood-thirsty killer. Shane and Semeneau once worked on similar research projects using the flora of French Guiana. The American's craving for recognition, however, led him to steal Semeneau's work and experiment with it. Plagued with the horrific consequences of the disease that is colonising his body and mind, he comes to Paris to seek Semeneau's help.

More than any of Denis' previous features, this film is a hybrid, a work whose densely intertextual quality signals a space of multiple becomings. For Deleuze and Guattari, 'becoming' is a state of in-between-ness, a process of metamorphosis, visible or invisible, that affects all forms of exis tence (Deleuze and Guattari 1987: 272). (I will come back to this in more detail in Chapter 3.) In Denis' work, it manifests itself in the make-up of the characters and diegetic space, as well as in the mutating film form in itself:

> Something profoundly amphibious characterises Denis' cinema. It is made from the point of view of women as well as men, from the point of view of the predators as well as from that of the prey, from here (France, with its freestone suburban villas, the Paris of Fantômas and Belphégor) and from elsewhere (the international dimension, Abel Ferrara, Hong Kong). It crosses genre (gore, horror, fantasy), genders (man/woman, animal/human) and does not settle anywhere. (Lalanne 2001: 24)

While its characters find it impossible to revert to an earlier state of existence, one where they could safely reconnect sensation and desire with love and affection rather than destruction, so too is the film's rich intertext acting as a wistful reminiscence, conjuring up some of the originary ghosts of cinema – the worlds and creatures of Gothic horror, Expressionism, Franju, Tourneur . . .). Before it is a film of horror or terror, *Trouble Every Day* is, like the eponymous song that haunts its sound-track, a film of melancholy. Creating an affective bridge between spectator and film world, the melancholy is a seductive, enfolding feeling, one that oozes from the exquisite photography and evocative sound-track and grows from the multiplication of possibilities suggested by the loose narrative threads.

Aesthetically, Denis' film is a work of fluctuation or, in Chauvin's words, a work of 'wandering-infiltration'. The editing weaves together sound-track and images so as to create variations in speed and slowness, distance and closeness, precision and formlessness. From stasis (Coré imprisoned in her room; Shane locked in the plane cabin) to movement (Shane and Coré roaming through the streets of Paris at night); from the exact ticking of rotating machinery to the horrific, inchoate noise of a victim's agonised cries; from the enigmatic call of a few, isolated electro-chords to the swelling, haunting melodies that unravel even as carnage takes over the screen; from the sterile order of the laboratories to the baroque chaos bred by monstrosity, vision and sound are far and intimate, tactile and distant, and the film drifts from one effect to the other, operating a series of passages as in a constant process of mutation.

Coré and Shane bear external signs of their 'becoming' from the start. These are inscribed on their body, in their features (and Denis does indeed play on the unusual looks of both Dalle and Gallo), and contradict the elements of social identity that define the characters as loving husband/wife or scientific specialist. Established generic clichés are thus recuperated and reworked into a 'becoming': not a copying or a pure transformation but, rather, a kind of morphing. In effect, like the virus that spreads into their very being, as they move through the body of the film, these two monstrous figures remain recognisable, yet they alter as if through a chemical reaction, just as their presence has a physical effect on the material appearance of a sequence.

For a brief instant, it seems we are looking at ('touching' with our eyes) the uneven surface of skin caught in extreme close-up; it is in fact (or, rather, it is also) a section of the wasteland close to the Parisian *périphérique* that we see, transformed into an outlandish expanse, a strange savannah bathed in the orange glow of tungsten lamps. Hidden in tall grass dripping with blood, Coré crouches like a wild beast. Or, a few sequences later: exposed to the crude light of the medical laboratories, Shane's face distorts; as he flies away from the place, the gaze of the camera catches his silhouette through the window, glimpsing it through the glass as if he were but one of the strange organic samples kept in the laboratory's glass vials.

The series of scenes that originally introduce this character similarly typify the sensuous and affective fluctuations that the film's assemblage of sequences effects. The first images are of perfect marital bliss: the young American couple, en route to Paris for their honeymoon, initially appears as in an old-fashioned cameo painting, framed by the soft edges of a plane porthole, and is then seen from within the plane cabin, engaged in a tender exchange of love vows. There is an intriguing cutaway in the midst of these shots, however: an abstract composition in a series of tiny dots, forming straight, geometrical patterns on a black background. Leaning over to look through the porthole, the young woman aptly compares this aerial view of the city of Denver to a 'computer chip' – the very image of modernity as controlled urban space.

Hence, it is not merely the clichés, but also vision as disengaged abstraction, that are destroyed in the subsequent shots, together with the safe distance that both initially establish. The atmosphere and visual economy instituted by the images are first discreetly offset by the presence of a camera that lingers too close, as if preying on the couple's intimacy, then violently disturbed in the passage to the horror and visual overflow of the dream sequence that follows. As the passengers drift into sleep in the dim, bluish glow of the plane cabin, Shane leaves his seat to seek refuge in the narrow confines of the toilet compartment. As an echo to the abstract motif of the aerial view, the familiar door sign, with its small pictogram of a woman and a man, lights up as he locks himself in. From the image of the young man crouching on the floor, the scene abruptly cuts to a close-up of a hand smeared in blood. Its caressing motion, mimicked by the camera's slow movement, renders the sight even more disconcerting. The vision remains obscure throughout and difficult to locate; at first, the images' slight throb and the sound of the plane engine, which bleeds over before turning into a higher-pitched hum, spatially connect it to the previous scene. But the gory composition that fills the frame yields no perspective or element of context, and the denial of depth and distance, as well as the intensely tactile quality of the photography, immediately undermine the possibility of detachment from these images. There is a wilfully Bataillean feel about them, in the merger between the horrific, the sensual and the sacrificial that they evoke: 'The lover annihilates the loved woman no less than the sacrificer annihilates the man or animal he immolates' (Bataille 1957: 100). In the dreadful images that follow, we recognise the face of the young wife, covered in blood yet looking back trustingly as the camera, mirroring the movement of a lover, lowers slowly towards her. In a subsequent shot, the camera follows the outline of her back, wrapped in a blood-soaked sheet. The shape of the body disappears in the meandering folds of the fabric, the gaze losing itself in their awful glistening wetness. A brief insert of the face in close-up deepens the sense of spatial confusion. In the last shot, the camera draws away, looking down at the young woman smiling peacefully with her eyes closed. Douglas Morrey compares the fascination for fabric displayed in several of the film's scenes with Deleuze's notion of the fold in Baroque art.

> Here again, the interest lies less in the narrative meaning of the fantasy . . . or even in its status as a fantasy, than in the sensuality of the image . . . This predilection for the pleats and wrinkles of tissue and fabric may be interpreted, I suggest, through an appeal to Deleuze's notion of the fold in his study of the Baroque. Following Leibnitz, Deleuze argues that matter is infinitely divisible, but not in discrete points on a linear scale: rather, matter divides into folds within folds . . . since each fold is the site of a nomad expressing a unique point of view on the world, or, better, the condition under which a subject may come to invest and actualise such a point of view. (Deleuze 1988: 7–9; cited by Morrey 2004)

From the composition of the images and sound-track to the rhythm and temporal variations of the sequences, the passage from optical perception at its most distanced and ordered to horror's baroque sensuality and haptic commotion founds the film's very make-up. Crucially, the two forms of vision are not merely opposed here; chaos is at the very heart of order.

In several instances, the film takes us into the sanitised space of scientific laboratories. The stereotypical opposition between the neon-lit, ordered cleanliness of these controlled, specialised environments and the sense of dreadful sensuality induced by the confusion and excessive violence of the horror scenes is heightened to the extreme. By focusing on inanimate objects and empty spaces, the photography creates a void in the middle of the image, pulling, as in the effect of *décadrage*, the gaze towards the edges of the frame, where chaos might be lurking. The systematic decentring of the human figure enhances the barrenness of the sets, and the horror filters in as if to fill the emptiness (Bonitzer 2001: 126; Beugnet 2004b: 169 and 172).

With the insertion of a microscopic point of view, the preamble to the first laboratory scene creates a multiplicity of connections within and beyond the film's own visual and temporal field. The image is one amongst a series of references to the matrix of all vampire movies: *Nosferatu*. In its play on scale and vision, and the transition from molar to molecular perception that it effects, however, it suggests a connection at the level of the image matter itself – as if, in a proliferation of cells, one film had grown out of the other. The microscopic picture, however, also comes as a counterpart to the brief cutaway to the aerial view previously described, and its likeness to a computer chip. The first shot is of a brain plunged in formaldehyde. The following images, set within the sterile-looking surroundings of a lab, show gloved hands neatly cutting through a slice of brain matter, arranging the pieces on a white slab with professional meticulousness. In the next sequence, a white-clad neuroscientist reaffirms the superiority of scientific investigation: 'We have been mapping out the human brain for years on end.' Under the lens of the microscope, however, the organic messiness overrules; like the aerial view of a planet, the brain cell shows the complexity and disorderly patterns of rivers and continent-like motifs. A similar effect takes place in one of the murder scenes (to which I will come back in Chapter 3), where the skin of a young man, scrutinised in extreme close-up by the camera, turns into a landscape or a constellation of planets.

Although in the following sequences exchanges take place between key characters, the frame at first excludes the human figure. Long, static shots of a glass bowl with a rotating mixer fill the screen. While the dialogues unravel off screen, the endless circular movement of the blender and its regular ticking noise impose their mechanical rhythm on the scene. When the scientist stops the machine, the conversation also comes to an end.

The neat regularity of the device encapsulates the denial of what the film, in its very material appearance and form – with its loose, peripatetic unravelling, its abrupt changes of rhythms and moods, and its brutal explosions of gore – helps bring to the surface again and again: the erratic, 'the contingent and the accidental – the historical in a word' (Ross 1999: 196). Hence, an aesthetic consideration of the film suggests that there is more to *Trouble Every Day* than the contemporary reworking of the rational/irrational opposition that is at the heart of the horror genre. Like in all fine horror, shock is the gateway between the plane of sensation and that of discourse.[19] In effect, connecting the film with Denis' previous works, the after-effect of France's colonial past is a discreet but key motif here; it is in Guiana that Brown, tempted by fame and profit, first experiments with a deadly virus. The illness that triggers the killings, and which seems to weave itself into the texture of the film just as it colonises the body of its characters, was thus brought back from a former French colony.

In her compelling account of the transformation of French society following the loss of its colonial status, Kristin Ross describes the speeded metamorphosis, shaped on the American model, from a 'rural, empire-oriented Catholic country into a fully industrialised, decolonized, and urban one'. In Ross's analysis, two connected facets of the mutation stand

---

[19] See, for instance, Jean-Marie Samocki's 1999 article on G.A. Romero's films: 'Du cannibale: un précis de décomposition', *Simulacres* 1, pp. 35–44.

out: the new cult of cleanliness and the safe relegation of its colonial history to the past. 'A dominant contemporary French perspective holds its colonial past to be an "exterior" experience, added on but not essential to French historical identity – an episode that ended, cleanly, in 1962.' Ross calls on Roland Barthes' commentary to underline how this process of separation went hand in hand with a new-found obsession with cleanliness: 'Decay is being expelled (from the teeth, the skin, the blood, the breath): France is forming a great craving for cleanliness' (Barthes 1957; cited in Ross 1999: 72).

In *Trouble Every Day*, the element of chaos, which destabilises vision, stirs up and deregulates the narrative thread and brings about the horror, is related to the archetypal, primeval nature of human desire, but also to closer historical realities caught in the (impossible) process of erasure. Whilst, in dialogues, the reality of the colonial past disappears behind discourses on profit and scientific progress, cleanliness appears an important and recurrent motif in the film; it weaves itself through the film's multiple narrative threads, from the cleaning of blood after the murders, to the tedium of the maid's job, as she tidies up room after room in the hotel where the Browns have settled, to the pristine and sterile environment of the laboratories. But the stain cannot be washed away for long, any more than the unravelling of time (historical time as well as filmic time) can ever be fully disciplined (into mechanical movement or into a neat linear historical or filmic narrative) and controlled. Here, horror, in all its dreadful sensuality and its messiness, is the event that prevents the relegation of the 'contingent and the accidental – the historical in a word – to the exterior' (Ross 1999: 196).

Ultimately, the horror in *Trouble Every Day*, as in the other films discussed in this book that use graphic violence, is like the horror that fills the media every day and soils our present and past history (collective or individual); it is the unbearable that cannot be wished away. In works like *Trouble Every Day*, *Sombre*, *La Vie nouvelle* or *Demonlover*, the violence is maybe better grasped in terms such as those used by Bataille to describe what he calls the '*part maudite*' – the 'accursed share' (Bataille [1949] 1988). The brutality of the vision presented by these works is not made 'better' with explanations and justifications; even if it offers a context, evokes the roots of a certain violence, it is a horror that denies the kind of functional-moral use that customarily befalls it in mainstream narratives. Hence, within the melancholy that imbues the world of Denis' film, the horror is simply the irreducible echo of the inexcusable suffering that takes place in our reality, the manifestation of that which remains in 'excess' of historical and moral reasoning.

The ambiguity of horror is that it lodges itself between two planes, that of pure sensation and that of discourse, maintaining the link between the two through the variations in rhythm and visual regimes that it effects, 'thinking' its way through binary oppositions, disrupting them, reconnecting the disconnected. What this brief exploration of *Trouble Every Day* suggests, then, is that where cinema becomes a cinema of sensation, the techniques and aesthetic choices can no more be reduced to generic determinants than their implications (and, by extension, the appraisal of the film in critical, ideological or moral terms) can be anticipated without emptying the film of its depth and meaning. The film exists first and foremost as an affective, sensory experience and its material form is the foundation as well as the vector of its signification.

Pornocracies: *Romance, À ma sœur, Baise-moi*

Few thinkers have upheld more adamantly than Georges Bataille the irreducible value of the wasteful, the non-productive and non-recuperable. In a post-capitalist world that seems entirely permeated and ruled by the laws of market and production, and where the female body in particular remains caught in a web of powerful production/exploitation forces, Bataille's theories acquire a particular resonance. Indeed, where the cinema of sensation is concerned, his ideas often help to move beyond allegations of empty sensationalism and see the pertinence of some of the more perplexing and disturbing visions offered by the films.

Thierry Jousse summarises the premise of Breillat's *Romance* (1998) as follows: 'What is the connection between the head and the sex, the face and the hole, the animal and the spiritual?' (Jousse 1999: 41). The increasing presence of graphic sex and violence in recent French cinema has gone hand in hand with the emergence of female figures who baffle common feminist understanding; in Catherine Breillat's work, as in Despentes and Trinh Thi's film, female characters defy the usual patterns of 'progressive' gender portrayals and have generated highly polarised debates. As Jousse's outline emphasises, it is the appropriation of themes and techniques generally associated with pornography that earned *Romance* its initial publicity. In itself, however, the way the critic phrases the question already makes Breillat's subversion of the pornographic vision implicit. The filmmaker uses the close-up in particular (an approach that will be discussed again in Chapter 3) – and often in a humorous way – to mark out the equivocal nature of human existence, torn between the rational and the animal. 'This face cannot possibly be connected to this cunt,' remarks Breillat's young heroine (Caroline Dulcey) while looking at reflections of her face and body.

Yet, even where the close-up fragments, the continuing flow of her voiceover commentary reconnects the parts. At the same time, however, her monologue makes no pretence of being informative or truthful, and takes the form of a meandering stream of consciousness, mingling clichés with contradictory assessments. Similarly, the close-up images of the young woman's body do not yield the investigative, unveiling thrust that characterises the pornographic image. Yann Lardeau talks of pornography's 'obsession with truth, with knowing everything . . . Hence the fascination that filmmakers have for female genitalia: this void, this nothingness . . . this presage of death . . . that must be covered with signs, with markers, so as to erase the threat' (Lardeau 2001: 140). With the meticulous composition of its close-up images, including images of female genitalia, its emphasis on the tactile, in-depth textures and fluids, Breillat's filmmaking directly addresses and demystifies not only the kind of clichéd perceptions of the feminine epitomised in pornography, but also conventional definitions of the female as abject as well as stereotypical notions of femininity as mystery. In so doing, the film debunks such representations of the female body that are as familiar as they are contradictory: a series of holes to be filled, an idealised object of desire or a medical object to be investigated. As the film itself moves through genres and registers, from the baroque *mise en scène* of erotic fantasies to the stylised and sanitised medical and domestic environments and the crude naturalism of documentary-like sequences, the body is shown as a body in the making, subjected to material and imaginary processes of metamorphosis, caught between the discursive (molar) forces that define and categorise and the material (molecular) process of 'becoming'.

In *À ma sœur* (2000), as in *Romance*, both films that feature sexual assault on a woman, the apparent 'passivity' of the female characters is, at first, deeply confusing. In the second instance, however, and even if the outcome arrives at the end of a complex exploration of the ambiguities of female desire (caught as it is in a web of social, cultural and economic determinants), the main character literally obliterates the young man who was the original source of her constant frustration and humiliation. At the end of *À ma sœur* on the other hand, the young Anaïs (Anaïs Reboux), who has been raped, insists that she knowingly submitted to this experience. Yet, this is not mere provocation on the part of the filmmaker; on the contrary. Through the main part of the film, which unravels like a slowed-down, out-of-sync version of a teen movie, Anaïs has been observing the ineluctable process whereby her (beautiful) sister Elena (Roxane Mesquida) is caught in all the stereotypical (social and cultural) trappings of romance. Led to subject herself wilfully to the 'loss' of her virginity, Elena becomes a typical victim of the understated, routine violence of heterosexual seduction.[20] The end of the film is thus as 'gratuitous' as it is meaningful, its sudden switch from teen movie to horror effecting the same radical disruption that the documentary footage of the birth sequence operates in *Romance* (see Chapter 2). Coming after the social 'taming' of her sister, Anaïs's own experience is but a manifestation of sexual economy's 'accursed share', with all the unfunctional, irrecoverable violence and excess that it implies. In assuming her experience as such, the young girl arguably reaches, as Maddock and Krisjansen propose, a state of 'sovereignty' that is further echoed in the film's denial of the kind of 'useful purpose' found in the 'educational', morally acceptable entertainment of conventional coming-of-age tales: 'What is the significance of the expression of sovereignty to *À ma sœur?* It is a significance that lies precisely in its particular preoccupation . . . saving this cinema from ever pursuing a useful purpose' (Maddock and Krisjansen 2003: 170).

In common with Breillat's characters, the trajectory of the heroines of Despentes and Trihn Thi's *Baise-moi* (2000) eschews rationalisation. Their actions do not appear calculated towards a social, moral, economic or cultural gain. Indeed, by confounding even the patterns of revenge that its rape-revenge premise called for, the explosion of brutality and the presence of graphic sex earned the film accusations of meaningless sensationalism. Yet, the film's critical edge lies precisely in its celebration of the non-utilitarian value of a chosen course that, in all the unbridled excess of its violence and sexual shamelessness, corresponds to Bataille's description of sovereignty: the enjoyment of 'the present time without having anything else in view but this present time' (Bataille [1949] 1988: 199).

'Hard-core', 'punk', 'electrifying'; an 'exuberant embodiment of excess' (Le Cain 2002); a film 'about girls having fun with sex and being able to laugh about it' (Vincendeau 2002: 38) or one with 'a sloppy *mise en scène* and nonchalantly written scenario' [that has] 'given feminist filmmaking a bad name' (Reynaud 2002) – in terms of polarised responses and controversy, *Baise-moi* is at least on a par with *Trouble Every Day*. The film, which contains graphic violence as well as sex, is a collaboration between writer Virginie Despentes (once a porn-shop assistant) and porn actress Coralie Trihn Thi, and its cast includes actresses who worked in pornography in leading roles. At its Cannes première, the film was received with

---

[20] Breillat's treatment of romance recalls the critique of romantic love as ideology found in the writings of feminist thinkers from Simone de Beauvoir to Shulamith Firestone, and classically summed up by Rainer Werner Fassbinder: 'Love is the best, most insidious, most effective instrument of social repression' (Fassbinder (1975), 'Six Films by Douglas Sirk', *New Left Review* 91, p. 92).

consternation, and for its general release, *Baise-moi* was initially granted an X certificate. Following the launch of a successful petition (headed by Catherine Breillat), however, it was later re-released under an 18 certificate.

Baise-moi follows the destinies of two young women – Manu (Raphaëlla Anderson) and Nadine (Karen Bach) – who are both initially involved in prostitution, then launch themselves into a murderous and sexual rampage: an ultimately suicidal run during which they develop a strong bond. The film recalls many other killing spree road movies and, indeed, makes knowing references to a series of cult films of the genre.[21] This self-referentiality, as well as the way the film constructs femininity as a constantly reiterated performance, has been discussed at length.[22] I am not going to engage with these already, often cogently, argued aspects of the film; it is to the effect of the film's 'molecular' aesthetics that I will turn.

Though the constantly expanding range of aesthetic potential offered in High-Definition Digital recording has become impressive, it is the 'dirty' look of the traditional format that *Baise-moi* exploits. Hence, if the film thus seems peculiarly out of sync with its own set of references – violent but stylised thrillers, rape-revenge films and road movies – it is because it was shot on characteristically low-budget, grainy video.

> The difference from Tarantino lies in the realism of the world they occupy. It is not stylised, postmodern genre playground . . . If *Baise-moi* was made on a larger budget with glossy techniques and an artificial look, it simply would not work. In fact, it would appear hideously gratuitous and self-indulgent. (Le Cain 2002)

As Le Cain's remark suggests, video is the format which does justice to the world that *Baise-moi* depicts, the world of the housing estates, of the poorest and most disenfranchised. But there is an additional dimension to the aesthetics of the digital video image, one that further accounts for its specific evocative power and its capacity to make the film event into more than a metaphorical or postmodern-reflexive exercise. *Baise-moi*'s images often lack sharpness and bear the distinctive grey-brown skin-tones and overall greyness or beigeness characteristic of the digital video mode.

---

[21] In particular, it was compared to, and/or includes quotes from, Gaspar Noé's *Seul contre tous* (1998), Quentin Tarantino's *Pulp Fiction* (1994), Ridley Scott's *Thelma and Louise* (1991) and Luc Besson's *Nikita* (1990).

[22] See, amongst other texts: Downing, Lisa (2004), 'French cinema's new "sexual revolution": Postmodern porn and troubled genre', *French Cultural Studies* 15:3, pp. 265–80; Camy, Gérard, Albert Montagne (2002), 'Baise-moi', *CinémAction* 103, pp. 217–22; Joyard, Olivier (2000), 'X, le retour', *Cahiers du cinéma* 548, pp. 16–17; Williams, Linda (2001),'Sick sisters', *Sight & Sound* 11:7, pp. 28–9.

Although the digital mode is based on encoding and not on impression, in this case, it is as if the video's porous surface has absorbed the grime and bleakness of the world it describes. This 'unclean' look is also what accounts for the video image's specific tactility, however; it is not from its content that it draws its typically tactile quality, but from its (skin-like) surface. Marks distinguishes between the effect of high-resolution film, where (as in Breillat's *Romance*) a wealth of content details and the high concentration of the textures and hues reproduced can create a tactile effect, and that of video's low density:

> Another source of video's tactile, or at least insufficiently visual qualities is its pixel density and contrast ratio . . . Graininess certainly produces a tactile quality, as the eye may choose between concentrating on figures and ignoring the points that make them up, or bracketing the figures and dissolving the points. (Marks 2000: 175)

Hence, video does not operate the same hierarchies between foreground and background, figure and ground as its higher-resolution, analogous counterpart. It is by now a topos of the discussion on digital aesthetics that it causes the human figure to lose the indisputable prominence it held in traditional film worlds, that the human form 'does not have the same face, or the same measure . . . is glued to the image as to a piece of dough, and as such, is subjected to a process of slowing down, of reduction that opens it, however, to forces yet unaccounted for' (Burdeau 2006: 10–11). In *Baise-moi*, there is indeed a sense that the two main female figures are caught in the thickness of matter, and that 'each act of sex and/or violence plays against a subtle though constantly palpable sense of a blankly indifferent world immersed in heavy, heavy time' (Le Cain 2002). To the effect of 'sticky', formless undifferentiation, then, and the 'burlesque apathy' (Brenez 2001) that permeates the film in between scenes of frenzy, responds the almost imperceptible tremor of the image's pixelated surface that seems to feed into the 'becoming-killing/fucking machines' of the characters. (Describing Anderson's performance, Le Cain talks of the 'kinetic intensity animating her every gesture'.)

The following comments by Pascal Bonitzer on the characteristics of the video image seem particularly topical here, in their evocation of the forces of anomy at work in the 'constant teeming' of the image surface – a 'swarming' force that is unleashed in *Baise-moi* in the 'becoming' of the two characters who pass through its electronic field. Yet, the film theorist, writing in the 1980s, does not merely overlook such 'unknown forces' at work in the digital mode of imaging, but further describes the image's lack of depth as the indisputable mark of the inferiority of video to film proper.

There is no hole in video, or, rather, there are only holes, a surface covered in holes that can be infinitely inlaid. All these holes are always already filled by what lays close to the surface . . . there is no empty space in video, the image is a swarming of animated dots . . . a space of constant teeming. (Bonitzer [1981] 1999: 31)

The space in video is pure surface . . . there is no depth layered through a play on different planes of scale, nor is there a peaceful or conflicting coexistence of bodies . . . there is but an undifferentiated inlay, a play of cut-out paper silhouettes as if all bodies were freed from depth and weight and spread out on the surface like cards. (Bonitzer [1981] 1999: 30, translation mine)

However, for the very reasons suggested by Bonitzer as the sign of its worthlessness, the effect of the video image's transformation of the profilmic into a depthless surface has forceful implications in the context of a film like *Baise-moi*. As Powrie notes,[23] Despentes and Trinh Thi's film

attempts to go beyond the spectacular, the surface of the body, the fetishised exterior, to begin to glimpse the possibilities of a transcendent and transparent embodiment, one where the outside, the exterior, is no longer separated from the interior, where the body is as much pure exteriority as interiority. For that to happen, old binaries must be dismantled. First, the male must not simply be role-reversed – as when one of the women's victims complains limply about their refusal of a condom – but he must be turned inside out: hence the shooting of the libertine through the anus, his insides being *shot through* quite literally so that the inside becomes the outside. (Powrie, forthcoming)

The use of video is crucial here precisely because of its much decried effect of neutralising depth; in comparison with high-resolution photography, the tactility of the video image undermines the kind of mastering gaze (that of the observer-consumer) encouraged in the traditional visual regime based on perspective. As Marks sums it up, 'When vision yields to the diminished capacity of video, it must give up some degree of mastery' (Marks 2000: 176). In fact, through the depthless porosity of the digital video image, it is our very conception of inside and outside that becomes confused:[24] as is further echoed through the film's dialogue and *mise en scène*, paradoxically (since digital video, as a low-budget medium, is favoured in pornography), it is an image that defies the more

[23] A topical comment in this context, even if the use of the term 'transcendent' goes against the definition of embodiment as experience (in opposition to symbolic representation or metaphorical accounts) upheld in further chapters.

[24] Sound often plays a similar role in confusing inside with outside in this film, as is the case in the scene of Manu and Nadine's first encounter. Manu is walking through an underground passage accompanied by the sound of a punk-rock track; suddenly pulled aside by Manu, she removes her headphones, revealing the source of the music as a diegetic (internal) one.

familiar terms of distanciation (objectification), appropriation (penetration) and consumption.[25]

'The most controversial section of *Baise-moi*', Le Cain remarks, 'is undoubtedly the rape scene – though even in the uncut version it is handled responsibly. "We did not invent rape," Despentes has said in interview. "I've been raped and one of my actresses has been raped . . . it's horrific, so I don't see why I shouldn't treat it that way"' (Le Cain 2002). In contrast with the stylised editing of later episodes of violence, the rape scene is mainly composed of long takes. It includes, however, an insert close-up of penetration. In the UK, the Board of Censorship condemned the shot as an eroticisation of sexual assault and yet, as suggested in the present discussion of the film, the absence of depth characteristic of the video image renders the sequence as a whole as untitillating as it is bleak and horrifying. In comparison with this graphic and repulsive portrayal of absolute violation, the sequence that follows is endowed with an eerie sense of calm. Initially caught in medium shot, the two women are sitting on the floor of the disused warehouse where they have just been attacked. The frame includes a large portion of the checked ground, covered in grime and dust, and through the flattening, colour-levelling effect of the video image, the figures seem to be crushed into their surroundings. Yet, Manu explains to her distraught friend, with remarkable self-control, that she does not care: 'It's like a car that you park in the projects: it's bound to be broken into, so you don't leave valuable stuff inside. It's the same with my cunt: I cannot keep fuckers from coming in so I don't leave anything precious inside.'

Like the video image on whose surface they appear, the female figures in *Baise-moi* remain elusive. They cannot be owned; they will not be used. Their actions will not be put 'into perspective'. As Despentes stipulates: 'They are outlaws. No excuses, no explanations, no intellectualisation. They are close to us because they are beyond judgement. Sensation, not thought.' It does not mean that *Baise-moi* is pure, meaningless nihilism devoid of critical impact, however. If the film is, in Brenez's words, 'not concerned with causes, but only with effects – suffering itself', this suffering is both suggested and graphically evoked at the beginning of the film, before it is externalised through the two women's foray into violence. *Baise-moi*, however, derives its additional critical force from its upholding of the value of purely unproductive energy; in a world where everything (lives, bodies, thoughts, desire, sex) can be manufactured, bought and sold,

---

[25] Indeed, the effect of depthless surface arguably accounts for the ineffectuality of much of pornographic film production.

where pornography is but one expression of the 'supreme capitalist' logic, *Baise-moi*'s two protagonists engage in a journey where desire cannot be bought any more than action can be harnessed to rationale.

> What is unbearable is the conversion of pleasure into a supreme capitalistic argu-
> ment. We still don't know very clearly what to set against this except anger and
> destruction, insofar as the individual conditions of access to pleasure – so perilous in
> themselves (cf. *Sombre*) – can definitely not become solutions, or values, or even con-
> tradictory forces, for fear of distorting immediately their wild, socially irretrievable
> and anti-economical aspects. (Brenez 2001)

As Brenez remarks, the logic of the capitalistic argument is such that it ultimately absorbs even the most anarchistic expressions of anger; the kind of 'socially irretrievable and anti-economical' experience that *Baise-moi* evokes cannot be anything else than short-lived. But if, like Anaïs in *À ma sœur*, Nadine, the surviving heroine of *Baise-moi*, ends up framed between two officers of the law, this does not take away the disruptive energy exuded by the film. Like Breillat's works, *Baise-moi* derives its significance precisely from the refusal of a useful purpose; but, whereas in Breillat's films it was the sudden shift into a different regime of imaging and the brutal disturbance of generic patterns that signalled the manifestation of violence or horror in its irrecoverable excess, in *Baise-moi* it is the video image that becomes its vector. Video becomes film's accursed sister; suffering and violence inscribed on the surface of its images, it carries the excess they generate through the grubby 'swarming' of pixels on its surface.

Liminal Visions[26]

It would be disingenuous to deny that films like *Trouble Every Day*, *À ma sœur*, *Baise-moi*, *Demonlover*, *Sombre* or *La Vie nouvelle*, like many of the other works that can be associated with a cinema of sensation, raise questions in terms of gender politics and the evocation of the 'other' in particular (namely in the *mise en scène* of woman as victim, and the significance attached to the presence of foreign territories and figures).[27] It would be

---

[26] Raymond Bellour talks of a cinema that attempts to evoke the '*bords marginaux*' ('the marginal edges') of our consciousness, this mental space where the endless stream of real horrors unravelled in the media is stored before our mind transforms it from mere, distant rumour into an actual vision (Bellour 2005: 16–17).

[27] Like that of their female counterparts, Assayas' and Grandrieux's choice and treatment of themes and characters generated heated discussions. In her review of *Demonlover*, Kate Stables talks of a film that 'titillates as efficiently as it disturbs', and finds it too ambivalent to be hailed as an authentic criticism of the exploitative world of international business it

equally short-sighted, however, to disallow the deeply sexist character of some avant-garde and neo-avant-garde films that are now canonised as classics of world cinema and heralded, in contrast with Assayas, Denis or Grandrieux's recent film works, as the 'true' artistic expression of subversion. More than ever, wilfully oppositional or transgressive forms of film-making occupy a shifting and ambiguous territory where it has become increasingly difficult to disentangle empty sensationalism from a genuine artistic vision. Thus, it appears crucial to consider whether conventional approaches and tools of film theory and criticism are indeed adequate where one seeks to build more than a superficial appraisal of contemporary film works.

Undoubtedly, as Claire Johnston pointed out in the early years of feminist film theory, whereas mainstream films flaunt stereotypes that are easily identified and debunked, the formal disguise behind which the same stereotypes and myths reappear unnoticed can transform art cinema into the most efficient of vehicles for reactionary discourses (Johnston 1973: 25).[28] On the other hand, what much of the contemporary critique also suggests is the existence of a particularly deep-seated suspicion towards the more formally exploratory and transgressive forms of cinema.

Discussing what three films that initially make for a disparate sample – Assayas' *Demonlover*, Noé's *Irréversible*, and Grandrieux's *La Vie*

---

describes. Writing about *Sombre*, Françoise Audé is similarly scathing about what she sees as a blind celebration of murderous impulses and the death drive presented in the style of pseudo underground counter-culture. Jonathan Rosenbaum also denounces the film for what he sees as the representation of a rapist and serial killer as a Dostoyevskian saintly figure (Audé 1999; Rosenbaum 1999). Evoking his own response to *Sombre*, Adrian Martin acknowledges the difficulty in finding an appropriate reaction to the film's disturbing images:

> How is one to 'take' this film, accommodate it within the normal, daily frame of one's values, experiences, politics? Is there really something unforgivably sadistic, or intellectually narrow, or regrettably anti-human in the film's project? (Martin 1999)

Yet, he adds, 'offence is a too easy – in fact, highly defensive – response to the singular force and power of Grandrieux's achievement'. Similarly, Jérôme Fabre sees in Grandrieux's work an affirmative sign of French cinema's continuing ability to reinvent its forms and widen its horizons:

> It is here [in the cinema of Grandrieux] that we find a young cinema, where directors think and make films that are free and raw . . . not in the narcissistic operating theatre and Rohmer-like prattle of the FEMIS babies. (Fabre 1999: 47, translation mine)

See also the supporting arguments offered by Serge Kaganski (Kaganski 1999).

28 Jean-Luc Godard is amongst the directors whose work attracted enlightening critical reappraisal by feminist film theorists (see, for instance, Claire Pajaczkowska's essay in Hayward and Vincendeau (1990); or Constance Penley's discussion of Godard and pornography in Penley 1988).

nouvelle – have in common, Olivier Joyard points to a shared attempt at experimenting with the material qualities inherent to sound and image in cinema. Yet again, in the journalist's opinion, the combination of graphic violence and sex is ultimately destined to mask the extent to which such repellent images amount to little more than a masquerade.

> Coming from almost opposed cinematographic horizons, the films of Oliver Assayas (*Demonlover*), Philippe Grandrieux (*La Vie nouvelle*) and Gaspar Noé (*Irréversible*) show a common willingness to be at the vanguard of 'contemporary' filmmaking. Work on the materiality of the image, equal importance granted to colours and sound; belief in a fragmented story-line; all three consider that cinema should be a violent, liminal experience. Yet, when they are confronted with the representation of a sexual act, it takes the form of a rape . . . It is incredible, but there it is: rape is a *trashy* and *chic* experience, the latest aesthetic looping, the black horizon of modernity . . . The flesh is sad, when it is not absent, since the place where a body's relationship with the other's desire occurs must be evacuated. (Joyard 2002: 11)

In the end, the article harks back to one of the most hackneyed arguments in French film criticism. Drawing on a pseudo-libertine legacy, it alludes to the right of the (male?) spectator to liberating and fearlessly hedonistic cinematic propositions, in order to dismiss all three films as depressing and bigoted visions of sexuality clad in modish aesthetics. In contrast, the author hails pornography in particular as the ultimate territory of the true expression of desire – the place where 'Sex is not put in the service of a discourse, it is a discourse in itself' (Joyard 2002: 12).[29] Modelled as it is on the conventional paradigm of gender difference, the definition of desire proposed in Joyard's text cannot account for the more diffuse, creative patterns of desire (and spectatorial enjoyment) offered by the films he dismisses. In effect, in at least two of the features put forward by Joyard as examples, formal experimentation acts as a counterpart to, and indeed, as a critique of, the sources (present in our everyday world) of the nightmarish visions that the films construct, wilfully taking the reverse course or proposing a critical and alternative vision of the culture of the body, desire and sexuality as it dominates our media-saturated world. Assayas and Grandrieux's films obviously respond to a context where pseudo-hedonistic images of the faultless body, endlessly matched to standardised forms of desire and

---

[29] To his initial sample of three films, Joyard opposes the more pleasurable ('*jouissifs*') films of pornographic director John B. Root and of cinema auteur Jean-Claude Brisseau. Brisseau's *Choses secrètes* in particular is hailed as the best counter-example (the article conveniently forgetting to mention that, aside from the hackneyed and rather ungratifying theme of female friendship ending in betrayal, Brisseau's otherwise remarkable film features a post-wedding gang rape).

forever engaged in the gratification of manufactured 'needs', have invaded all the facets of our largely visual culture where they wage an unfair challenge to equally standardised images of suffering and world catastrophes. In contrast with the facade of normative perfection offered by advertisement, television and mainstream cinema, the films concerned evoke the ill-defined and threatening sense of desire and sexuality that imbues a reality where exploitation and greed are the rules.[30]

The emergence of alternative aesthetic projects certainly responds to the need to explore anew the affective potential of an art form too often recuperated and limited to the illustration of mainstream discourses. By extension, using the affective-transgressive power of the cinema as cinema of sensation, some filmmakers strive to offer a critical questioning and, possibly, the beginnings of a response to the process of normalisation and image recycling at work in our Western society of the spectacle. Describing *La Vie nouvelle* as 'a survey of the human psyche at the beginning of the 21st century', Nicole Brenez outlines the wider significance of the issues raised by the film:

> As Jean Claude Pollack explains it well, such an ethical journey takes the form of a nightmare. But it is a collective nightmare, not a small, private daydream. It is the actual nightmare in which we are all plunged since the revolutionary ideals were revealed as non-viable, leaving a world devoid of hope sunk in a state of material as well as moral devastation. (Brenez 2005: 21)

---

[30] Like the director's first feature, *Sombre*, the nightmarish vision offered in Grandrieux's recently released *La Vie nouvelle* raised a number of polarised responses that fed mainly into the debates on art cinema and the use of violence and sex. To reject certain critical readings is misplaced because missing out on the fundamentally archetypal dimension of the films and characters is arguably easier with *Sombre* than with *La Vie nouvelle*, where most of the characters carry the vestiges of a social, national or economic identity. It is the geographical and political setting in particular, and the evocation of the recent conflicts in the Balkans, that triggered a number of angry reactions, as with Quandt, for instance, for whom Grandrieux's cinema 'arrogates political, social, and historical horror for a fashionista vision of the apocalypse' (Quandt 2004). However, given the formal challenge that *La Vie nouvelle* represents, Quandt's legitimate questioning of the film's ethics is usefully qualified when compared to a comment by the producer of the award-winning series *Sex Traffic* (2004), Hugo Cassavetti, who spent months in pre-production and casting in Ukraine, Moldavia and Bosnia. Cassavetti provides an interesting angle on the public response to, and long-term effect of an older, pleasantly idealistic feature on prostitution: 'The film *Pretty Woman*, extremely popular in East European countries, has had a devastating effect. Young girls believed in this glamorised vision of prostitution, with the pretty whore played by Julia Roberts who finds her Prince Charming. They tell themselves that it is not so terrible, that it is worth taking the risk' (Cassavetti 2005: 90). A similar remark can hardly be levelled at *La Vie nouvelle*'s nightmarish, experimental vision. Yet, while *Pretty Woman* is widely thought of as harmless entertainment, the harshness of some of the reviews of Grandrieux's feature seems to go well beyond the issue of the greater expectations one might have of an art movie.

In their formal aspiration as well as their imagery, some films seek to probe into the degraded forms created by the reductive and exploitative channelling of the chaotic force of human desire on the widest collective plane as well as the private level. In that sense, the cinema of sensation does indeed reconnect film practices with the possibility of the kind of alternative path called for by Artaud. However, whereas the early avant-gardes hailed the affective and sensual dimension of art, and called on the powers of the unconscious partly as a reaction and defence against a rational system and culture that brought about the catastrophe of World War I, today's filmmaking is informed by all that has taken place since. Writing about contemporary art in the late 1990s, Hal Foster links the persisting shift of artistic practices towards the abject and the traumatic with the staggering scope of continuing violence and worldwide destruction that, in spite of the precedents set by two world wars, unravels throughout the late twentieth century. Some artistic practices, he comments, question the traditional function of art as a shield, a screen against a real understood as traumatic, and reject the 'age-old mandate to pacify the gaze, to unite the imaginary and the symbolic against the real' (Foster 1996: 140).

In *Cinema 2*, Deleuze had associated the postwar shift in cinematic practices with the need to respond to the after-effects of World War II, the difficulty of finding adequate forms of expression to make sense of or, simply, to evoke situations and spaces that bear the mark of devastation and spell dehumanisation (Deleuze 1989: xi). As we move from the twentieth to the twenty-first century, these 'situations' and 'spaces' continue to haunt contemporary films, only they have been further diffracted through the unrelenting, catastrophic after-effects of decolonisation and the post-conflict devastations that affect our world with their correlation of exploitative, dehumanising practices (genocide as generalised war strategy, exclusion replacing immigration policy, the displacement of populations, new forms of slavery, sex traffic, routine violence . . .). They have also been rendered dangerously more unreal by the levelling effect of globalisation and standardised media coverage. Where discourse, and film structured as discourse, increasingly fails to offer adequate ways of addressing and evoking such realities, the cinema of sensation arguably represents an attempt at accounting for and thinking through some of these issues, and questioning the role of the moving image in relation to them, via the operations of film itself.

By bringing to the fore the materiality of the cinematic image and suggesting the possibility of a more multi-sensory experience of film, the techniques at work in the cinema of sensation not only facilitate a blur of identities, but tend to undermine the very distinction between subject and object. It brings out the 'intertwined and reversible structure' (Sobchack

2004: 294) of body and world; indifference, detachment, are thus offset by sensual empathy and embodiment – the inscription of that which is other, distant, unrelated, into the subjective space, on to the subjective body. Graphic violence and sex are a part of this process, in the same way that pleasure and a sense of self-expansion are. In effect, if the cinema of sensation is not reducible to a sensationalist cinema, neither is it definable as a territory apart from the rest of cinema. Rather, where the majority of cinematographic practice takes place at the level of representation and discourse, the cinema of sensation brings its images into the interstices of molar and molecular planes, consciously seeking to engage the viewer at both levels. In turn, this shift in filmmaking practices renders film theory's conventional analytical tools inadequate or, at least, insufficient.

What needs to be considered, then, are ways of addressing the unfamiliar visions embodied in certain films without disconnecting them from the work on the materiality of the image: that is, from an approach to filmmaking where the moving image is not merely, to paraphrase Joyard's comment, 'in the service of a discourse, but a discourse in itself' – and an embodied one at that.

The Art of Sensation

Grandrieux, who started as an experimental filmmaker and film essayist,[31] described his foray into feature-fiction cinema partly as an answer to his wish to reach a wider public, to see his work shown outside of the museums (Grandrieux 1999a). Encapsulated in a few sentences, his conception of what cinema is about singularly echoes Artaud's initial claims:

> Cinema is made with images, sounds, rhythm, cuts, light, bodies, movement, framing – rather rudimentary components in the end . . . cinema was not created to construct stories in the psychological sense. (Renaud et al. 1999)[32]

In recent interviews following the release of *Flandres*, Bruno Dumont puts the point forward even more succinctly – 'I am interested in sensation, not

[31] Grandrieux is the author of a series of experimental films and documentaries, including *La Peinture Cubiste* (1981) in collaboration with Thierry Kuntzel. He also produced *Studio Live*, an experimental programme inviting artists to produce single-take films for Arte.

[32] Grandrieux also insists on the importance of the film experienced as an event in itself:

> What I am interested in is the issue of experience – the experience you have when watching a film. A corporeal, physical, human experience. The cinema that moves me is a cinema of sensation. I am moved by what the film transmits as sensation – and not just emotion – through the images, the sounds, the editing, the bodies, the actor . . . and the story must be caught within cinema's highly material presence. (Béghin 2001)

sense' (Rouyer and Tobin 2006: 90). As with the other directors whose
work is concerned with the materiality of film, this principle is constantly
reiterated in defiance of the scenario-based tradition predominant in film
criticism as well as in filmmaking practices.

> There is this sentence that Bruno Dumont keeps repeating in his interviews, as if he
> was brandishing a banner: 'Cinema is for bodies, cinema is for emotions'. Whether
> we agree with him or not, this motto, applied by the filmmaker from Bailleul, resulted
> in the most *startling* films created in the past ten years. Dumont's cinema is a cinema
> that shocks – a visceral cinema. (Darras 2006: 15)

Here, the primacy is thus explicitly returned to the very fabric of
images and sounds, to the effect of the cinema as audio-visual movement:
light, colours, textures, lines and shapes, amongst which the human
figure features as a changing, mutating, element. 'My film has nothing to
say' (Rouyer and Vassé 2003: 20) – for all its provocative directness,
Dumont's statement is not a denial but, on the contrary, is a reaffirmation
of cinema's distinctive capacity to produce sense, and as such, a reasser-
tion of the cinematic experience as the unique fusion of body and mind.[33]
Rather than mapping pre-existing discourses on film, or analysing it as
the expression of ideas that exist otherwise, Deleuze saw the cinematic
thought process taking place through an assemblage of film and spectator, where the film event 'moves' the spectator into thinking (Deleuze
1989: 156). Representational and narrative functions are secondary; film
needs not derive its meanings from those predetermining frameworks; it
'thinks' in moving images and sound. A similar awareness of cinema's
potential as an art form that addresses the interpretative mind through
the senses is at work in the cinematography of a number (and, I would
argue, amongst the most interesting) of contemporary French directors.
Recent work by Claire Denis, Philippe Grandrieux, Vincent Dieutre,
Bruno Dumont and Catherine Breillat, amongst other directors, suggests
a shared desire to return to cinema as an art of sensation and to explore
the medium's distinctive capacity to weave together the sensual and the
conceptual.

In turn, this loose community of sensibilities is mirrored in the development of a wider community of people; to study the cast and crew as well

[33] A former philosophy teacher, Dumont explains:

> with cinema, I try to use only the material found in the real. Philosophical systems
> concern one part of our beings only – the head. Yet, our instincts, our body, our very
> presence on earth determine our thoughts . . . [Characters] should not be mouthpieces,
> means of expression, but expression itself. (Guichard 2006: 28, translation mine)

as production credits of these films is to become aware of the recurrence of certain names amongst French actors and actresses, technicians and producers as well as scenarists or writers.[34]

Still, produced separately, without manifesto or expression of a common purpose, these films initially form a highly diverse collection; in terms of authorship, themes, narrative elements and critical reception, they show as many contrasts as similarities. Even stylistically, there is a wide variety of approaches in evidence here. But in all instances, cinematic corporeality – the materiality of film, bodies in film and film as embodiment – is key. In turn, this reaffirmation of cinema's corporeal dimension determines certain concordances: loose, open forms of narrations, disregard for genre boundaries, a proliferation and collage of a diversity of visual and sound material.

In addition to adopting a feature-film format, the majority of the works discussed here retain at least a rough narrative outline and include characters that, even when they are not fully fledged characters in the conventional sense, can usually be identified as the main protagonists of the film. The loosening of the narrative causal chain and of the corresponding filmmaking functions simultaneously allows for, and grows from, the greater involvement with the sensual dimension of the pro-filmic material; visions born out of familiar perception are thus heightened and altered and the conventional narrative framework is overruled by, or combined with, more radical strategies. The starting point, then, remains that of a pro-filmic reality captured, at least initially, in its commonly perceived figurative appearance, but whose distortion, whether it is punctual or systematic, allows for the film to come forth in its material actuality, as an event in itself. As will be explored and illustrated in the following chapters, before or beyond the spectacle of human figures enacting a story, images and sounds impose themselves as matter, the fabric of the film, moulded and shaped into colour and rhythmic fields. Given precedence, the sensual and affective effect tends to pre-empt and largely condition the discursive and representational dimensions. Vision and hearing bring into play the other senses, moving the figurative and perspective-based organisation of the filmic space towards an amorphous, sensory-based reality, allowing for the traditional relation between subject and object to become drastically destabilised.

---

[34] Actors Laurent Lucas and Michael Lonsdale, directors, scenarists and actresses Marina de Van and Coralie Trinh Thi, writer Emmanuelle Bernheim, philosopher and essayist Jean-Luc Nancy, artistic directors and camerawomen Caroline Champetier, Agnès Godard and Josée Deshaies, to name but a few, are amongst the names that appear repeatedly in the cast and crew lists of the proposed corpus.

The filmmaking practices discussed in the following chapters take us beyond the vision afforded by the primarily functional, sleek or unobtrusive *mise en scène* and camera work of traditionally realistic feature films. They betray, instead, an underlying sense of affinity with the Baroque sensibility,[35] a fascination for the layered and perplexing quality of compositions in the folds of which the eye might eventually be caught in death's own gaze, unless it loses itself in the teeming multiplicity of matter itself.

[35] See Deleuze's exploration of the fold in Deleuze, Gilles (1988), *Le Pli: Leibnitz et le baroque*, Paris: Minuit. Descriptions of Baroque forms of expression often resonate with the evocation of the effect of the aesthetics of sensation at work in the cinema of the senses. In *La Littérature baroque en Europe*, Didier Souiller typically describes Baroque art as an art *of* movement and *in* movement. It 'addresses emotion and imagination rather than reason and logic'; in a 'time dominated by instability', Baroque forms operate a 'passage from the certain (exemplified by imitation, unity and closure) to the unknown, the multiple, and the opening on the infinite' (Souiller 1988: 263, translation mine).

CHAPTER 2

The Aesthetics of Sensation

What would be really surprising is that sound should be unable to suggest colour, that colours should be incapable of inspiring melody, and that sound and colour should be unsuited to the translation of ideas; given that things have always expressed themselves by means of a reciprocal analogy, since the day when God called forth the world as a complex and indivisible whole. (Baudelaire [1866] 1976: 784, trans. Mary Breatnach)

A few minutes into Grandrieux's *La Vie nouvelle*, there is an image that lasts but an instant – the blurred shape of a human silhouette, running forward, as if trying to emerge from the sticky, engulfing matter that surrounds it. It is like a stain on the celluloid, moving to a distant humming sound, its distorting contours on the brink of dissolving in the trembling, snowy texture that fills the screen.

To foreground the materiality of the film medium is to unsettle the frontier between subject and object, figure and ground – the basis of our conception and representation of the self as a separate entity. 'Hapticity' and the denial of perspective perturb the visual hierarchy that tends to designate the human figure as a self-standing, autonomous entity at the centre of the representation. Not all the films discussed here give precedence to haptic visuality, but all include key moments at least where the establishment of a detached and objectifying gaze merely intent on making sense of the representational content of a shot is precluded and gives way to a different viewing experience. Cinematic synaesthesia and correspondences – the evocation, through images and sounds, of other sensual affects as well as concepts – the close-up, as well as an array of techniques that foreground cinematic corporeity through visual and sound alterations, all work to generate haptic forms of visualities. In effect, intriguingly, recent French cinema offers particularly vivid illustrations of how such techniques have the potential of radically renewing our experience of watching, sensing and thinking through film.

As if echoing Artaud's call for a 'third path' (the claim for an alternative to psychological/narrative cinema on the one hand and abstract cinema on the other), in his seminal reflection on figuration and abstraction, *Logique de la sensation*, philosopher Gilles Deleuze sets out to develop an alternative route. Deleuze considers how modern art can go beyond figuration, yet not turn into abstraction – how the image can evolve between the purely figurative and the purely abstract: 'It is thanks to the extraordinary achievements of abstract painting that modern art could be extracted from figuration. Is there not another path, however, a more direct, *sensitive* one?' (Deleuze [1981] 2002: 19, translation and italics mine). Intended to describe the evolution of painting and serve as a premise to a study of Francis Bacon's work, Deleuze's analysis seems equally, if not more, applicable to the medium of moving images because film is, first and foremost, a medium of time and change, where image and sound are in constant mutation. Deleuze's description of the ways by which an art form can escape the figurative, illustrative and narrative rule thus offers indubitable resonance in the context of a cinema of sensation:

> There are two ways of moving beyond figuration (that is, beyond the illustrative as well as the narrative): it means either moving towards the abstract form or the Figure. This path of the Figure, Cézanne gave it a simple name: sensation. The Figure is the sensitive form related to sensation. (Deleuze [1981] 2002: 39, translation mine)

Here, the differentiation between figure and figuration points to the construction of an environment where the (human) figure is present and at least temporarily identifiable, but appears out of the conventional narrative and perspectival spatio-temporal structure.[1]

Hence, Deleuze's study of Bacon's work is still based on the figure, but it is a figure that is initially caught in a grid that isolates it from a wider, potentially narrative context. Furthermore, it is the figure presented in a non-perspectival space, where its relation to the background is not one of depth, but one of coexistence on the same plane – a 'corrélation de deux secteurs sur un même plan également proche' ('a conjunction of two areas on the same plane and in equal proximity') (Deleuze [1981] 2002: 14). Such considerations, which anticipate discussions by contemporary theorists on the passage from a modernist formalism to a postmodern 'formlessness' (Krauss 1985; Foster 1996; Krauss and Bois 1999), prove relevant not only where experimental film proper is concerned, but also, as will we see, in the context of a 'cinema of sensation' that appears to create a bridge between experimental and feature cinema. What is at stake is the passage from or, rather, the fluctuation between figuration and figure rendered possible by

---

[1] I will occasionally use the term 'figural' to suggest this passage and describe the sphere of the figure caught in endless mutation, as defined here. Its meaning will thus differ from that assigned to the term in the writings of, amongst others, François Lyotard and, more recently, David Rodowick.

THE AESTHETICS OF SENSATION

the elaboration of a haptic regime of the gaze, and the multi-sensory perception and understanding of the cinematic matter.

Blurring or overload of photographic precision, extreme close-ups, superimpositions, under-exposure or over-exposure, variations in sound pitch and intensities: when cinema becomes a cinema of the senses it starts to generate worlds of mutating sounds and images that often ebb and flow between the figurative and the abstract, and where the human form, at least as a unified entity, easily loses its function as the main point of reference. One way or another, the cinema of sensation is always drawn towards the formless ('*l'informe*'): where background and foreground merge and the subjective body appears to melt into matter.

The Haptic and the Optical

In the current critique of Western epistemological systems, much space is given to the questioning of a primarily 'optical' mode of visual understanding and representation. Based on the establishment of a perspectival space and on the distinction between figure and ground, optical vision arguably posits a Cartesian, rational subject gaining knowledge and mastery of the world through the exercise of a detached, objectifying gaze.

> If we can talk of classical representation, it is as part of the conquest of an optical space, where vision is more distant and never frontal: form and ground do not belong to the same plane any more; the planes have become distinct and their depth is traversed by a perspective that connects background and foreground . . . the outline ceases to be a common limit on a shared plane to become the form's own delineation, establishing the primacy of the foreground . . . Art can then become figurative, yet we can see that this was not what art was initially and that figuration is but a consequence. (Deleuze [1981] 2002: 118, translation mine)

In effect, art theorists generally stress the historical dimension of this model. Marks, like Deleuze, draws on the work of early art historians[2] (in particular, the writings of Alöis Riegl who coined the term 'haptic') to trace back to late Roman and Byzantine works the emergence of art forms that would increasingly privilege a spatial construction based on distance and depth. This had characteristic implications, both in terms of the organisation of the picture plane itself and the relation between the perceiver and the art work.

---

[2] 'Riegl and Auerbach . . . described how Western art came to achieve sensuous similarity to its object through representation, rather than through contact. Riegl, especially, argued that increasing abstraction, or increasing membership in the symbolic, characterises the history of the Western art' (Marks 2000: 167).

It is important to note that the creation of abstract space in Byzantine art made it possible for a beholder to identify figures not as concrete elements on a surface but as figures in space. By contrast, haptic space is concrete, in that it seeks unity only on a surface. The rise of optical representation marked a general shift toward a cultural ideal of abstraction, with significant consequences. Abstraction facilitated the creation of an illusionistic picture plane that would be necessary for the identification of, and identification *with*, figures in the sense that we use 'identification' now. In other words, optical representation makes possible a greater distance between beholder and object which allows the beholder to imaginatively project him/herself into or onto the object. (Marks 2000: 166)

Whereas optic images set discrete, self-standing elements of figuration in illusionistic spaces, haptic images dehierarchise perception, drawing attention back to tactile details and the material surface where figure and ground start to fuse. Haptic images thus encourage a mode of visual perception akin to the sense of touch, where the eye, sensitised to the image's concrete appearance, becomes responsive to qualities usually made out through skin contact: 'we can speak of the *haptic* each time vision discovers in and by itself a tactile function that belongs to vision and vision alone and is distinct from its optical function' (Deleuze [1981] 2002: 146, translation mine).[3]

Contemporary theorists tend to reject the theological view that holds the optical as the logic stage put forward in a process that leads unavoidably to the establishment of Renaissance perspective as the arch-model. They point, instead, to haptic vision as a continuing alternative that has been given more or less attention depending on the period. As mentioned earlier, there currently is, in artistic practices as well as in theoretical trends, a critique of the Western ocular-centrism and Cartesian subjectivity and a marked shift towards sensuous, embodied forms and epistemologies. With

[3] Deleuze adopts a term (*haptique*) first coined by Alöis Riegl ([1902] 1995). As in his study of the 'figure' mentioned above, what makes Deleuze's classic description of the optic and haptic modes in painting equally resonant in the context of film is the notion of a passage from one to the other and the importance of movement (and the following quotation thus creates intriguing echoes with the process of 'becoming' discussed more fully in Chapter 3):

The more the hand is . . . subordinated, the more vision develops an 'ideal' optical space and tends to capture its forms through an optical code. But this optical space, at least in the beginning, still holds references to the manual with which it is thus connected: we can call *tactile* such visual references, such as depth, outline, volume, etc. This loose subordination of the hand to the eye can give way, in turn, to the true insubordination of the hand: the picture remains a visual reality, but the formless space and restless movement that now impose themselves to the eye are uneasily fathomed by vision and put the optical space out of joint. (Deleuze [1981] 2002: 146, translation mine)

Deleuze's analysis operates a gradual categorisation which also involves what he calls an 'optic-tactile' space ([1981] 2002: 146).

its exploration of fragmentary subjectivities and concrete forms, the modernist period, however, paved the way for this return of the material. Already in 1915, Heinrich Wölfflin was writing about Rembrandt in characteristically synaesthetic terms:

> As our attention progressively moves away from the represented figure as such, our awareness of the surface of things, of the bodies as they are perceived through touch, becomes more and more acute. The way the flesh is presented to us . . . it becomes as tactile as silk, its weight palpable. (Wölfflin [1915] 1996: 43)

Wölfflin's description could easily apply to a number of the film sequences discussed below. Indeed, watching some of the extracts described in the following pages (and, more powerfully, when watching them on a big screen and being immersed in the image), I experienced the intense tactile impression that Marks describes as 'brushing the image with the skin of my eyes' (Marks 2000: 125). Yet, as Marks reminds us, it is not the pro-haptic qualities of cinema that are generally endorsed in common filmmaking practices.

> Like the Roman battle of the haptic and the optical, a battle between the material significance of the object and the representational power of the image was waged in the early years of cinema. . . . As the language of cinema became standardised, cinema appealed more to narrative identification than to bodily identification. In theories of embodied spectatorship, we are returning to the interest of modern cinema theorists such as Benjamin, Béla Balázs, and Dziga Vertov in the sympathetic relationship between the viewer's body and the cinematic image, bridging the decades in which cinema theory was dominated by theories of linguistic signification. (Marks 2000: 171)

In mainstream practices, then, cinematic vision is bound to the requirements of narrative exposition and tends to be constructed according to a strict optical organisation; to watch a film is to distinguish objects and human forms (characters) at the level of representation, already distinct and encoded. The return – much in evidence, as we have seen, in recent French film and French theory – of filmmaking and theoretical approaches that give prominence to the corporeal dimension of the cinema has allowed for the pro-haptic dimension of the medium to be reinvested, not merely in experimental practices, but also in feature filmmaking. The creation of haptic forms, and the unsettling of optical vision, are at the very heart of the aesthetic of sensation developed by the French filmmakers discussed here. Changes in focus, unusual angles and framing, long shots alternating with close-ups and extreme close-ups, graphic editing and the combination of different media (8mm, 16mm, 35mm, high- and low-definition digital footage) with their variations in ratio and graininess and so on: the choice of techniques operates a constant passage from optical to haptic perception, where the material presence of the image competes with, and often supersedes, its representational power. Indeed, as Marks stresses, haptic images tend to 'resolve into figuration only gradually, if at all' (Marks 2000: 163). Beyond the needs of narrative clarity, the cinema of sensation thus plays on the material qualities of the medium to construct a space that encourages a relation of intimacy or proximity with the object of the gaze, privileging primary identification with the film as event, rather than identification with characters caught in plot developments. The effect is an unsettling of the conventional vision-knowledge-mastery paradigm, in favour of a relation where the spectator may surrender, at least partly, a sense of visual control for the possibility of a sensuous encounter with the film – where the subject affectively yields into its object. It comes as no surprise that horror cinema should make great use of haptic images; there is something both appealing and potentially threatening in the way haptic perception undermines the strategies of distanciation at work in conventional optical perception. In the most radical instances (as we will see when we consider certain uses of the close-up, for example) the shift from optical vision to de-subjectified perception operates a strange, unsettling effect of reversal, where the subject appears caught in the field of vision of the object, as if the gaze originated in the inanimate.

This ambiguity at the heart of corporeal cinema, between the pleasures of sensuous communion and the terror of self-integrity decomposing, accounts for the highly polarised response that this kind of filmmaking generates depending on the theoretical line of approach. Approaches inspired by psychoanalytical models, and by the kind of dark surrealism at work in the writings of Georges Bataille in particular, have focused on the terror aspect, the pull of the void and the systematic dismantling of conventional notions of subjecthood that the passage from figuration to indifferentiation or formlessness can affect. In contrast, Merleau-Ponty's phenomenological thinking and the Bergson-inspired writings of Deleuze, and of Deleuze and Guattari, form the basis for more positive extrapolations.

From Formlessness to Immanence

It is as if this art wanted the gaze to shine, the object to stand, the real to exist, in all the glory (or the horror) of its pulsatile desire, or at least to evoke this sublime condition.
(Foster 1996: 140, italics in original text)

In *The Return of the Real*, Hal Foster identifies a cluster of related terms which hold particular significance in the understanding of artistic practices that reject the function of art as a shelter against 'the real', a buffer that renders the gaze harmless. Amongst those terms, and in spite (or maybe, because) of the difficulty in defining them unambiguously, Bataille's *informe* (Bataille 1929) and Lacan's related concepts of the real and the gaze (Lacan 1978) have become primary notions in contemporary art theory and criticism.[4] The common point between these related notions (and Lacan is indebted to Bataille's impressionistic theories for the development of a number of his own ideas) is the radical attack on subjectivity and the beholding of chaos, the pull of the senseless, as the irreducible and most powerful threat to the construction of the subject. A provocative denial of the process of transcendence and idealisation at work in formal discourse and art, Bataille's concept of the *informe*, or 'formless' as defined by Hal Foster, corresponds with the optic/haptic paradigm: '[Bataille's *informe* is] a condition where significant form dissolves because the fundamental distinction between figure and ground, self and other, is lost' (Foster 1996: 149). The notion of the *informe* pre-empts Lacan's elaborations on the concept of the real as one of the three orders – the imaginary, the symbolic, and the real – that structure human existence. The real is neither synonymous with external reality, nor is it solely defined in opposition to the imaginary (the recapturing of a lost sense of unity and wholeness) or the symbolic (reality interpreted and ordered through discourse and systems of prohibition). The real 'is not simply the antonym of the imaginary. It exists outside or beyond the symbolic, is menacingly homogeneous, and is not composed of distinct and differentiated signifiers' (Macey 2000: 324).

Stressing the similarities between Bataille's and Lacan's concepts, Foster further extends his argument to two connected aspects of Lacanian theory: the traumatic and the gaze. Trauma, the 'missed encounter with the real' (Lacan 1978, quoted in Foster 1996: 132), signals the failure to make sense of certain experiences that are too horrific, are too threatening, and remain beyond understanding and articulation. Lacan describes the real as *traumatic*; though language, culture and art offer frameworks and screens through which the real can be conceptualised and mediated, the real (as in the case of Barthes' *punctum*, Foster argues) can 'poke' through those screens. Closely tied with vision, the traumatic real is inseparable from Lacan's discussion of the gaze, where he attempts to conceptualise the most extreme condition of threat to the subject as unified being and master of the (perspectival) gaze. An intuition of the gaze in the Lacanian sense is the presentiment that the gaze can be experienced in a disembodied form, that

---

[4] The additional reference here is Nietzsche, whose seminal reflections on the 'real' are discussed at the beginning of Chapter 3.

the subject ceases to stand as the beholder of a dominant point of view, to fall under the gaze of the object itself and become but a 'stain' in the 'spectacle of the world' (Lacan 1978: 97, quoted in Foster 1996: 138–9). Such concepts find an increased resonance both in thematic and formal terms, Foster remarks, in those art practices attuned to that part of the contemporary human condition that is over-present in today's information-saturated world, yet most difficult to make sense of – death, violence, war, persistent poverty and illness: '*This shift in conception – from reality to the real as a thing of trauma – may be definitive in contemporary art, let alone in contemporary theory, fiction, and film* . . . For with this shift in conception has come a shift in practice' (Foster 1996:146, italics in original text).

Such a shift is noticeable in the work of many of the filmmakers discussed in this book, its effects woven into the texture of their films, as well as in the filming and viewing experiences themselves. For Brenez, the achievement of this kind of cinema rests specifically on the willingness to use film to approach these borderline experiences of the human condition that both Lacan and Bataille explored in their writing. Interestingly, Brenez reclaims terms usually associated with the psychoanalytical field to combine them with concepts linked to post-Lacanian approaches.

> The image is no longer given as a reflection, discourse, or the currency of whatever absolute value; it works to invest immanence, using every type of sensation, drive and affect. To make a film means . . . confronting the sheer terror of the death drive, or the still more immense and bottomless terror of the unconscious, of total opacity. (Brenez 2003)

Whereas Bataille celebrates the creative/destructive power at work in the passage to formlessness, the limitation of the psychoanalytical project is that it ultimately rests with the reinstatement of selfhood. Accordingly, film theories purely based on psychoanalytical models have tended to look at the passage from optical to haptic vision in terms of the passage from misrepresentation (an illusory sense of identification) to abjection and alienation. Current Deleuzean-based reappraisals have developed in complete disagreement with the psychoanalytical school and the notion that vision is the arch-means of identification and self-construction, and, in turn, inherently alienating. In her cogent critique of both traditional psychoanalytical models and the 'masochistic models of spectatorship' proposed by contemporary theorists such as Stephen Shaviro, Marks thus underlines that 'We need not respond with dread to cinema's threat/promise to dissipate, or even wrench away, our unified subjectivities. A tactile visuality may be shattering, but it is not necessarily so' (Marks 2000: 151). Sobchack starts from Merleau-Ponty's questioning of 'the limits between the body and the world' and uses the philosopher's concept of the world as 'flesh'[5] to uphold a 'desire to enfold other subjects and objects (and, often, the world itself), to know their materiality and objectivity intimately and, indeed, to embrace their alterity *as our* own'. Here, the experience of the 'diminution of subjectivity' does not translate as a terrifying sense of impending annihilation but as one of 'sensual and sensible expansion' (Sobchack 2004: 288, 290). In the same vein, Braidotti rejects the 'semiological cage' set by psychoanalysis, but hails Deleuze as the most viable alternative:

> Very much a thinker of the outside, of open spaces and embodied enactments, Deleuze encourages us not to think in terms of within/without, but rather as levels of expression and sustainability of unfamiliar forces, drives, yearnings or sensations; a sort of spiritual and sensory stretching of our boundaries . . . I see it rather as a way of making the contemporary subject slightly more familiar with and consequently less anxious about the yet untapped possibilities that his or her living, embodied and embedded self can empower him or her for. (Braidotti 2002: 147)

Whether they lean towards Merleau-Ponty's phenomenology and his intuition of the 'world as flesh' or Deleuze and Deleuze and Guattari's elaboration of the concepts of immanence and becoming, both Sobchack and Braidotti, however, acknowledge the inherently composite experience, gratifying and violent, posited by the radical questioning of objective, distanced perception.

> Put in terms that suggest existential ease or horror, awesome or awful encounters with inanimate 'things', inherence in the world or alienation from it, this question [Merleau-Ponty's query 'of the limit between the body and the world'] interrogates the *objectivity* of subjectively embodied and sensate being. (Sobchack 2004: 286)[6]

[5] Sobchack refers to Elena del Rio's description of 'flesh' as that which

> designates the manner in which subject and object inhabit each other by participating in a common condition of embodied course . . . *Flesh* connotes the structure of reversibility whereby all things are at the same time active and passive, visible subjects and visible objects, the outside of the inside, the inside of the outside . . . The concept of *flesh* is precisely what allows . . . a renewed notion of subjectivity, one which introduces *alterity* into the very definition of 'selfsameness'. (del Rio 1996: 103–4)

Jana Millroy offers a complementary definition of Merleau-Ponty's 'chiasm':

> the Merleau-Pontian idea of the chiasm, where being in the world, the becoming self is fleshed out of the oscillations between self and other, reading the other in touching across the text in which the distinction between word and thing, language and experience, has not yet been made. (Millroy 2005: 545)

[6] Braidotti further comments:

> This [Deleuze's concept of becoming animal as the pull towards the unformed] raises ethical questions about how far to go in pursuing changes and stretching the boundaries

In setting one trend of thought (psychoanalysis and related approaches) against the other (phenomenology, Deleuzean 'nomadology'), theorists have often struggled to account for the paradoxical pleasures of films that raise the issue of limits in terms of vision and affects, or, conversely, to make sense of the destructive streak that often runs through those films which formal or thematic characteristics appear to fit most closely with a Deleuzean terminology in particular.[7] Looking at the shifting aesthetic fields and unusual viewing experiences that recent French cinema has to offer, I would suggest that those theoretical strands that have been deemed incompatible can nevertheless respond to each other. As I describe some of the techniques at work in the elaboration of an aesthetic of sensation and in the passage from optical to haptic vision, I will also shift focus, supplementing, as it were, one approach with the other.

Synaesthesia

In one chapter of his *History of the Devil* entitled 'Towards a history of the senses', Robert Muchembled outlines how, in the passage from the medieval to the modern order, the 'Western civilising process' promoted the sense of sight to the detriment of the other senses:

> The civilising process then under way taught people increasingly to conduct themselves in a decent and modest manner, avoiding both violent gestures and untimely bodily manifestations. . . . In this context, the senses of proximity – smell, taste and touch – were more controlled than sight or hearing. Each country evolved in its own way, but Western culture as a whole now advocated keeping a greater distance between people. (Muchembled 2003: 98)

As we have seen, in cinema, vision as distanced, objectifying perception has become the favoured mode of representation; other visual regimes and

---

Footnote 6 (*cont.*)

> of subjectivity. The issue of 'too much' also raises the question of pain, even violent emotions or excess. Deleuze's becoming animal leads to his reappraisal of a Spinozist ethics of sustainability. It is a call for experimenting with limits and with possible levels of subversion. It is also a way of challenging a conceptual creativity so that we can find non-negative and non-pathological ways of expressing the intensities we experience 'within'. (Braidotti 2002: 145–6)

[7] As Powell admits in her Deleuzean study of horror cinema:

> The conceptual frames of Deleuze and Bergson are primarily life-affirming and politically progressive. Because horror fantasy overtly presents that which blocks, damages and destroys human life and potential for happiness, I produce literal and sometimes deliberately skewed applications, to elucidate both concepts and films. (Powell 2005: 9)

other senses (hearing included) have tended to be overlooked, and we do not readily associate viewing film with the senses of touch, smell and taste. Yet, for all it is an audio-visual medium, cinema's synaesthetic powers of evocation are undeniable. In its discussion of the synaesthetic effect of vision and of the visual perception of movement, the following description, by Merleau-Ponty, of the complex interrelation that connects the senses, could be the depiction of series of film shots:

> The form of objects is not their geometrical shape; it stands in a certain relation to their specific nature, and appeals to our other senses as well as sight. The form of a fold in linen and cotton shows us the resilience or dryness of the fibre, the coldness or warmth of the material . . . In the jerk of the twig from which a bird has just flown, we read its flexibility or elasticity . . . One sees the weight of a block of cast iron which sinks in the sand, the fluidity of water and the viscosity of syrup. (Merleau-Ponty [1962] (2002): 229)

Synaesthesia, where 'the stimulation of one sense cause[s] a perception in another' (Cytowic 1993: 52), is not, as Vivian Sobchack reminds us, 'mere rhetoric': 'Philosophy aside, recent developments in neuroscience have indicated that "the boundaries between the senses are blurred"' (Guterman 2001: A17, cited in Sobchack 2004: 70). Similarly, Merleau-Ponty insists on the commonly overlooked effect of correspondence that sensual perception implies:

> The unity of the object will remain a mystery for as long as we think of its various qualities (its colour and taste, for example) as just so much data belonging to the entirely distinct worlds of sight, smell, touch and so on. Yet modern psychology, following Goethe's lead, has observed that, rather then being absolutely separate, each of these qualities has an affective meaning which establishes a correspondence between it and the qualities associated with the other senses. (Merleau-Ponty [1948] 2004: 60)[8]

Caught in the habit of privileging an optical, interpretative understanding of the world, however, we are not always aware of the epistemological richness afforded by a largely unconscious synaesthetic perception:

---

[8] Merleau-Ponty also refers to Sartre's explorations of the way the attributes of specific objects permeate their multi-sensory perception:

> The lemon is extended throughout its qualities, and each of its qualities is extended throughout each other. It is the sourness of the lemon which is yellow, it is the yellow of the lemon which is sour. We eat the colour of a cake, and the taste of this cake is the instrument which reveals its shape and its colour to what may be called the alimentary intuition . . . The fluidity, the tepidity, the bluish colour, the undulating restlessness of the water in a pool are given at one stroke, each quality through the others. (Sartre 1943: 186, cited in Merleau-Ponty [1948] 2004: 63)

> Synaesthetic perception is the rule, and we are unaware of it only because scientific
> knowledge shifts the centre of gravity of experience so that we have unlearned how
> to see, hear, and generally speaking feel, in order to deduce, from our bodily organ-
> isation and the world as the physicist conceives it, what we are to see, hear, feel.
> (Merleau-Ponty [1962] 2002: 229)

In cinema, 'scientific knowledge' translates as the organisation of a film
as a system of representation; mostly, we are expected to comprehend it
as such – an already encoded narrative space – 'by-passing' or playing
down, as it were, the sensuous experience of film watching (or, as in
action and horror genre films, praising the special effects for their 'realistic' feel), subsuming it to the logic and coherence of the scenario and
the realism of the representation and characterisation. Yet, cinema's
synaesthetic power of evocation turns the viewing of certain films into
primarily affective, multi-sensory experiences. To engage with such
works arguably allows the viewer to transform into what Sobchack
describes as a '*cinesthetic* subject': a spectator who can experience a
film not merely as an exercise in the mastery of a representational system,
but as the triggering of a 'pre-logical non-hierarchical unity of the
sensorium' (Sobchack 2004: 69).

In effect, as Marks underlines, there currently seems to be a 'Western
cultural longing to rediscover sensuous knowledges, evident among schol-
ars, artists and consumers' (Marks 2000: 144), in which film as a multi-
sensory experience has a crucial role to play: 'Although cinema is an
audio-visual medium, synaesthesia, as well as haptic visuality, enables the
viewer to experience cinema as multi-sensory' (Marks 2000: 22–3).
Mimesis, as 'a form of yielding to one's environment rather than dominating it', and embodied memory, she argues, are key processes in the acti-
vation of a sensuous cinematic experience: 'a work of cinema, though it
only engages two senses, activates a memory that necessarily involves all
the senses' (Marks 2000: 140). Through very simple as well as elaborate
operations, cinema can thus reawaken or make the viewer conscious of
sensual correspondences. Through framing, camera movement, light and
contrast, the grain of the image and the mix of different film stocks, as well
as the variations in sound and visual intensities, the effect of the audio-
visual footage extends to touch, smell and taste, and, in turn, operates as a
relay between the sensual and the emotional – the diffuse but pervasive
multi-sensory evocation of pleasure, desire, longing, fear and terror.

In some of the examples discussed below, the deployment of synaesthetic techniques partakes in the vivid evocation of desire as a multi-
sensory, embodied experience; in others, it is connected to a critique of
the dominant systems of Western epistemology; through synaesthetic

techniques, film then 'thinks' its way through common strategies of historical amnesia and exclusion.

Les Invisibles

Halfway through Thierry Jousse's *Les Invisibles* (2005), one key sequence operates, through a very simple reversal of the conventional hierarchy of sensory effects, a delightful unsettling of the relationship between sound and vision. *Les Invisibles'* main character, Bruno (Laurent Lucas), is a musician and composer of electronic music, who, while surfing on a telephonic network, falls in love with the misty voice of a mysterious woman. Lisa (Margot Abascal) agrees to meet him but refuses to be seen; their rendezvous should always take place in anonymous hotel rooms and in darkness. Bruno, however, secretly tapes each of their encounters, replays his recordings obsessively and starts using them in his musical compositions. One morning, after spending the night with the young woman, the musician wakes up with a start and finds himself alone in an unfamiliar bedroom. He retrieves his miniature recorder from under the bed, puts on his headphones and plugs them in. The noise of a door opening suddenly fills the sound-track with uncanny realism, and as the young man turns his head to look, so does the camera turn towards the original source of the sound, settling on a close-up of the bathroom door left ajar after Lisa's departure. In a slow circular panoramic, the camera then follows the young woman's invisible body as she is heard wandering through the room, the sound of her slight footsteps accompanied by her soft humming of the distinctive tune (Prokofiev's *Peter and the Wolf*) that connotes her presence throughout the film. A medium-shot insert of Bruno shows him now mimicking the progress of the camera's travelling movement and staring intently at the empty space as he tracks the ghostly presence. The course of the camera slows down briefly near the valet, where we listen to the ruffle of fabric, then continues its course to the main door where it pauses expectantly. The final shot is a medium close-up of the inert doorknob – we hear the noise of the door opening and closing, then silence. What makes this brief sequence memorable is the remarkable power of evocation that the sound-track alone acquires; in the end, we not only hear, we *see* the doorknob turn as if in the grip of Lisa's hand. Yet, in the dull light of the early morning, the bedroom, with its glum palette of brown and beige colours, has initially offered a perfectly unremarkable sight. The hotel room commonly represents an 'any-space-whatever' as well as, in Marc Augé's designation from which Deleuze initially draws, an in-between space, as interchangeable as the hotel room occupied for a few hours by the lovers of

Claire Denis' *Vendredi soir* (2002). Here, it also recalls Deleuze's own characterisation of the 'any-space-whatever' as a space where connections 'can be made in an infinite number of ways', a space that is not given whole; in this sequence of *Les Invisibles*, the camera may pan around the room, yet it offers only a low, horizontal section of it – presumably, at the level where Lisa's hands would have appeared. In that sense, the film constructs a space that recalls Deleuze's description: 'Space has left behind its own coordinates and its metric relations. It is a tactile space' (Deleuze 1986: 109).[9] The couple's previous meetings had taken place in almost complete obscurity, with the camera moving slowly, in caressing movements, to outline the forms of their barely visible silhouettes. Hence, lost in the surrounding darkness, the hotel rooms where they met were but mere chiasms of shadow destined to hold the bodies of the lovers.[10] Yet, in the morning of the last encounter, and for the duration of a fleeting moment, this banal, disconnected space regains some kind of homogeneousness; it becomes literally inhabited, the body of the young woman effectively materialising through the combination of sound and camera movement, creating, through the pleasure of synaesthetic recognisance, an elusive instant of sensory plenitude. Here, sound functions like a fetish, demonstrating what Marks describes as cinema's power to reawaken our sensual memory. Yet, at the same time, there is a discreet epistemological and ethical value attached to this mysterious miniature portrait in movements and sounds. Crucially, this sonorous image of the young woman yields none of the powers of objectification that an actual gaze would have implied (in that sense, it is the very antithesis of the obsessive gaze in which Simon, in Chantal Akerman's *La Captive*, tries to imprison his lover). Like Ariane in *La Captive* (2000), Lisa is a figure of flight; for all that the apparatus estab-

---

[9] In his discussion of the close-up as an element of suture, Pascal Bonitzer remarks:

> It is not pure coincidence if Bazin uses the image of the close-up on a door knob: it is because where the camera operates in a studio or in a closed room, the close-up, which constitutes a limit of the optical system integrated to the Hollywood type of editing (diffraction and suturing of the vision) marks the edge, the knob of the door that opens onto the unknown. (Bonitzer 1999: 24)

In the extract from Jousse's film, the construction of such a finite space, where the 'spectator is fixed to a very precise spot', is countered by the uncanny effect of the choice of framing and the atemporal audio-visual synchronicity.

[10] Sobchack remarks: 'Chiasm is the term first used by Merleau-Ponty in "Eye and Mind" to indicate a "unique space which separates and reunites, which sustains every cohesion". In general phenomenological usage it is used to name the ground of all presence against which discrete figures of being emerge as such' (Merleau-Ponty (1964) 'Eye and Mind', trans. Carleton Dallery, in James Edie (ed.), *The Primacy of Perception*, Evanston, IL: Northwestern University Press: 187, cited in Sobchack 2004: 294).

lished by *Les Invisibles*, with its audio-voyeurism and suspenseful quest, initially seems to give the filmmaker the power of a 'deus ex machina', the loose narrative frame does not allow the device to 'pierce through the mystery, only to use it as its spring-board' (Burdeau 2005: 40). Ultimately, the only lines of dialogue uttered by the lovers in daylight generate nothing more than an exchange of clichés; in a modern rendition of the myth of Psyche, the cost of Bruno breaking his vow and contemplating the young woman in her sleep is the disappearance of the object of his fantasy. Cut short halfway through the film, the love story gives way to chronicling the elaboration of a musical composition whose sensual, sonorous environment actually grows to form the fabric of the film.

Jousse's long-standing involvement with electronic and noise music, and his collaboration with the musician Noël Akchoté in particular, account for the remarkably intricate quality of *Les Invisibles'* sound-track. As the opening credits roll, a dense, feverish layering of voices, male and female, interspersed with telephonic jingles, fills the sound space then combines with electronic sounds. In effect, in the dehierarchisation of sounds, then of sound and visual matter, that the film operates, Jousse applies techniques borrowed from electro and noise music. As sounds are recorded, scanned, sampled and edited by Bruno, the human voice loses its prevailing status to become, alongside the noise of creaking gates, crushed dead leaves and purely abstract electronic chords, just another component of the rich sonorous matter that forms the film's sound-track. At the same time, there is an unusual sense of redundancy to the film's visual treatment; the first images are close-ups of sampling disks. The opening credit sequence further intersects with shots that meticulously explore the complex surfaces of an editing suite and then cuts to a close-up of the back of Bruno's head, the camera moving slowly away to reveal him sitting in front of his sampling desk, bare-chested, with headphones on. Such footage abounds in the film: partial close-ups of a character showing the nape of a neck, an ear, as well as detailed still-life-like shots of recording equipment. In the same way as Marks underlines how 'unnecessary' filmic images of hands are 'in terms of evoking a sense of the haptic' (Marks 2000: 171), Jousse's insistent return to visual evocations of sound and hearing may seem merely tautological. Yet, like the extracts of dialogue, which the obsessive replaying, sampling and mixing transform into musical patterns, these images of sensory involvement, in their superfluous, descriptive nature, participate in reappropriating the representative or discursive into the filmic matter. With its limited range of motifs as well as colour tones, but also its emphasis on the textured surface of things – steel and plastic, fabric, flesh – the filmmaking, thus, takes attention away from the narrative. Encouraging the spectator's immersion in the film's sonorous and tactile environment, it strives to evoke, by way of this sensuous involvement, a mental space structured around a musical perception of the world.

Jousse associated Emmanuelle Bernheim, a writer whose factual style has been compared to that of the *Nouveau Roman* authors, with the elaboration of the scenario of *Les Invisibles*. In effect, in its emphasis on phenomenological description, Bernheim's writing could be characterised as 'cinematic', and it is not surprising to also find her name in the credits of some of the films of Claire Denis, whose works offers fine explorations of cinema's synaesthetic power.

Nénette et Boni

I have described elsewhere how Denis' work, in particular through her collaboration with director of photography Agnès Godard, has gradually moved further into the territories of the cinema of sensation (Beugnet 2004b). Amongst her films, *Nénette et Boni* and *Vendredi soir* stand out in their conscious privileging of the exploration of cinema as an art of sensation over narrative elaboration, as well as in the vivid web of correspondences that they succeed in creating which collapse the effect of cinematic synaesthesia into the evocation of subjective states of mind. *Nénette et Boni* brings together, through the contrasted portraits of a brother and a sister, two opposite experiences of the world; where Nénette (Alice Houri) stands for the distrust of the physical, Boni (Grégoire Colin) exudes a sensuality which, in some sequences, literally radiates through the body of the film. Thus initially, it is the body of Boni – not an adolescent any more, yet not quite a young man – that serves as the locus of an intense, and often witty, exploration of cinema's sensuous power of evocation: 'Boni is an essentially physical being whose existence is, so to speak, reduced to a body that the director films at every moment of the day. She shows a body in pain or in ecstasy, a body expanding, emptying itself, pouring out' (Garbaz 1997: 39). Badly camouflaged behind his naïve show of machismo, Boni's hypersensitivity translates into a filmic universe that is awash with sensations – audio-visual sensations that the filmmaking converts into feelings of touch, smell and taste. Sensations are sometimes evoked through representation (we witness Boni kneading pizza dough, crushing soft brioches between his fingers, eating fresh bread, awaking to the smell of percolating coffee, or, simply, returning the camera gaze with his own piercing stare), or even through dialogue (as in the long sequence in the shopping mall where Boni meets the baker woman (Valeria Bruni Tedeschi) outside a perfume shop and listens, mesmerised, as she describes the hidden powers of body odours).[11] However, multi-sensory evocations emanate most compellingly from the filmic matter itself. In blocks of colour or in small bright touches, the heightened hues that characterise the young man's environment bring the material surface of the image alive, rendering it more tactile. The crude ingenuousness of Boni's erotic obsessions is captured through a series of unashamedly obvious metonymic figures that contribute to the film's sensual overload; surrounded by freshly baked buns and breads, or outlined by the fluffy pink material of her nightdress, the voluptuous figure of the baker woman, the object of Boni's desire, is the very incarnation of softness and warmth. Early in the film, a series of characteristically haptic images (director of photography Agnès Godard uses a similar approach for a number of sequences in Denis' *Trouble Every Day* and in Sébastien Lifshitz's *Wild Side*, discussed later on in this chapter) draw a sensuous portrait of the young man through a humorous yet powerful combination of effects that bring the five senses into play.

The scene cuts directly from a shot of Nénette walking into the cold, wet night. At first, all we see is a heap of bright and colourful flowery patterns; the frame is filled with a view of Boni's bedcover. Godard's camera travels slowly over the fabric, its sinuous movements mimicking the complicated, swirling motifs that adorn the cloth. The sequence then cuts to a close-up of exposed flesh – a fragment of Boni's naked back, over which the camera lingers in a slow caressing movement before settling on the nape of his neck and ear, his face remaining averted, half-buried in the pillow. Throughout, Boni's whispering voice mingles with the noise of softly rustling fabric and the expectant sound of a few muted guitar chords; Boni is masturbating while dreaming about the beautiful baker woman. The young man's fantasy materialises in a brief insert of dislocated, obscure shots where he dreams up an encounter with her. Then, in a sudden cut, the frame appears filled with abstract motifs: a combination of moving organic and geometric patterns in various shades of yellow, like sun-beams refracted through a piece of patterned glass – a pure evocation of warmth. A strange gurgling

---

[11] In their wilful exploration of cinema's synaesthetic pleasures, films such as Jousse's and Denis' thus encourage a dehierarchisation of sensual perception. In his chapter in *A History of the Devil* entitled 'The Devil and the Body', Robert Muchembled stresses how one of the effects of the promotion of sight, which led to the demoting of other senses, was the demonising of smell.

> Sight, in the minds of educated people, was increasingly associated with masculinity, God, clarity, beauty and reason, particularly after Descartes. It was civilised, distancing itself from the eye of the witch that bore the mark of the diabolic toad . . . But while the mechanism for a promotion of sight was being established, smell was experiencing a descent into hell. (Muchembled 2003: 99, translation mine)

noise accompanies the shot and bleeds over a further cut, to an image of Boni sitting against a concrete wall, exposing his face and torso to the sun. The next cut is a medium close-up of Boni waking up in bed to the sound and smell of filtering coffee and leaning over sideways to stroke the percolator. This series of sequences form a vivid evocation of a progressive, pleasurable passage from deep sleep to being awake. Framing, light and editing wilfully render the audio-visual footage confusing, relinquishing its expository function in favour of a multi-sensory evocation – the concrete and the crude merge with the dream-like; complete abstraction combines with images of the most banal of objects to form a moment of purely sensuous cinematic experience. The way the body of the film folds itself around the body of the actor works like a cinematic equivalent of Merleau-Ponty's chiasm, 'where being in the world, the becoming self, is fleshed out of the oscillations between self and other [before] the distinction between word and thing, language and experience' (Millroy 2005: 545). In effect, in *Nénette et Boni*, as in her later, eloquently titled feature, *L'Intrus*, the yearning for a relation with the world that would not be an experience of alienation but one of sensory plenitude incarnates itself literally in the body of the newborn baby. The shots that depict Boni holding his sister's baby do not merely capture the feelings of warmth and softness that emanate from the still amorphous body that the young man cradles; coming at the end of the multi-sensory filmic experience that *Nénette et Boni* offers, these images also evoke the kind of sensuous, pre-linguistic perception that cinema, maybe, sometimes, in that interstice between the physical impact of a film and its interpretation, can offer to the spectator with whom the film then becomes but one assemblage – a kind of 'body-without-organ'. The conclusion of the scene, however, should help us keep in check the element of pomposity that such theorising could generate: the baby pees on Boni.

Vendredi soir

Adapted from Bernheim's eponymous novel, as in Jousse's film, the premise of *Vendredi soir* is the chance encounter of two strangers who become lovers for one night. Driving through Paris during a freezing winter evening, Laure (Valérie Lemercier) is caught in a massive traffic jam. She lets a passer-by climb into her car, and the film depicts, almost without dialogue, the development of their mutual attraction. With its minimalist story- line, its limited use of places and near-unity of time, *Vendredi soir* was generally described as a formalist exercise (Kaganski 2002: 36). Yet, it is precisely by eschewing plot development to construct, instead, a temporal space that is like a suspended moment, an 'enchanted parenthesis', that Denis can, in turn, create the vividly sensuous world that is *Vendredi soir*. In *Les Invisibles*, Jousse portrays a young man whose stubbly chin and compulsive eye-rubbing denote a constant state of tiredness. In *Vendredi soir*, it is the sweeping long shots and dreamy music of the opening sequence, the long still takes joined by dissolves and slow-travelling shots that describe the traffic jam, that concur to evoke this in-between state, between sleep and awakeness, where one's body drops its guard and surrenders itself to the sensory impact of its surroundings. As in Jousse's film, the feeling that *Vendredi soir*'s diegesis is created out of a temporal parenthesis is associated with the presence of a number of locations that evoke the Deleuzean 'any-spaces-whatever'. Yet again, the characters are not merely 'seers', as in Deleuze's description of the inhabitants of these cinematic spaces (Deleuze 1989: xi); hence, in *Vendredi soir*, the enigmatic insert which shows the disembodied floating vision of a deserted subway station is but the prelude to an intensely embodied and sensuous experience. Accordingly, the exiguous space of the car, in which much of the film's first half is spent, is not a trap but a shelter, its cosiness directly contrasted with the cold wetness of outside, and its restricted geography precluding the establishment of an inclusive, overseeing gaze.

In conventional film language, fragmented images of the body tend to be used to objectify a character (sexually) or to stress a gesture that is crucial to the progression of the plot. But in *Vendredi soir*, this fragmentation, often dictated by the configuration of the space, participates essentially in the progressive invocation of the bodies. The camera tends to focus on unexpected details. In close-up, it follows the outline of a neck, the shape of a thigh under a tight skirt, the movement of a mass of hair in front of a fan. In turn, the fragment becomes a sensory extension, the close-up a focalisation on a particular sensation. The rough texture of the hotel room's carpeted floor is evoked by the contrast with Laure's bare feet which she rubs against it; the shyness and impatience of the first embrace, like the contrast between cold air and warm skin, are encapsulated in the images of hands slipping under the thick layers of winter clothes (Beugnet 2004b: 192).

Entering Laure's car as a stranger, Jean (Vincent Lindon) is immediately scrutinised at close range, the camera capturing images and sounds[12] that are evocative of smells, textures, volumes and even densities – the outline of the young man's profile, his ear, his sturdy hands as he lights a cigarette,

[12] Denis had the opportunity to mix the sound with an SR surround system that recreates a rich and textured sound and generates a heightened feeling of being enveloped in it (Péron 2002: 18).

but also the open neck of his shirt under a leather jacket that makes rich creaking noises as he settles in the seat. Denis has stressed the importance of translating these sensations as vividly as in Bernheim's writing: 'Emmanuelle Bernheim has described this well, the weight, the space occupied by the man who enters the car. So it needed to be felt in the film, that it was not an idea of a man, but a man who has a weight' (Denis 2002, translation mine). Similarly, Bernheim acknowledged Denis' ability to activate cinema's power of evocation: 'As soon as he enters the car, he smells good. You almost feel like you are smelling him, exactly as I tried to describe it in my book' (Bernheim 2002, translation mine). In effect, as in *Nénette et Boni* and *Trouble Every Day*, in *Vendredi soir*, the characters' physical presence imprints itself in the reality around them and seems to linger on after they depart. Laure's body leaves a dent on the mattress that she playfully bounces on at the beginning of the film. Jean leaves the smell of his body, after-shave and cigarettes in Laure's car. The young woman breathes in deeply, touches the wheel to feel the warmth of his hands and sits in the seat shaped by the weight of his body. But the memory and imprint of the other's body carry an element of threat. Laure suddenly withdraws when she feels Jean's teeth closing on the skin of her shoulder. This instinctive reaction of defence recalls *Trouble Every Day*'s evocation of desire's darker dimension. In Laure's case, however, it is also a reminder of the proximity of her 'other' life, a reality where she cannot afford to carry the visible memory of the adulterous embrace. In effect, in Denis' film-making, synaesthetic perception plays fully on the effect of correspondence, that which encompasses the passage from physical sensation into affects and abstract thought. Without recourse to a voiceover, and with hardly any dialogue, the film constructs a vivid sensory world to which corresponds a web of emotions as well as internal reflections: attraction, fear of the unknown, panic and pleasure (Beugnet 2004b: 192–4).

La Blessure

Whereas it was the writing of Bernheim that served as a catalyst for both *Vendredi soir* and Jousse's *Les Invisibles*, Denis' latest release, *L'Intrus* (2005), shares its initial source of inspiration with Nicolas Klotz's feature, *La Blessure* (2004). Both films take their cue from the eponymous book of philosopher Jean-Luc Nancy, whose interests and research have developed across the fields of politics and psychoanalysis, around notions of otherness and selfhood, community and multiculturalism. What attracted Denis and Klotz to Nancy's writing, and in particular to the text of *L'Intrus* (though the relation between text and films is much looser than one of adaptation or even transposition), is the way it brings into play the 'embodied' experience. The autobiographical part of Nancy's book, which describes the repercussions of coronary malfunction and the aftermath of a heart transplant (whether the transplant, though necessary for his survival, might be rejected by his body), serves as a basis for a reflection on the issue of exclusion in its many contemporary guises.[13]

In the films, the embodied dimension that informs Nancy's thinking is assumed by a wilfully synaesthetic approach and the privileging of a haptic form of visuality. Crucially, in both cases, as the embodied evocation of displacement and alienation, cinematic synaesthesia does not merely work as an implicit but concrete critique of the principle of exclusion that the films evoke, but simultaneously denies the potentially abstracting, generalising effect of the metaphorical. As Braidotti points out:

> Being nomadic, homeless, an exile, a refugee, a Bosnian rape-in-war victim, an itinerant migrant, an illegal immigrant, is no metaphor. Having no passport or having too many of them is neither equivalent nor is it merely metaphorical, as some critics of nomadic subjectivity have suggested. These are highly specific geo-political and historical locations – history tattooed on your body. (Braidotti 2002: 3)

Synaesthetic, embodied evocation may be one of the ways by which film can 'think' its way concretely through the most burning of contemporary issues, tackling strategies of historical amnesia and exclusion through its own operations. Both uncompromising and richly poetic, Klotz's description of the arrival of African asylum seekers in France makes just such a use of filmic synaesthesia to affecting consequence. Indeed, *La Blessure*

---

[13] Nancy's writing emphasises the paranoia at the heart of Western societies by stressing how medical terminology and the vocabulary of diseases is used to describe other spheres of the modern condition and, in particular, transnationality and the circulation of people.

> I (who is 'I'? that is precisely the question, the old question: who is the subject of the uttering, always a foreigner in the midst of its own utterance, where this subject is necessarily the intruder and yet also the originator, the initiator, the heart?) – I have, then, almost ten years ago, received someone else's heart. I got a transplant. For some unclear reason, my own heart had become useless. In order to live, I needed to receive someone else's heart.

> My heart became my foreigner: foreign precisely because it was inside . . . A strangeness appears 'at the heart' of that which is most familiar.

> One thing at least emerges: identity equals immunity, the one becomes identified with the other. To weaken one is to weaken the other one . . . We are overwhelmed with recommendations regarding the external world . . . but the most active enemies are inside: the old viruses hiding in immunity's shadow, the intruders that were always there, since there always were intruders. (Nancy 2000: 13, 17, 33)

comes close to the kind of works that Marks explores in *The Skin of the Film* and that she defines as intercultural cinema. Shot mainly in hidden parts of Roissy's airport and in a Parisian squat, the film abounds with the type of space that Deleuze evokes in his now classical description of 'any-spaces-whatever'.

> The fact is that, in Europe, the post-war period has greatly increased the situations which we no longer know how to react to, in spaces which we no longer know how to describe. These were 'any-spaces-whatever', deserted but inhabited, disused warehouses, waste ground, cities in the course of demolition or reconstruction. And in these any-spaces-whatever a new race of characters was stirring, a kind of mutant: they saw rather than acted, they were seers. (Deleuze 1989: xi)

Denied their status as asylum seekers, the characters of *La Blessure* are herded into rooms that belong to the airport's 'limbo' land – the indeterminate space that lies between the landing strips and the arrival gates, and seems to fall under the sole jurisdiction of the police. There, the asylum seekers are indeed reduced to waiting and watching, but also, in the denial of intimacy that their detention by the police implies, to being watched (as well as interrogated and subjected to regular body searches). I would, thus, contend that Klotz's film offers a cogent basis for a reconsideration or updating of Deleuze's concept. As Marks puts it:

> These any-spaces-whatever are not simply the disjunctive spaces of post-modernism, but also the disruptive spaces of post-colonialism, where non-Western cultures erupt into Western metropolises, and repressed cultural memories return to destabilise national histories. In this case 'the new race . . . kind of mutant' to which Deleuze refers (in terms that suddenly take on a rather xenophobic cast) describe the very real conditions of migration, diaspora and hybridity. (Marks 2000: 27)

In effect, the multi-sensory, synaesthetic quality of certain scenes of *La Blessure* comes as a form of resistance to the dehumanising effect of a space dominated by the surveillance gaze. It is the relief offered by the presence of other forms of sensual engagement that provides a space – a different, tactile sort of space – where a different kind of contact, relation, speech (unlike the predetermined one-way communication that takes place between the incomers, the police and airport staff) can unravel.[14] The film includes several monologues in which asylum seekers recount their experience of leaving their native country and arriving in France. The first of

---

[14] In that sense, Klotz's project recalls the famously provocative premise contained in the title of Spivak, Gayatri Chakravorti's 1988 article 'Can the Subaltern Speak?', in C. Nelson, L. Grossberg (eds), *Marxism and the Interpretation of Culture*, Urbana: University of Illinois Press, pp. 271–313.

these monologues takes place at the airport, during the night, and plays on the evocation of touch and taste as the premise for a painful work of reminiscing. The sequence starts with a medium shot of Blandine (Noëlla Mobassa), the central figure of the film, who lies in bed wounded, in a cell she shares with another, pregnant, woman; the camera focuses entirely on one or the other woman, the intimacy of their exchange effectively excluding the option of an establishing shot. Blandine, who is peeling an orange, offers a piece of the fruit to her companion. The gesture is the catalyst, stirring the other young woman to rest her head on the bed and start talking. The rest of the sequence is composed of one single long take, during which the framing – a medium close-up – remains unchanged. The soft light, outlining the volumes and textures (skin and fabric), contributes to the feeling of closeness created by the scene, as does the hushed tone of the voice. The frame includes a large chunk of the bedcover, with its muted colour and soft-looking surface, as well as part of Blandine's arm, thus creating an internal frame around the slightly off-centre face of the young woman. Halfway through, Blandine's hand moves into sight, first to lie on the shoulder of her companion, then to rest soothingly on her cheek. The young asylum seeker recounts how she was driven out of Kinshasa, how she first lost track of her husband and was harassed and pursued by the police till she managed to escape the Republic of Congo with forged papers. At the end of her tale, she eats the section of orange and buries her face in Blandine's lap. The sequence comes brutally to an end as the door suddenly opens, letting in the corridor's harsh light, while a policeman calls the two women using the names on their forged passports.

Throughout the film, synaesthetic evocations create similar moments of reprieve, painful but cathartic, so that Blandine herself eventually breaks her silence and confides her angst to her husband. As will be discussed again in the following section, in *La Blessure*, the senses of touch and taste, the collecting or the preparation, as well as the gift and the sharing of food, create embodied expressions of those untold memories and experiences which are granted no space in the visual field opened by the reality of exile and exclusion.

L'Intrus

With *L'Intrus*, Denis creates an elliptical evocation of the postcolonial, transnational zeitgeist that is literally incarnated in the body of Trébor (Michel Subor), a white, middle-aged man with a shady past and a fortune of questionable origins. As the choice of name underlines, the significance of Trébor/Subor's body as the locus of metaphorical and embodied evocations of the issues initially addressed in Nancy's writings exceeds the diegesis; early on, the actor's career was linked with those (rare) examples of French cinema addressing its colonial past,[15] and Denis had already co-opted his charismatic presence for *Beau Travail* – her enthralling tale of the French Foreign Legion (Beugnet 2004b; see also the discussion of the film in Chapter 4). Though I will come back to *L'Intrus* in the course of the following chapter, there is, in this unusual work, a scene that stages a blind, almost silent encounter between two cultures that I would like to describe here in connection with cinematic synaesthesia and the previous discussion of *La Blessure*. The episode occurs halfway through the film and has little-to-no narrative value as such; what it does is literally map out, on a character's body, the traces of a traumatic past (individual and collective) and evoke the experience of 'estrangement' that its materialisation generates. The sequence takes place in Geneva, in the hotel room where Trébor is resting after undergoing a heart transplant. It cuts directly from shots of the streets under falling snow, a dull, cold vision of the city as an any-space-whatever, to the inside of a darkened room; the silhouette of a woman opening the curtains to let in the light is outlined sharply against the window. As she makes her way back from the window towards the centre of the room, we only get a glimpse of her older Asian face; the camera follows her but focuses on her hands, detailing the way she lays her bag down carefully before taking off her coat. The camera stays with her hands as she feels her way towards Trébor, who is sitting on the nearby bed. The scene is almost silent, the old woman indicating by the pressure of her hands how she wants Trébor to lie down and move his body. So far in the film, Trébor had been portrayed as a predator. The sense of vulnerability that his abandoning of his body to the hands of a stranger implies is compounded by insert close-ups of his wary face, then of his knife laid out on the patterned bedcover like a strange exhibit. Yet, it is the point of view or, rather, the positioning of the old woman, that the camera relays, looking down on to her hands as she starts massaging Trébor's body. This body appears only in fragments, creating vivid evocations of localised contact as the masseuse's fingers dig into the nape of his neck, lightly touching his ear before moving on to legs and feet. Only towards the end of the sequence does a counter-shot offer an image of her face, and the confirmation that the old woman is indeed blind. This shot occurs just before she motions

---

[15] In *Beau Travail* (1999), the Foreign Legion officer played by Subor could have been an older embodiment of the character he acted in Jean-Luc Godard's *Le Petit Soldat* (1961) 40 years before. Similarly, in *L'Intrus*, he appears like the older personification of a character from *Reflux*, a feature shot by Paul Gégauff in 1965, when Subor was in his twenties. For a fuller discussion of the intertextual components of *L'Intrus*, see Beugnet 2005a.

Trébor to lie down on his back, revealing his scars – straight, linear folds of reddened flesh cutting through his torso to form a dreadful geometrical marking. The hands of the old woman feel the raised skin lightly, following its furrow hesitantly. A close-up on Trébor's eyes shows him squinting with pain as the old woman asks whether he is suffering. The sequence then cuts to its first inclusive view, showing Trébor's body laid out on the bed and the old woman kneeling next to him with her hand on his leg, waiting, as if taking stock. The following scene puts the sense of empathetic exchange created by this brief moment in check, however; it shows Trébor paying the old woman for her service. Still, through the vivid, tactile quality of its camerawork and *mise en scène*, the scene calls to mind Marks' description of exiles as 'seers', endowed with a 'third eye' that allows them to see the scars woven into the history of an amnesiac postcolonial West:

> These people are 'seers' in the metropolitan West, aware of violent histories to which its dominant population is blind. They possess what Fatimah Tobing Rony (1996) calls a third eye, which allows them to perceive the dominant culture from both inside and outside. (Marks 2000: 26)

Feeling alienation

Cinema's evocation of the other senses is a powerful way of making us 'feel' alienation, either by evoking, through an unspoken, physical contact, a connection that was severed, or by revealing its absence. Touch without empathy is the sign of a lost link with the other and with the world, the ultimate expression of dehumanisation. Hence, for instance, Breillat's critique of modern medicine as the 'investigation' of the (female) body: medical students being instructed to feel the inside of a pregnant young woman at the hospital, forming a grotesque line-up in front of her open legs. It is the most shocking, and certainly the most pornographic, of the scenes in a film that features 'real' sex (though Breillat's account derives its force from the ability of the heroine to seemingly turn the situation to her advantage). Hence also Grandrieux's vision of contemporary human traffic: Boyan moving along a line of naked men and women, looking and touching, evaluating their worth in the manner of a horse-dealer (*La Vie nouvelle*).

In effect, if Grandrieux's filmmaking operates the most radical destabilisation of the conventions of feature cinema's visual economy, the synaesthetic power of its images brings little of the sense of reprieve or catharsis suggested in Klotz or Denis' films. Indeed, in *La Vie nouvelle* (2002), Grandrieux's own dystopian vision of the after-effects of war and exile operates like a progressive descent into hell where the growing sense of estrangement and powerlessness is compounded by a progressively more powerful confrontation with the meaninglessness of matter. This process of inexorable, unspeakable alienation that infuses the film's audio-visual make-up culminates in the sequence of the inferno towards the end of the film.

Here, synaesthesia initially operates through the technology itself, in the way the images are recorded. Grandrieux used a thermo camera to shoot these sequences; what impresses the film is not light, but heat, transformed into a scale of greys. The result is a vision of ultimate abjection; bodies metamorphose into monstrous creatures, eyeless, translucent silhouettes, part-human, part-animal, howling and hovering blindly in the dark, and tearing up each other's flesh – a scene of utter chaos, filled by an inchoate mix of rumbling noise and distorted yells. The figures, some of them still bearing, in the blurred outline of familiar features, the disappearing traces of an identity, contort under the strain of their monstrous metamorphosis. It is the pull of the formless in its terrifying, Bataillean horror that this evokes – a reminder of film's powerful capacity to conjure up and then annihilate the human figure by swallowing it back into the images' matter. There is also a strong sense of 'becoming' here, in the way the transformation of the figures seems to occur as if in an exchange of 'particules', through the mutation of their very 'molecular' make-up (Deleuze and Guattari 1987: 272). Yet, even if we behold the aesthetic shock that such images create, it is difficult to equate them fully with the positive, life-expanding dimension of Deleuze and Guattari's concepts. As well as to the theory of 'becoming', Grandrieux's vision relates to Deleuze's comments on expressionist cinema (and on Worringer's theories of expressionism) where he describes its 'formlessness' and 'disorderly convulsion' as the evocation of a 'world chaos' from which (in Worringer's opinion) modern man must emerge with 'the cry' as the ultimate expression of his predicament (Deleuze 1989: 51–4 and 225 n34). Strikingly, the sequences that follow the descent into hell demonstrate that metamorphosis is no less effective when it results not from manipulation of the recording conditions, but merely from the movement of a body and the angle of shooting: the film concludes on a horrific cry of despair – a Bacon-like vision that deforms the main character beyond recognition.

Close-up[16]

The camera enters the mayhem, weaves its way between the distorted shapes, brushing against flesh that ripples like white magma; a distorted face fills the

---

[16] See my article for Nottingham French Series, Beugnet (2006).

screen, its eyes and mouth gaping like dark craters. What exacerbates the horror of the infernal vision at the end of *La Vie nouvelle* is the way the haptic images bring us amongst the monsters, suggesting contact. Prominent in the kind of aesthetics of sensation that emerges through that part of recent French cinema I am interested in, the close-up is a key cinematic figure here, one that dramatically emphasises the ambiguous nature of the process at work in cinema's haptic vision. In the way it orchestrates a passage or a rupture from optical vision into haptic visuality, the close-up epitomises how cinema's incessant processes of metamorphosis ultimately entail a sense of radical desubjectivation. It is here, at the point where the boundary between subject and object of the gaze appears to dissolve, that cinema most power-fully evokes a sense of loss of self, where the cinematic experience offers itself most strikingly as an exultant combination of pleasure and terror.

The close-up is one of the most potent techniques through which film 'thinks' through the issue of the construction of the subject and object (and the possibility of inter-subjectivities), and, where cinema becomes a cinema of sensation, these issues are paramount. Alternating between two poles – the contemplation of the imperceptible, of the micro-life, or the dramatic engagement with the body in mutation, the device offers nour-ishment for the haptic eye rather than psychological information or narra-tive linkages; it chronicles the metamorphosis of the body rather than reassert identity as the continuity and coherence of sameness.

In one of his articles on the evolution of filmmaking,[17] critic Pascal Bonitzer talks of the 'passion for close-up vision' as part of a new way of looking, where the eye is 'completely free . . ., an eye that does not operate according to the classical perspective, a tactile eye, or, better, a "haptic" one'.[18] The history of the close-up is interwoven with that of the construc-tion of the body; scale in film, and the typology of the shots, have trad-itionally been established and measured in relation to the scale of the human body. However, the close-up is also a fundamental element in the 'develop-ment of the cinematic body' ('*la formation du corps cinématographique*'). The 'cinematic body' should be understood here in the sense of bodies on screen, of film as body, as well as of the cinema as a whole, and in that latter sense, both diachronically, as an array of potential historical developments, and

---

[17] Bonitzer [1982] (1999), *Le Champ aveugle*, Paris: Cahiers du cinéma. Although Bonitzer cites Deleuze – and in particular bases his definition of hapticity on Deleuze's study of Bacon – his article on the close-up pre-empts the publication of the first volume of Deleuze's books on cinema where Deleuze develops the concept of the affection-image.

[18] Bonitzer 1999: 28. The terms of the description are reminiscent of Stan Brakhage's often quoted introduction to 'Metaphors on Vision', first published in *Film Culture* 30 (Autumn 1963).

synchronically as the sum of effects and experiences it offers (Bonitzer 1999: 16). Indeed, in many ways, the destiny of the cinematic close-up seems to encapsulate the history of the 'battle of haptic and the optical' (Marks 2000: 171).[19] Bonitzer recalls the intensity of the debates that took place around the function and meaning of the close-up and suggests that the history of its application coincides with the denial of crucial aspects of cinematic expression. In particular, he outlines the development in classical narrative cinema of strategies of containment for what he calls the 'poetic anarchy', called forth by the close-up's inherent power of rupture. In effect, the close-up shot initially generates a spatial, temporal and figurative as well as perceptual disruption. It dis-locates the object of the gaze, fragments it and carves it out of its surroundings. Against Griffith's synecdochal use of the close-up, however, Sergei Eisenstein and Béla Balázs famously insisted that the device derived its powerful impact from its ability to establish itself as an entity in itself, appearing outside of notions of relative scale and realist space (Eisenstein [1940] 1974: 229; Balász [1923] 1972: 57),[20] to *abstract* [its object] *from all spatio-temporal co-ordinates* (Deleuze 1986: 96).[21]

By the same token, the close-up thus also ruptures the body of the *récit* and brings the narrative flow to a halt, almost like a still picture. Combined with the effect of isolation or abstraction and the impact of scale afforded

[19] The close-up shot is one of the techniques whose emergence marks the move from early cinema to forms of modern cinema. With techniques such as the close-up, cinema ceased to be a kind of 'filmed theatre', where the point of view of the camera and, by extension, that of the spectator, were more or less fixed at a specific angle and distance (and, in fiction film, where the *seen* corresponded to the whole *scene*).

See also Walter Benjamin's classical description of the new vision afforded through film's operations:

Our taverns and our metropolitan streets, our offices and furnished rooms, our railroad stations and our factories appeared to have us locked up hopelessly. Then came the film and it burst this prison-world asunder by the dynamite of the tenth of a second, so that now, in the midst of its far-flung ruins and debris, we calmly and adventurously go travelling. With the close-up, space expands; with slow-motion, movement is extended. The enlargement of a snapshot does not simply render more precise what in any case was visible, though unclear: it reveals entirely new structural formations . . . Evidently, a different nature opens itself to the camera than opens to the naked eye . . . [T]he camera introduces us to an unconscious optics as does psychoanalysis to unconscious impulses. (Benjamin [1969] 1986: 236)

[20] As he vividly summarised it: '[A] cockroach filmed in close-up seems on the screen a hundred times more terrible than a hundred elephants captured in a long-shot' (Eisenstein [1940] 1974: 112). Similarly, in his analysis of the facial close-up, Balázs stresses how in the close-up vision 'a dimension of another order is opened to us' (Balázs [1923] 1972: 57).

[21] As we will see in Chapter 4, in *Zidane*, the use of the close-up as part of a process of 'sculpting in movement' questions the traditional dichotomy of close-up as autonomous entity or as linkage.

by the cinema screen,[22] this endows it with a force of *interpellation*; the close-up insists, calls on and directs the attention of the viewer. As such, it (forcibly) brings the eye where it would not normally look. Destroying the customary effects of unifying perspective, erasing the elements of localisation provided by the wider context, it places the viewer, in André Gardies and Jean Bessalel's words, *en position de proximité absolue*.[23] The close-up thus creates uncanny intimacies and shows us the body as we rarely dare look at it – as an organic mass bearing the marks of a process of decomposition that is barely visible to the naked eye. Ultimately, the extreme close-up brings us beyond the point of recognition, where the body becomes matter and falls into the realm of the unnameable.

The close-up derives its unsettling effect from an ability to call on the most powerful of drives: scopophilia, curiosity, the endless desire to see and to know. The repulsive/compulsive paradox is no better illustrated than in the experience of being presented with the relentless reality of the abject[24] in close-up – the magnified image of the body deformed or metamorphosing that suddenly fills one's field of vision, or the vertigo of the gaping hole that appears to draw the gaze of the camera towards the void, recalling Bonitzer's remark: 'In the cinema, the hole is always dramatic. It is a well, a wound, a key-hole for the sly gaze of the voyeur. . . . it is a black hole, an anus, an open sex, a gaping belly, an abyss' (Bonitzer 1999: 31, translation mine).

Bonitzer does not mention sound, yet the close-up is sonorous as much as visual; as exemplified in the extract from *Les Invisibles* discussed earlier, physical closeness can be evoked by sound in the absence of images. In the films discussed here, sound plays an essential role in the construction of a haptic space. Synchronous or asynchronous, precise and hyper-detailed or inchoate, the audio close-up pulls the viewer in and envelops him or her with a sensuous or uncanny sense of intimacy or gives full power to the feelings of repulsion brought forth by excessively close contact with the abject (and, where the image does not show, the sound's synaesthetic presence feeds into the viewer's imagination and gives materiality to the invisible).[25]

[22] And this is where the impact of *interpellation* of the film image, projected on a large cinema screen, exceeds that of the televised image, for instance. See John Ellis (1993), 'Broadcast TV as Sound and Image', in *Visible Fictions*, London: Routledge, pp. 127–44.

[23] André Gardies Jean Bessalel (1992), *200 mots clefs de la théorie du cinéma*, Paris: Éditions du Cerf, p. 100.

[24] In Kristeva's now classic definition, the abject is that which dissolves the 'I', or 'pulverises the subject', an 'ever present' that 'repels but beseeches', that which disrupts identity, systems, order. What does not respect borders, positions, rules' (Kristeva 1982: 4).

[25] As Ann Powell remarks, sound remains an under-studied dimension of the cinema and Deleuze only mentions in passing the possibility of considering 'the sound image for itself' (Powell 2005: 206).

Strategies of containment

Although filmmakers from the early avant-garde movements had explored different effects of the close-up in conjunction with the fragmentary nature of film, the device was developed primarily as part of cinema's classical continuity system. Dramatisation and narrative organisation, shot/counter-shot and cause-and-effect links, all worked towards suturing the gaps opened by the close-up, re-establishing the illusory impression of unified bodies and identities, promoting character identification and the spectator as omniscient observer. Whereas in its poetic effect of disruption, a close-up of a head or part of the body is a monstrous apparition or a fantastic landscape, in mainstream practices, the close-up image draws its meaning only in connection with the full shot of the body in action. It functions as one element in a totality that forms a finished narrative. The head stands for the whole body (the rational in control of the physical), the face is a signifier of subjecthood and individuality, and the expression is an element of a narrative logic, to be explicated by the counter-shot that provides an image of its cause or effect.[26]

Bonitzer stresses how, ultimately, the 'terror of the close-up', as he describes it, is appropriated and contained within the boundaries of genre conventions, as in the horror film and the thriller (Bonitzer 1999: 22). But pornographic films as well as scientific and medical documentaries are equally relevant in this context.[27] Indeed, the device's various effects of fragmentation are commonly cited as central stylistic features of porn, gore and horror films,[28] and arguably, by virtue of the

[26] In synecdochal mode, the cause-and-effect system and strategies for creating suspense in particular take their full force thanks to series of connections where facial expressions – horror, surprise, delight – are isolated by the close-up and preceded or followed by an image of their cause (delays and inversions – effect before cause – helping to build the suspense). In his description of the 'affect' image, however, Deleuze, in agreement with Eisenstein and Balázs, insists on the importance of the close-up as an entity in itself, resulting in the suspension of such links (Deleuze 1986: 100–1).

[27] On the connection between scientific and pornographic discourses, see, for instance, Hansen, Christian, Catherine Needham, Bill Nichols (1991), 'Pornography, ethnography and the discourses of power', in Bill Nichols (ed.), *Representing Reality: Issues and Concepts in Documentary* (Bloomington: Indiana University Press), pp. 201–29.

[28] In its common format, the pornographic film characteristically multiplies close-ups and does away, as much as possible, with the narrative dimension, which is only reintroduced when the film fails to 'deliver', recommencing endlessly the same minimal story with small variations. Partly in opposition to such uses of the close-up in relation to the female body in particular, long shots dominated in many of the 1970s non-action-driven films of feminist filmmakers. The section entitled 'Body-landscape', however, describes alternative approaches, developed in recent cinema, that revisit the link between narrative stasis and close-up.

direct impact that they aim to effect on the body of the spectator, call into question the viewer's status as detached observer.[29] The strategy, however, appears mainly as a derivation and an intensification of mainstream cinema's chief stylistic figures. The itemisation of the body and its fetishistic treatment become first and foremost a tool for the objectification, visual possession and consumption (or erasure) of the 'Other'. In this context, the much-debated premise of feminist film theory, concerning the construction of the gaze in film as primarily 'male' and as a discourse of power, remains as useful as ever; in the majority of cases, the body investigated, attacked and dehumanised is that of the woman.[30] A parallel thus emerges between the recuperation and containment of the disruptive effect of the close-up, and the attempt, alternatively, to mark out or deny difference: that is, contain and/or assimilate the body of the 'other', in particular female.[31]

As a cinema of sensation, however, contemporary French film provides some potent counter-examples of stylistic and thematic forms of reappropriation, where a renewed exploration of the disruptive power of the close-up appears coextensive with the remapping of the cinematic body through haptic vision.

---

[29] Though he grounds the premise of his discussion of pornographic cinema in characteristically psychoanalytical terms, Paul Willemen makes an unusual remark with interesting implications as far as film and embodiment are concerned; the construction of the gaze in pornography, he argues, is not necessarily limited to a strategy to override the fear of castration. 'The specular relation is dependent on the emphatic direct address interpellating the viewer as possessor and donor of the phallus, the one who is required *to complete* the picture, as it were' (Paul Willemen (1992), 'Letter to John', in Caughie, John, Barbara Creed, Annette Kuhn (eds), *The Sexual Subject: A Screen Reader in Sexuality*, London: Routledge, pp. 171–83), p. 176.

[30] It is a well-known argument that even female pleasure has become a fetish in porn movies, as if the classical close-up on the hero or heroine's face is translated here as the close-up on the woman's face at the moment of orgasm. On this subject, Claire Pajaczkowska's enlightening study of Godard's *Sauve qui peut (la vie)* (1980) provides interesting parallels with the uses of the voiceover in *Romance* discussed later in this chapter (Claire Pajaczkowska (1990), 'Liberté, égalité paternité!: Jean-Luc Godard and Anne-Marie Miéville's *Sauve qui peut (la vie)*', in Hayward, Susan and Ginette Vincendeau (eds), *French Film: Texts and Contexts*, London: Routledge, pp. 241–8).

[31] Unsurprisingly, genres where the close-up abounds have long been considered essentially male directors' territory and, with the exception of the melodrama, where the close-up conventionally functions as part of a general system of 'emotional shock tactics', as implicitly intended for mainly male audiences. However, with a large proportion of women amongst its successful filmmakers and technicians, contemporary French film, where it explores the territories of a cinema of sensation, emerges as a potent example of reappropriation of these areas of the cinematographic body (Beugnet 2006).

The Body-landscape

Significantly, in many of the films considered here, the temporal and spatial parenthesis created by the close-up at the level of the shot seems to operate already at the level of the overall narrative organisation. It is as if the filmmakers had sought to remove the bodies of their characters from the flow of the 'mouvement-image', to take them away from the action-driven narrative in order to create a kind of stasis that, in turn, induces the regime of the close-up.[32]

In Klotz's *La Blessure*, the immobility enforced by the containment of the bodies (locked up in narrow cells at the airport and later trapped in crowded squats) is never elided. Where outward reality seems little else than barred horizons, however, the close-up helps to suggest that inner spaces elude closure. A sense of inaction is also key to Catherine Breillat's controversial tale of sexual awakening, *Romance* (1998), whose cyclical narrative includes scenes of bondage sessions during which the body of the main character is tied up and immobilised. As we have seen, Claire Denis' *Vendredi soir* takes place during a general transport strike when the whole of Paris is brought to a standstill during a cold winter night; filmed in floating tracking movements and slow motion, the city appears to fall gradually into a sort of trance, like a gigantic body becoming frozen. Since the two main protagonists spend the first part of the film in the restricted space of a small car, Denis recounts that, at times, director of photography Agnès Godard and herself 'also had the impression of living through a love story. In the end, we knew the very texture of their skin' (Beugnet 2004b: 193). Paradoxically, since the film is, after all, a road movie, a similar effect of narrative stasis operates in Dumont's *Twentynine Palms*, which accumulates any-spaces-whatever (hotel rooms, petrol stations, the edges of the speedway . . .) and combines long takes with the absence of action proper to the point where it ultimately feels as if the narrative itself 'were becoming static' (Rouyer 2003: 15).[33]

In such cases, the tight framing does not operate as a narrative complement to the medium or long shot or as a means of objectifying and

---

[32] A precursor in this area of filmmaking, Agnès Varda explained how, when making what she calls 'neighbourhood documentaries', she played on the spatial and temporal restriction implied by pregnancy and motherhood. She famously shot *Daguerréotypes* (1974) within the space allowed by the electric cable that connected her camera to her house, describing it as 'an umbilical cord' (Alison Smith (1998), *Agnès Varda*, Manchester: Manchester University Press, p. 73).

[33] 'In *Twentynine Palms*, days follow days and resemble each other. It is the same endless car journey, the same hotel room, the same innocuous discussions. It feels as if the narrative itself were becoming static (*le récit semble faire du 'sur-place'*).' Rouyer uses the French term *récit*, which does not merely signify the elements of a story but the way a story is narrated.

investigating the body. On the contrary, freed from the imperatives of plot developments and conventional fetishism (the necessity to insert a visual cliché – the close-up image of a breast or leg – as the signifier of desire or sexual availability, for instance), the close-up creates a different space for the camera to linger, opening to the gaze the realm of the 'body-landscape'.

The importance of Agnès Varda's filmmaking in this context has been outlined before.[34] Varda herself has commented on the way she uses long panoramic close-ups to transform a body into an 'immense landscape onto which one wanders'.[35] This motif appears in many of her films, but in *Jacquot de Nantes* (1990) it yields a particular poignancy because the body depicted is that of her husband, Jacques Demy, who was then dying of cancer. In a key sequence, Varda's camera moves slowly along the skin of his arm, showing the hair, veins and blemishes, mapping out the vulnerability of the human body. Through montage, she then compares these images to a landscape from Demy's youth: an estuary with sinuous, reedy banks. In *Les Glaneurs et la glaneuse* (2000), discussed below, Varda comes back to this concept of the body as a repository of visual memory where, filmed in close-up, the body escapes the purely representational order to belong to a new ('molecular') plane, and becomes an element in a temporal unity or cosmology.

Such visual exploration of the body is also prominent in the films of Denis, especially when she collaborates with Agnès Godard (who, significantly, also worked with Varda and took part in the shooting of *Jacquot de Nantes*). Denis and Godard use similar visual tropes to construct the vivid sensory worlds of their films, and the extensive use of close-ups is crucial in creating the synaesthetic correspondences that transform *Nénette et Boni* and *Vendredi soir* into the sensuous viewing experiences I previously mentioned. As discussed earlier, those senses that the cinema cannot offer, like smell and touch, are evoked through the meticulous exploration of part of a body, of the skin surface, or by filling the frame with the colour and texture of a piece of clothing, as well as through the rich rendering of sound details.

Expectedly, in the cinema of sensation, physical love often belongs to the realm of the 'body-landscape'. Yet, rather than being a strategy to merely create a sense of heightened sensuality, this particular approach to the imaging of the body seems to operate as part of a haptic visual mode which,

---

[34] Guy Austin (1996), *Contemporary French Cinema* 'Manchester: Manchester University Press; Sandy Flitterman-Lewis (1990), *To Desire Differently: Feminism and the French Cinema*, Urbana: University of Illinois Press; Smith 1998.

[35] Agnès Varda (1994), *Varda par Agnès*, Paris: Cahiers du cinéma, p. 279.

in opposition to the voyeuristic or investigatory gaze, privileges uncertainty.[36] By the same token, rather than isolating it, it integrates physical love to the body of the film. In the love scenes at the end of Laetitia Masson's *En avoir (ou pas)* (1994), the camera[37] films the bodies of a heterosexual couple at such close range that it becomes impossible to differentiate the body of the man from that of the woman. Accompanied by the sound of the waves, the composition seems to hover between abstraction and the formation of a moving seascape (Beugnet 2000: 220). In *Wild Side* (2004), a story that involves a trio of lovers, Sébastien Lifshitz, working with Agnès Godard as director of photography,[38] sought a similar effect; when he films his characters making love, the three bodies are interwoven and shot so that they cannot be told apart, and the sound-track fuses the sound of their breathing.[39] Like *En avoir (ou pas)*, *Wild Side* operates a striking contrast between the scenes of prostitution (disconnected fragments, obscene in their mechanical gesturing, or scenes of staged intercourse coolly observed by a distant camera) and the scenes of physical love, where the bodies are included into an overall composition, just as the act is included in the characters' lives.

Yet, in these cases, the close-up emphasises physical love as a moment of reprieve, of *différance*,[40] a parenthesis where one 'loses oneself'. In contrast with the body caught in action in medium or long shot, filming in close-up makes it possible to evoke a body that is temporarily freed from its function as social, cultural and even gender signifier – a body that escapes the conventional order of male/female dualism. Although, as we will see, the pull of the undifferentiated is connected with the most fundamental of anxieties, the suspended moment of undifferentiation, as it is exemplified here, thus also potentially signifies a positive liberating experience.

[36] The opening shots of Alain Resnais' *Hiroshima mon amour* (1956) remain the reference here.

[37] The film was shot by Caroline Champetier.

[38] See also Agnès Godard's camerawork in the recent films of André Téchiné (*Les Égarés*, 2003), and Laurence Ferreira Barbosa (*Motus*, 2003), a contribution to the ARTE series *Masculin-Féminin*.

[39] In the film's press release, Lifshitz comments:

> I am conscious that the film is based on three stereotypes of marginality: a transsexual prostitute, a young *beur* who drifts and also prostitutes himself, and an illegal immigrant from Russia . . . But I was precisely interested in starting from such stereotypes, from what we all think we know about them . . . and reveal the human part of it, the lived experience which is common to all of us.

[40] If I somewhat divert the eloquent Derridean neologism from its accepted applications to suit this particular context, it is because the term conveys so vividly an active, wilful dimension in the preserving of the gap between a sign and its meaning (that is, in this case, between a body and its identity as established through a web of social, cultural, geographical and gender signifiers).

Wild Side starts with a boldly celebratory nude portrait that introduces the main character specifically in the terms just described. With its ten close-up shots, the opening sequence forms a kind of cubistic ensemble, though its lushness of colour and texture comes closer to the luminous quality of a Renaissance painting. The alternating off-centre compositions show fragments of a body laid out on a crimson silk bedcover and lit so as to outline their faultless surfaces; the skin literally radiates light and softness. Throughout the series of shots, we hear the androgynous melancholic voice of the singer Antony, singing a love song about a dead boy. Its chorus is a simple line, endlessly modulated – 'I ask him, are you a boy or a girl?' This is the question that haunts the whole film, and to which the introductory images, however, already form the silent answer: a refusal to choose.

The first image shows the curve of a back with the start of the buttocks. The shot is perfectly still, and only the almost imperceptible breathing movements reveal that these are live images. Cut to: a slim hand with long, painted red nails.[41] Cut: a shot of the back, filling the right-hand side of the frame this time, with the beginning of the curve of a breast. Cut: slender feet with red nail polish. Cut: the shoulders, a mane of curly hair filling the top part of the frame. Cut: the curvature of the buttocks and the beginning of the legs. Cut: the inside of the elbow. Cut: the hips, turned upwards, revealing the small crater of the navel and underneath a small triangle of hair, and male genitals. Cut: an extreme close-up of the navel, the skin heaving slowly, the rest of the frame filled by shadows. Cut: the last image shows the top of the torso with the small, perfect mounds of the breasts exposed. Each of the shots has been composed and lit so carefully that every single one of the images stands as an entity in itself, rather than as a mere fragment of a disconnected whole. And, indeed, through montage and framing, but at the opposite end of the spectrum set by pornographic visual fetishism, what film can intimate here is the possibility of a figure that is more than the sum of its parts, of a body that is more than one thing – the embodiment of indetermination as more.[42] The same melancholy haunts *Wild Side* and *Tiresia*, and in both films, the issues of foreignness and displacement (in *Tiresia*, the central character comes from Brazil; in *Wild Side*, each of the three main protagonists is, in one way or another,

---

[41] Here, in particular, the sequence recalls the camerawork for the sequence that introduces Camille, the androgynous character of *J'ai pas sommeil* (1995), a Denis film with Godard as camerawoman.

[42] As Tiresia, the transsexual character of Bonello's film, puts it: 'It is true, I have something more. It is a great joy, but also a desperate feast, and that is what you cannot see.' Tiresia speaks these lines in Portuguese, and her captor answers that he does not understand what she says.

geographically displaced, in exile from the place where they grew up) are woven together with that of transsexuality as an embodiment of exile. At the same time, these images suggest that there is more to embodiment and identity than what the 'molar' order of perception offers. The imperceptible breathing movement that animates, ever so slightly, the surface of the body also seems to animate the surface of the image; as the circulation of the micro-movement of a 'molecular' plane is thus rendered palpable by the cinematic image, it intimates the possibility, allowed by the close-up haptic imaging to sense an affinity between different planes of existence.

Faces and heads

In the same way that it allows for moments of *différance*, the decontextualisation operated by tight framing, however, always implies the risk of creating ahistorical bodies. In effect, in the conventional system of representation and dramatisation, the close-up on the face in particular tends to induce a specific ideological dimension. It does not merely relegate the wider context to the out-of-field but, by the same token, works to foreground a transcendental or singular dimension of the human figure, to evoke an ideal or identify the hero as a free agent.[43] In the works of the directors cited here, however, this function of the close-up is often shunned or implicitly questioned. Claire Denis, for instance, plays on the concept of archetype at the beginning of *Beau Travail* (1999), where her series of close-ups on the faces of legionnaires of mixed ethnic background, rather than bringing out a sense of individuality, illustrates an obsolete ideal of colonial and military assimilation.[44] Strongly defined features, racial differences and scars singularise the soldiers' faces, yet ultimately, as the close-ups follow one another, the repetition works to create a sequence of images linked primarily by a relation of contiguity and resemblance (Beugnet 2004b: 108). Here, the close-up operates a metonymic play that conveys but one underlying cliché: the archaic, illusory sense of timelessness and parity maintained by the army. To this

---

[43] See, for instance, Roland Barthes' classic 'The face of Garbo', in (1975) *Mythologies*, New York: Hill & Wang, pp. 56–7; Judith Roof (1999), 'Close encounters on screen: gender and the loss of the field', *Genders Online Journal* 29, www.genders.org/g29/g29_roof.html; Vivian Sobchack (1979), '*The Grapes of Wrath* (1940): thematic emphasis through visual style', *American Quarterly* 31:5, pp. 596–615.

[44] Jane Sillars and Martine Beugnet (2001), '*Beau Travail*: time, space and myths of identity', *Studies in French Cinema* 1, Spring, pp. 159–65. In *Beau Travail*, the military's economy of the Same is contrasted with the changing diversity exemplified by the look and demeanour of the Djiboutian women.

economy of the Same, one could contrast the sequence of the concert in the transsexuals' café at the beginning of *Wild Side*, where the camera envelops the crowd of listeners in a slow travelling shot, capturing individual or groups of faces in medium close-up, emphasising the sheer diversity of types, the baroque beauty and flamboyant multiplicity of looks in evidence amongst the audience.[45]

In its most common function, as a fragment rather than an entity in itself, the close-up on the face, with its effect of temporal stasis, often stands as the denial of the process of continuous mutation that is inherent in the medium of the moving image.[46] In contrast, in *Tiresia*, multiplicity and difference – as opposed to selfsameness as the definition of the character as individual – are encapsulated in the mutation of the character's appearance, to which the close-up of the face bears witness, its conventional function as the epitome of the affirmation of individual singularity and sameness thus reversed. The passage from one regime of the *récit* to the other (from one of Tiresia's destinies to another) is actualised in the close-up on Tiresia's face (we only get a glimpse of her unchanged body). The film starts with a long close-up of the androgynous face of actress Clara Choveaux as Tiresia. At the beginning of the second half, the wounded Tiresia is first filmed in medium-long shot, lying motionless in the bed of Anna, the young girl who rescued her/him. In the following sequences, the camera gradually approaches the ailing Tiresia, offers a close-up of the back of her/his head, then cuts to a medium close-up of his face, now that of actor Thiago Telès. Part of the process of acceptance

---

[45] Indeed, here, the close-up works as the opposite of the voyeuristic gaze, creating a sense of intimacy that combines with the evident pleasurable fascination suggested by the slow movement of the camera. In contrast, in the deliberate tracking shots of the transsexuals working the night at the Bois de Boulogne, found in *Wild Side* but also in Bonello's *Tiresia* and in Akerman's *La Captive*, the flamboyant beauty of the transsexuals is still very much at the heart of the vision, but the *mise en scène* is more ambiguous. Traversed by a strong voyeuristic undertone, the sequences emphasise the status of the object of the camera gaze (and of the gaze of the male drivers that cruise along the alleyways of the Bois) as a spectacle.

[46] Where characters are concerned, Thomas Docherty stresses as cinema's distinctive property the way they might be 'transfigured' from one scene or one shot to the next. Films like *This Obscure Object of Desire* (Buñuel, 1977) thus arguably redouble what is an inherent property of the cinematic character. In *Tiresia*, however, the device puts an interesting slant on Docherty's definition of postmodern fiction. Docherty contrasts earlier forms of fiction, where change was 'something that happened at the level of the individual rather than in the wider socio-political formation itself' with a postmodern approach seeking to 'return the dimension of history which earlier modes of characterisation, or the theoretical understanding of character as "identity", deny' (Docherty 1996: 55–7 and 59). Foreign, illegal immigrant, transsexual and incarnated in the bodies of two performers, *Tiresia* does challenge conventional patterns of characterisation on both the individual and the historical plane; in the way the character literally/concretely embodies the issue of otherness/acceptance that underpins the film, it is not reducible to a metaphorical figure.

of the character, with her uncertain gender, status and fate, goes through the admission by the spectator of this alteration in the character's appearance which takes place in the absence of further narrative elucidation; in effect, it is not so much Tiresia who has changed but rather the kind of gaze to which she/he is subjected. In contrast, one actor (Laurent Lucas) plays the role of a deranged voyeur who imprisons Tiresia, and later appears as the priest who questions Tiresia; the one who has the investigatory, fixing gaze is, thus, fated to reappear in the same body, with the same fixed features. 'A feature of faceity [*visagéité*] is no less a complete close-up than a whole face. It is merely another pole of the face, and there is as much intensity expressed by a feature as there is quality by the whole face' (Deleuze 1986: 97). Whereas Tiresia's faces and changing features are an invitation to engage with a non-voyeuristic all-encompassing gaze, the character of her captor is summed up by the extreme close-up of his eye – a vision of frenzied obsession where the eye becomes a monstrous entity, a grotesque apparition with a life of its own.

The Denial of Disclosure

In the cinema of sensation, the close-up is rarely synonymous with the image as a 'given', but nowhere more acutely than in the facial close-up does this represent a break away from conventional practices. The ostensibly inexpressive faces of Dumont's (unprofessional) actors in particular epitomise the wonder of the face as an entity, as the 'combination of a reflecting, immobile unity . . . and intensive micro-movement' (Deleuze 1986: 88).[47] Here, as with the body filmed in close-up, it is the tactile quality of the image that is foregrounded, and the face is offered to the gaze as a self-contained landscape to be explored.[48]

In many of the films discussed here, the close-up resists even further the principle of exposure and the anchoring of meaning (or the denial of change) that it conventionally stands for; the face eludes the gaze, turns away, remains averted or cast in shadows. In a previous discussion of this strategy, I called it the 'denial of disclosure',[49] and described it in relation to the striking

---

[47] Matthieu Darras describes Dumont's approach in eloquent terms: 'Not to understand. To present the gaze with a mystery, or mysteries; present them to the spectator who may be able to pierce through them' (Darras 2006: 98).

[48] 'The face is a surface: features, lines, wrinkles, length, shape – square or triangular – the face is a map, even if it is applied and unfolded onto a form, even if it is surrounded by and borders cavities that, as a result, only appear as holes. Even as a human head, a head is not necessarily a face. The face appears only when the head ceases to be encoded by the body' (Deleuze and Guattari 1980: 208).

[49] The '*stratégie du retrait*' in Beugnet 2000.

alternation of exposure/resistance to the gaze that operates at the beginning of *En avoir (ou pas)*. The opening of Masson's film plays on the effect of the medium close-up in the *mise en scène* of power relations. It starts with a series of medium close-ups of young women who are being subjected to a job interview. While each candidate in turn is filmed facing the camera, with the repetition of similar shots and framing outlining a dehumanising process of professional and human exchangeability, the interviewer remains an ominous presence, a disembodied voice emanating from outside the field of vision. In contrast, in subsequent scenes and comparable set-ups, the face of the film's main character, also a young female worker, appears to elude the camera's gaze. In effect, throughout the introductory sequences, as she is filmed working or in discussion with the factory manager, we have to contend with images of the back of her head and partial glimpses of her face in profile (Beugnet 2000: 217). Similarly, in *Vendredi soir*, although the camera, trapped in the narrow confines of a car, lingers on fragments of bodies, the faces of the main protagonists are not fully presented until well into the film. Dumont operates under similar constraints of *mise en scène* in *Twentynine Palms* (2003), though here the car is less a shelter than the enclosed theatre of an increasingly tense, sparsely dialogued *huis clos*. In one typical driving sequence, the characters exchange a few words that are shocking in their appalling yet revelatory banality: 'What are you thinking about?' 'Nothing.' Shot from the back of the car, outlined against the washed-out desert landscape that unfolds in front of them, their heads become two mere black shapes, blotting out the view. This troubling visual trope creates a connection with Dumont's following feature, *Flandres* (2006). At the end of the first love scene between Barbe (Adelaïde Leroux) and Demester (Samuel Boidin), the lovers lie still, literally crushed into the ground by the camera's high-angle gaze, together yet utterly lonely. While the young woman confronts the camera with her unflinching stare, at her side, Demester's head, clad in a black woolly hat, is but a dark hollow; it is as if the lovers belong to separate planes of appearance. This figure – the human shape as a stain, a gaping hole in the midst of the image – is a recurrent one in the cinema of sensation. It is, as we will see, a key element of composition in the images of Grandrieux and des Pallières. The evocation of a subjectivity dissolving under the stare of the real, it recalls Lacan's description of the subject as a 'mere stain in the spectacle of the world' (Lacan 1978: 97).

Abjection or the Body in Metamorphosis

In the examples mentioned above, the function of the close-up thus challenges the conventional principles of exposure and scrutiny; from a classic element of exposition and fetishism, the close-up becomes a pivotal figure in a critical reworking of vision as power and of visual representation as the hallmark of self-identity.

In effect, in the way it pulls in the gaze, the close-up is the perfect tool for capturing the process of metamorphosis of a body passing from form to formlessness, becoming a deformed and unrecognisable entity from which, in turn, form emerges. Unsurprisingly, in works where the close-up is part of an exploration of the ambiguous, elusive territories of the abject, the body metamorphosing – transsexual, pregnant and ageing, in particular – becomes a recurring motif. In *Le Pornographe* (Bonello, 1999), a porn director, played by Jean-Pierre Léaud, proposes including a birth scene in one of his films – a suggestion met with disbelief and utter disgust by his producer. Such could be the reactions of certain viewers misled by the title and controversy created by *Romance*, since at the end of the film, Breillat introduces, precisely, a graphic sequence of a birth shot in close-up. The traditional porn-movie close-up on the face of the woman lost in ecstasy is replaced by that of the woman in the pain of childbirth, and the images of holes being filled are replaced by images of spilling out. At the same time, offsetting the sequence's documentary-like description, the close-up shots are highly tactile, capturing through light, colour and volume the monstrosity, but also the wonder, of the workings of the female body. Furthermore, both the symbolic significance of the images and the disruptive power of the close-up, already exemplified in the eruption of documentary-style images of an actual birth in the territory of the fiction, are echoed in the montage; before leaving for the hospital, the young woman has orchestrated the death of the father of her child. The close-up shot of the baby coming out of the womb is directly followed by images of the explosion that signals the death of the young man; it does not only literally blow away the narrative thread that was based on that particular character, but creates a jubilant image of the abolition of the Law of the Father already rendered obsolete by the dynamic chaos of the birth images.

In *Opéra Mouffe* (1958), Varda had also depicted the body becoming the unknown, famously comparing, in a succession of close-ups, the belly of a pregnant woman (herself) with that of a melon being gutted. Forty years later, in *Les Glaneurs et la glaneuse* (2000), the evocation of the body as alien is part of the director's on-going reflection on subjectivity, authorship and ageing. Armed with a small Digital Video camera, she films one hand with the other, closing in on the devastated surface of her skin and commenting: 'Entering horror. . . . I feel I am a beast. It is worse. I am a beast that I do not recognise.' Connecting the microscopic to the macroscopic, Varda links these unusual images of the female body to a whole economy of consumption and refuse (throwing away the old and misshapen and replacing with the new) where images of ageing are systematically excluded from the cinema screen in particular. Yet, she is not discouraged but inspired by her explorations. As Mireille Rosello stresses in her analysis of the film, the hands are those of a creative woman establishing herself as subject and author through her images (Rosello 2001: 29–36).

'To force oneself to only see beauty in the world is a deception in which even the most clear-sighted readily fall.' This motto from writer Louis-René des Forêts appears as part of the opening credits of Dieutre's *Leçons de ténèbres*, superimposed with a detail from a Caravaggio painting: the close-up of a profile, focusing on the ear. Death and decay – that which, in the words of Léo Bensani with whom Dieutre is seen in conversation halfway through *Leçons de ténèbres*, literally 'in-forms' our destiny and our body – haunt every single one of the film's images. As in Varda's case, the Digital Video camera is a privileged ally here, its haptic gaze exploring the surface of art work and live bodies both lovingly and anxiously. Throughout, the close-up shot partakes in the relentless chronicling of both physical intimacy and of the signs of death at work, which the camera tracks on the painted bodies of the Renaissance works as well as on the real bodies of the narrator's lovers: in the wrinkles that line the painted figures' faces beneath the hairline cracks in the varnish, and, beyond the levelled-out surface of the video image, in the marks left by time on the lovers' bodies and faces.

> Of course, these 'wrinkles' evoke a premature and unnatural ageing that relates to the AIDS epidemic. And, of course, since this is a filmed painting, the montage precedes the shooting and, by reaction, the framing undoes the frame. What we see is like a superimposition of tracing paper and surfaces: skin, painting, screen, thought flattened by fear. (Sylvain Coumoul, commenting on the surfaces of skin and painting in Gregg Araki's *Mysterious Skin*; Coumoul 2006: 22)

In Dumont, the close-up also probes reality's material surface, seeking to catch the almost imperceptible movements of that which might be 'really happening under the surface of appearances' (Balázs [1923] 1972: 56). Indeed, in spite or because of his anti-idealist attachment to the material dimension of the pro-filmic, Dumont tends to be alternatively described as a religious director (because of the way he appears to search for sublimation on the most ordinary concrete aspects of the reality he films[50]) or denounced for his entomologist-like approach:

---

[50] In a recent interview, Dumont describes the constraints imposed by the sets of *Flandres* as a 'material given that is non-ideal, and therefore needing to be elevated' (Henric and Millet 2006: 33).

[Dumont's films] give you the feeling that you are observing people reduced to their lowest common biological denominator, in pristine laboratory conditions: every handsome scope shot is perfectly centred for maximum legibility. But even though the clinical is always threatening to overwhelm the poetic, it never quite happens. (Jones 2000: 73)

In effect, as with the previous examples of Varda's work in particular, Dumont's filmmaking is maybe best considered in terms of an existential quest. Following Merleau-Ponty, Sobchack draws on Sartre's writing to describe the encounter with the inanimate world as the nauseating confrontation with the subjective objectivity of one's own body. Such moments of realisation are vividly evoked in *Nausea*: 'If you existed, you had to exist *all the way*, as far as mouldiness, bloatedness, obscenity were concerned' (Sartre 1964: 128, quoted in Sobchack 2004: 303). The intense stare of Pharaon de Winter (Emmanuel Schotte), the painfully sensitive policeman of *L'Humanité* (1999), betrays his incapacity to distance himself from the world's meaningless, organic obscenity: hence, the grotesque close-up shots of the bloated body of Pharaon's chief, the camera lingering over his sweat-soaked neck or framing his hand limply placed over his crotch; hence, the close-up on the murdered girl's genitalia,[51] and, also, the close-up on her leg on which tiny insects climb as if it were a hill. Dumont's filmmaking pushes banality, and the banality of horror, to its limits; his camera investigates the concrete surface of things relentlessly, the long take extending the possible meaning of the images well beyond their denotative and connotative functions, to the point of total defamiliarisation, where the categories are upturned and the banal turns into the repulsive and the uncanny, and, more rarely, the repulsive into the absorbing and moving. The close-up is a primary tool for this insatiable quest, exploring bodies in particular for infinitesimal signs of decay and life that escape the common span of attention and scale of vision, or, in Balázs's characteristically poetic style, 'the hidden mainspring of a life we thought we knew very well' (Balázs, [1923] 1972: 55). The sound of boots sinking in the mud, of the characters' breathing, of a plough cutting through heavy soil: the synchronous sound-track, with its 'audio close-ups', is essential, bringing a supplement of materiality and a sense of weightiness to the image, evoking, in Merleau-Ponty's terms, the 'stickiness' of the 'world as flesh' (Merleau-Ponty [1948] 1964 and [1962] 2002: 61).[52] The sense of

---

[51] A horrifying evocation of Courbet's *L'Origine du monde* echoed by a later scene where the main female character exposes herself to Pharaon.

[52] In an interview, Dumont justifies his use of mono sound to capture the inherent 'dirtiness' of live sound: The camera was running and I followed the character with the boom. No

closeness elicited by sound is also crucial to the process of '*visagéification*' (where the inanimate acquires human, face-like features – 'faceification': Deleuze 1986: 87–8) that Dumont's use of the scope creates. Hence the striking opening to *L'Humanité*, where the character is a mere speck on the horizon, but the sound of running and panting fills the sound-track; in the course of the long take, scale becomes an effect of the sound. It is the landscape that breathes.

> It is through sound that the depiction of the desert in *Twentynine Palms* diverts from its traditional representations. In contrast with Hollywood cinema, sound has depth here, it wraps itself around the characters. (Darras 2006: 15)

> Scope takes in so much that it brings the background to the fore; it makes it impossible for the figure to dominate. I wanted to shoot from far away, to minimise the characters as much as possible, and integrate them to the background. (Dumont 2003: 20)

In a number of the sequences in *Twentynine Palms*, as in *L'Humanité*, the combination of the audio close-up and scope format thus effects a decentring of the human figure and, in a paradoxical reversal of scale, turns the desert into the vision of a monstrous entity on whose skin the characters seem to wander.

Such play on scale is also crucial to the elaboration of the strange filmic body that constitutes Claire Denis' *Trouble Every Day*, and to the evocation of the paradoxical coexistence of the human with the animal, of the subject with the abject, that is central to the film. As we have seen, Denis simultaneously draws on the conventions of gore and on the universe of dark fairy tales to evoke archaic fears and, in particular, the fear of the kiss that turns into a bite – the terror of being eaten alive. In this context, the 'body-landscape' motif is a premise for the exploration of the kind of extreme forms of eroticism evoked by Georges Bataille, where pleasure is derived from the annihilation of the self in the other.[53] One of the film's most debated scenes is one of murder, where a young woman tears her lover's body up with her teeth and nails before devouring it. As the couple first embrace, the camera slowly travels along the young man's torso, from the armpit to the nipple and belly button, recreating through the

post-synchronisation. A sound editor redid the steps and even added bird cries. He cleaned up the live sound, which is always dirty. He idealised it by putting in stereo, but all that did was make me realise how much it diluted the image. I put back in a bit of live, mono sound behind the image, which is something nobody does anymore' (Henric and Millet 2006: 33).

[53] 'It is precisely because we are human, because we live under the sombre prospect of death, that we know the exacerbation of violence, the desperate violence of eroticism' (Bataille 1961: 22).

magnified features of his pale flesh an image evocative of a map of the plan-
etary system or of an aerial shot of a landscape.

Drawing on the writings of Lacan and Kristeva, Barbara Creed has
stressed how horror films, by staging in graphic detail the metamorphosis
and annihilation of the body, play on the obscure feeling that we are never
in full control of our own selves, that the sense of being a unified, self-
knowing individual is but an illusion.

> The horror film puts the viewing subject's sense of a unified self into crisis, specifi-
> cally in those moments when the image on the screen becomes too threatening or hor-
> rific to watch, when the abject threatens to draw the viewing subject to the place
> where 'meaning collapses', the place of death. (Creed 1986: 65)

Well before psychoanalysis exposed it, the question of the fragility of the
human self had been sensed and played out in this way in those popular literary and art forms from which Denis drew inspiration for her film. From
these long-standing traditions of horror, terror and supernatural fiction,
she retained in particular the intuition of the ambiguous nature of the
abject, of the creative and the destructive being irremediably enmeshed,
which, as we have seen, is felt through the primary engagement with the
film – the engagement with the beguiling sensuousness of the film's synaesthetic imaging, with its enthralling, pulsing rhythm and the pregnant sense
of melancholy and awful passion that combine in its sound-track. Creed
accounts for such a sense of ambivalence when she remarks how Kristeva
'emphasises the attraction, as well as the horror, of the "undifferentiated"'
(Creed 1986: 48), and, in this aspect, rejoins Bataille in his celebration
of the eradication of the subject in eroticism. The consciousness of the
eventual dissolution of the self is understood here not only as inherent to
being human, but also as an intrinsic condition to desiring and to pleasure.
For Bataille, the erotic, which always borders upon death, is one of
the processes whereby subjectivity, pulled towards the realm of the
undifferentiated (orgasm as *la petite mort*), is at risk of being annihilated; in
order to experience *jouissance*, I must accept, albeit temporarily, dissolving
and merging into the other. As in death, those who give themselves up completely to the erotic drive cease to exist primarily as 'discontinuous' individuals and experience an archaic sense of continuity (Bataille 1957: 24).[54]

---

[54] Bataille's concept of continuity thus complements, rather than contrasts with, Deleuze's
extrapolations on desire and immanence. As we have seen, in opposition to psychoanalysis's
characteristically 'negative' definitions of desire, Deleuze defines it as creative process, constitutive of a continuum – the plane of immanence – where subjectivity exists as a fluid process
of becoming (Deleuze and Parnet [1987] 1996).

This confusion[55] is key to *Trouble Every Day's* bloodthirsty scenes of 'consummation'. If the association of desire and sexuality with death and horror is a somewhat hackneyed topic in cinema, *Trouble Every Day* nevertheless manages to imbue it with a strangely bewitching sense of poignancy. In the episode of the young man's murder, conventional shock tactics are denied by the length of the takes shot in close-up, by the increasing obscurity of the image, and by the sound-track, which combines a graphic evocation of pain with the haunting tune of the *Tindersticks'* music. As kisses turn into bites, the sound, like the image, veers towards the formless. The young man's cries turn from begging for mercy into an incoherent howl that mingles with his killer's moans. The sequence thus partly draws its forceful impact from an unsettling of the spectator's position, the framing and scale of the images, as well as the light and the heightened sound effects challenging familiar patterns of orientation and the sense of a definite, superior point of view. In turn, the continuous play on scale and on the effect of '*visagéification*' creates uncanny echoes across the spatio-temporal spectrum of the film and opens the door to patterns of identification and embodiment that further unsettle the distinction between pleasure and terror. Well before the scene of murder that I have just described, the shots of the no-man's-land, across the *périphérique* where, at the beginning of the film, Coré is seen hunting, predict subsequent close-up visions of physical annihilation. Though captured in long shot, for a fleeting moment, with its hair-like blades of grass, the ground, awash with yellowish light, resembles a close-up image of skin. At that moment, it is as if the kind of assemblage that spectator and film can form was made visible: as if the film was revealed as a monstrous body in itself, and as if, through our eyes, we were making contact with its skin.

In its eloquent characterisation of cinema as a cinema of sensation, Wilson's description of Breillat's work seems equally topical to the films I have just discussed. Breillat's work, Wilson explains, 'disrupts the relations of distance and control, on which viewing has been seen to depend, by her emphasis on the tactile. She refuses merely to offer us images of the body's surface, of its integrity and wholeness' (Wilson 2001: 151). Wilson stresses the sensual aspect of the filmmaking, yet simultaneously insists on the intellectual dimension of Breillat's films, a combination equally characteristic of the work of the other directors discussed here. In these films, the remapping of the body appears coextensive with a remapping of the cinematic territory, where the function and use of the close-up in particular mark a desire

---

[55] In *Carnal Thoughts*, Sobchack reminds us of the revealing etymology of the word confusion, preceding fusion with a prefix that means both 'with' and 'against' (Sobchack 2004: 303, n36).

to do away with the usual binarisms and blur the frontiers between the inside and outside, masculine and feminine, figurative and abstract, sensory and conceptual, subjective and objective.[56] Freed from the imperative of narrative realism and the omniscient gaze, their close-up vision encourages multi-sensory perception, where close-up images and sounds evoke the other senses and flirt with the abstract, both visually and through the further connections such audio-visual perception creates with feelings, atmospheres and concepts. As in Deleuze's classic assertion, then, the body (of the characters on screen and of the spectator as assemblage with the film) ceases to be 'the obstacle that separates thought from itself'. It is, rather, 'through the body (and no longer through the intermediary of the body) that cinema forms its alliance with the spirit, with thought' (Deleuze 1989: 189).

In the works discussed here, the body in close-up is represented neither in terms of objectification or fragmentation, nor, conversely, as the stable anchor of subjectivity. Metamorphosing or deformed beyond recognition, the body in close-up evokes a subjectivity in a state of flux – a subjectivity in the making or in the process of dissolution.

The Gaze of the Inanimate

In the aesthetics of sensation, the journey from optical to haptic vision works against the psychoanalytic understanding of the self as a conscious-ness that projects itself (and, caught in a process of misrecognition, alien-ates itself through vision). In the way haptic visuality re-actualises and, indeed, renders tangible the question of the 'limit between the body and the world' (Merleau-Ponty [1964] 1968: 138), however, it is a regime of the image that evokes existential horror – the pull of the senseless, the encounter with the 'real' as nothingness, the nullification of the self caught in the gaze of the inanimate, as well as the possibility of existential pleni-tude. What is at stake, then, which film, as the medium of sensation, 'thinks' through so vividly, is the evocation of the complementary poles that define the relation of the subject to the world, caught as it is between the daunting sense of the void on the one hand, and the sense of a diminu-tion or temporary loss of subjectivity as an all-embracing experience of the world on the other. Indeed, cinema as a cinema of sensation captures most acutely the alternation between the experience of being in the world as one of sensory plenitude or as radical alienation and sense of loss, where the

---

[56] As such, this remapping implicitly denies obsolete gender binarisms that traditionally associ-ated the female body with the inability to transcend and conceptualise.

inanimate, the object as beholder of the gaze, represents the ultimate challenge to the self-standing subject, the subject in control of his or her environment and vision. As with cinematic synaesthesia, this ability of film to
evoke that which cannot be fully described in words – the experience of
losing one's subjectivity – becomes crucial where film addresses one of the
most acutely topical facets of today's human condition: the experience of
exile.

In effect, in many of the films, the evocation of the gaze of the inanimate
and the description of exiles as 'seers' are intertwined. It is this combination that helps to come to grips with the violent, angst-ridden universe
constructed by Philippe Grandrieux's *La Vie nouvelle*, for instance. It
unquestionably resonates with the striking vision of displacement that the
film's enigmatic opening sequence offers: the preying gaze of the camera
roaming a barren land and crashing against the wide-eyed stare of a group
of night wanderers. The stare of the 'seers' corresponds to the unfathomable gaze of the inanimate, of the landscapes, objects and buildings that
bear witness to that which, in Deleuze's words, 'we no longer know how to
react to'.

It is in its beholding of the commensurate existence of an objective and
subjective world that cinema can help make sense of that which standard
discourse fails to grasp. Here again, the close-up holds a key function, in
its capacity to grant the content of the image a status of autonomous entity
and endow the object or landscape with a face-like quality, to behold the
inanimate object as that which 'returns the gaze'.

As Deleuze stresses, when a thing 'has been treated as a face [*visage*]',
when it has been 'envisaged' or rather 'faceified' [*visagéifiée*], 'in turn, it
stares at us' (Deleuze 1986: 87–8).

> Even an object is faceified [*visagéifié*]: a house, a tool, an object, a piece of clothing,
> etc. We can say that *they are looking at me* not because they resemble a face, but
> because they are caught in the process of . . . faceification. The close-up in cinema
> applies to the knife as well as to a cup, a clock, a kettle, which is looking at me.
> (Deleuze and Guattari 1980: 214)

Suffering, Sobchack notes, 'enhances the awareness of oneself as a subjective object: a material being that is nonetheless capable of *feeling* what it is
to be treated *only* as object' (Sobchack 2004: 288). It is this sense of interrelation that is conveyed through the presence of inanimate objects in *La
Blessure*. In the passages on synaesthesia, I mentioned the film in connection with Marks' study of the cinema of exile, and with the importance of
objects as repositories of memory, in themselves or through particular
sensory qualities or gestures that are associated with them. Marks quotes

Hamid Naficy as he stresses the multi-sensory character of the experience of exile: 'The exiles produce their difference not just through what they see and hear but through their senses of smell, taste and touch. Indeed, these aspects of the sensorium often provide, more than sight, poignant reminders of difference and separation from homeland' (Naficy 1993: 152–3, quoted in Marks 2000: 111).[57] In *La Blessure*, the asylum seekers that succeed in entering the French territory have few, if any, belongings left. There is almost nothing to fill their sparse squat, but, in its attention to certain objects and its patient recounting of the way these inanimate objects are handled and seem to bear witness to the exiles' suffering and resilience, the camerawork recalls Balázs's description of the close-up as that which 'shows the speechless face and fate of the dumb objects that live with you in your room and whose fate is bound up with your own' (Balázs [1923] 1972: 55).

One of the film's most unassumingly affecting sequences starts with a silent, extended close-up shot of a handful of dead gilt-heads. The fish are floating in a bucket of water, and the greenish tones of the liquid recall the dreary light of earlier sequences: the dull shine of tungsten lamps that infused the dehumanised spaces of the airport at night, when the asylum seekers were seen being brutally herded on to a plane set to leave the French territory. A hand eventually comes into the frame and, to the clear-cut sound of rippled water, seizes one of the fish. We then listen to the fish being prepared off-screen (the sound of the knife gutting it, then scraping the scales). Soon afterwards, we hear the voice of a man who starts telling of his arrival in Paris. Throughout the long monologue, long takes showing the fish in still close-up are intercut with medium shots of two men (Blandine's husband Papi and another African asylum seeker) sitting, one preparing the fish in measured, deliberate gestures, the other one looking on, smoking and talking. For each of the fish prepared, the hand dips into the water to clean the gutted body and knife, and the water, mingled with the blood and remnants, gets increasingly cloudy. The gestures punctuate the account of the asylum seeker's trials. The young man describes his discovery of Paris in the middle of the winter: the cold; the quest for a roof over his head; how he was robbed of his few possessions, slept rough and experienced the squalor of temporary shelters populated with drunks

---

[57] In his article about 'Lazareen art and film', Max Silverman underlines how, in post-World War II films, as in literature, objects gain an ambiguous status as witness and memory holders, as well as materialisations of the unnameable. Silverman, Max (2006), 'Horror and the everyday in post-Holocaust France: *Nuit et Brouillard* and concentrationary art', *French Cultural Studies*, 17:1, pp. 5–17.

and 'mad people'; how he still goes for days without eating; how he feels he has lost a part of himself.

The initial vision elicits contradictory feelings: repulsion, yet also comfort, and a cathartic feeling created by the mimetic linkage between image and dialogue. The sight of the dead fish generates a feeling of alienness, with its synaesthetic evocation of the cold weight and inanimate texture of the wet bodies. At the same time, through the sheer length of the take, the persistence of the vision, the shots convey the impression that these humble forlorn shapes do indeed return the gaze, while the act of them being progressively hollowed out accompanies the tale of destitution that fills the sound-track. The cathartic character of this embodied narrative offsets the initial repugnance, as does the feeling of comfort that the preparation of food, and its sharing, generate, particularly in insecure living conditions; even in this desolate setting, in this most destitute of situations, Papi's gestures testify to a wealth of habits and know-how that is not lost. In the following sequence, his eating of the scraps from his ailing estranged wife's plate suggests understanding and a sharing in her pain.

The Inclusive Gaze and the Evil Eye

Where cinema becomes a cinema of the senses, the haptic encounter with the object can elicit a sense of revulsion as well as a sense of appeasement or at-oneness-with-the-world – a confusion of which the films offer potent examples. 'Visagéified' by the gaze of the camera, the inanimate world becomes a homologous entity whose presence is either threatening or comforting. Conversely, the human figure that falls under the gaze of the inanimate (benevolent and non-judgemental or relentless and nullifying) enters the uncertain field of the figural; through changes in framing and focus and the play on precision and blurredness, on heightened or low light and colour contrasts, the figure that is beckoned by its surroundings appears alternatively incorporated into a field of sensual inclusiveness or drawn into a formlessness that annihilates it.

There is the Morpheusan embrace of the immobilised body of the city that welcomes the lovers in *Vendredi soir*, and the playful presence of the anthropomorphised objects that populate its streets (anchovies smiling on the face of a pizza, numbers changing places on car number plates, a forlorn glove abandoned on the road like Cinderella's shoe . . .). There is Varda's gentle celebration of the found object (and, indeed, of the found image) in *Les Glaneurs et la glaneuse*; or, in the second part of Bonello's *Tiresia*, the inclusive gaze of the camera, its panning and to-and-fro movements, embracing the natural surrounds and the objects and gifts in Anna's sparsely furnished house where the now-blind Tiresia finds temporary refuge. There is the effect of the zoom that presses Lady Chatterley's silhouette into the welcoming embrace of the forest in Ferran's film; there are the changes in focus that fuse the figure of the player with the pitch and the crowd in Gordon and Parreno's *Zidane*. But there is also the sense of relentlessness elicited by the laboratories' sterile environment and the close-ups of scientific equipment in *Trouble Every Day*; the oppressive formatting frame imposed on the body by the workstation as the material extension of the office environment in de Van's *Dans ma Peau* (discussed in the following chapter); the overwhelming presence of the monster-like machine at the beginning of des Pallières *Adieu*. There is the powerful appearance of the giant windmills in *Twentynine Palms*, the awesome, inexorable force of their endless rotation.

As Jones underlines in the case of Dumont's films, terror breeds where the object, though it seems to return the insistent questioning gaze of the camera, yields nothing:

> Dumont does the typical shot/counter-shot move, but he stays on the object seen for an uncomfortable interval, and it never yields anything: unlike 99% of the movies you see, there's no mental or poetic correlative between the looker and the looked at. There's a terrific power to these moments, a basic, brutally elemental longing for the world to explain itself. (Jones 2000: 73)

It is in the filming of the contemporary city or, rather, of the anonymity of the bleak estates and high-rise developments that seem increasingly to overshadow urban centres and swallow their surroundings, that the effect of '*visagéification*' and of the return of the gaze are at their most disquieting. Here, the long shot acquires the status of the close-up with particularly unsettling results; it turns an expanse of dull grassland on the edge of the city bypass into a monstrously enlarged vision of skin (*Trouble Every Day*), or beholds the blind gaze of endless rows of windows, transforming the mournful facades of colourless buildings into sinister faces, ominous in their opaque, massive presence (*L'Intrus*, *Wild Side*, *La Vie nouvelle*).

Even more than the *mise en scène*'s physical annihilation, in the films discussed in the previous pages, the ultimate subversion of the subject position thus takes the form of a dematerialisation – the 'hollowing out' of the subjective body turned into a mere 'stain', a hole in the concrete matter of the image – as if the human form belonged to a different plane of appearance or molecular speed than its surroundings. The 'counter-shot', as it were, to the image of a hollowed-out subject is a shot that beholds the inanimate as that which 'returns the gaze' – a gaze that works to nullify the occurrence of the human figure caught in the field of vision. Such is the basis of the 'aesthetics of chaos': a clash of visual regimes – distorted images, blurred-ness and the detailed precision of high-density photography – and the visu-alisation of a world where, around the disaggregating human figure, the inanimate appears to achieve a concrete, inexorable presence.

> In the end, all figures of otherness boil down to just one: that of the Object. In the end, all that is left is the inexorability of the Object, the irremediability of the Object . . . The Object's power and sovereignty derive from the fact that it is estranged from itself . . . The Object is an insoluble enigma, because it is not itself and does not know itself. (Baudrillard 1993: 172, quoted in Sobchack 2004: 305)

The Aesthetics of Chaos

Two works stand out as highly singular amongst recent French cinema releases; Philippe Grandrieux's *La Vie nouvelle* (2002) and Arnaud des Pallières' *Adieu* (2003) are films that offer remarkable and unsettling explo-rations of what Deleuze describes as the 'unbearable. . . . inseparable from a revelation or an illumination, as from a third eye . . . forcing us to forget our own logic and visual habits' (Deleuze 1989: 18). The directors share a common investment in using film to address that which constantly defies our level of tolerability, all that fills the news and historical records and that which we tend to put to the backs of our minds: violence and madness, war and displacement, exclusion, exploitation and dehumanisation. At the same time, these experiences, that surface through liminal images as if recalled from indifference or forgetfulness, are not treated as separate. An 'aesthet-ics of chaos' makes visible relationships that are severed in standard repre-sentations of events, it stresses the coexistence of distinct durations and realities, the porous borders that connect sheltered spheres and war-ridden territories, radical evil and banal everyday life. Hence, the alternation, inherent to the films' attempt at remapping the confusion of the era, between any-spaces-whatever (roads, no-man's-lands and soulless urban spaces) and 'originary worlds' (the virgin forest) 'composed of unformed matter', where 'radical evil' rules (Deleuze 1986: 123; see also Chapter 3).

As we have seen, Grandrieux's first feature, *Sombre*, an atypical road movie about a serial-killer, is set in France. *La Vie nouvelle*,[58] on the other hand, takes place in and around a nondescript city in the Balkans, a space of post-conflict urban desolation surrounded by forests. Its elliptical story-line revolves around a young American (possibly a soldier on leave from

[58] Prior to the making of *Sombre*, Grandrieux had worked on a documentary on Sarajevo. A further stay in the Balkans and time spent in Sofia after the release of his first feature film provided the initial material for *La Vie nouvelle*.

Kosovo), Seymour (Zachary Knighton), who becomes obsessed with a prostitute called Melania (Anna Mouglalis) who 'belongs' to a local slave-trader, Boyan (Zsolt Nagy).

Des Pallières' *Adieu* interweaves two separate narrative threads: the story of Ismaël, an Algerian dissident who leaves his country illegally and seeks refuge on French soil, and that of a family of French farmers, the father and three sons, confronted with the death of a brother/son. It is the voiceover monologue of Ismaël, recounting his journey to his absent daughter, which constantly reconnects the two threads.

There are echoes of similar thematic concerns in des Pallières and Grandrieux's work, and most importantly, a common practice of cinema as cinema of sensation. By venturing into (*Sombre, Adieu*), or immersing (*La Vie nouvelle*) the viewer in, aesthetic territories traditionally associated with the experimental, these directors use the resources of filmmaking to turn the filmic world as a whole into a process of constant becoming, where the human form is endlessly confronted with 'the *passivity* of immanence and the *opacity* of the material' (Sobchack 2004: 304).

Sombre and *La Vie nouvelle*[59]

One of *La Vie nouvelle*'s most terrifying sequences is devoid of action and human presence. Filmed in one of the featureless corridors of the hotel-brothel where most of the interior scenes take place, it takes the form of an extended, perfectly paced forward camera movement. Shot from a slightly high angle, it starts at the back of the corridor, taking in the walls on each side, and zooms slowly towards the bare window that cuts through the wall, centre-frame, in the distance. It is absolutely fixed and steady, an ineluctable movement that creates a powerful chilling effect of entrapment. A desolate urban landscape appears, precisely framed by the window's dark surround, and as sharply defined and still as if in a high-resolution photograph. As the camera closes in, the view eventually fills the frame, an endless layering of tall concrete buildings that seem to return the gaze of the camera with the dead stare of countless rows of blind windows puncturing their dismal grey facades. The sequence cuts to a view of the same corridor, but this time it includes the silhouette of the main character standing against the light, a mere dark outline, as if on the verge of being cancelled out by the world's unblinking gazes concentrated through the eye of the window.

This motif of the human form caught in the figural field as if trapped halfway between two planes of appearances is a recurrent one in

---

[59] See my 2005 article for *Studies in French Cinema* (Beugnet 2005b).

Grandrieux features: the visualisation of the human form's disjointed violent relation to the world that surrounds it.

Neither *Sombre* nor *La Vie nouvelle* is constructed like a progressive movement from a familiar reality into the darker realms hidden beneath its surface. Rather, the mutations that affect the films' audio-visual make-up create a reality in constant flux, as if constructed in layers of different speeds and consistency through which the characters seem either to disintegrate or function as *passeurs*.

Though Jean, the killer of *Sombre*, is obsessed with orifices, with the mouth and female genitals, it is he who, by his presence, creates a hole in the visual texture of the film; the image often offers shots of the back of his head or head and shoulders forming a blurred shape that obscures the view. In *La Vie nouvelle*, bodies and faces are almost always truncated, partly swallowed by the light or the engulfing darkness. More than any of the other protagonists, however, the female character, Melania, seems irremediably caught in a web of conflicting gazes and desires. An elusive figure, she casts a thin, dark frame against the pale daylight, and eventually vanishes, turning into a swirling, flame-like shape while dancing, to reappear only as a monstrous creature, half-woman, half-beast, at the end of the film.

Ultimately, it is the border between the imaginary and the real, as well as reality and fiction, that becomes porous. In *La Vie nouvelle*, Seymour does come back from the sub-human vortex where Boyan leads him to face again the horror of the present. And while *Sombre* offers to the spectator a foray into a nightmarish tale, the exploration of the dark world of his wolf-man, it also retains a different, more familiar way of looking at the world: that of the spectators of the Tour de France, familiar static figures waiting to see the cyclists race past, unaware of the killer's presence. The other reality is 'like the absolute counter-shot to the film. The external world exists, we will return to it when leaving the film' (Grandrieux 1999c: 39). But as the vulnerability of the human form suggests, neither here nor there is reality a given, an objective world existing merely 'for us'. Moving between the inexorable concreteness of photographic hyper-precision and the confusion of blurredness and superimpositions, the filmic matter evokes a reality in constant flux, where figure and ground, the inside and the outside, the subjective body and its objective surroundings are alternatively out-of-sync or fused. Hence, the approach to filmmaking that founds Grandrieux's work: a rediscovery of the cinematic image as visual and sound textures – a form of sculpting in movement.

'His films are rich in shots that work the image like a sculptor works the clay.' This remark, by Laurent Le Forestier (2004), describing the work of

Jean Epstein, could easily apply to Grandrieux's filmmaking. The pace of Grandrieux's films is based on long takes, during which the images are conjured up, shaped and altered. The work on light and sharpness is paramount in generating the films' affecting atmospheres. It also plays a crucial role in creating visuals that are at once composed, modelled, yet simultaneously evocative of the pull of the 'formless'. The films' images are fluid and changing, often hovering on the border between the figurative and the abstract, their surface alternatively obscured and animated as if by the pulse of the wider field that lies beyond their frame. Not only is the image subjected to all forms of distortion, but these transformations often occur in the course of the take, the variations in the speed of recording, in lens and distance, as well as in lighting levels, creating unusual effects of chiaroscuro, and heightened contrasts of sharpness and blurredness. As with the images, Grandrieux describes the composition of the sound-track in modelling terms, as a process where the sound is 'constructed in strata, successive layers, working sound like a clay in which the film is wrapped' (Grandrieux 2003: 27). *Sombre* has little dialogue and *La Vie nouvelle* does away with dialogue almost completely; few of the sequences in the films are shot and edited with direct sound. Freed from its conventional function as accompaniment or narrative support, the sound-track is thus an intrinsic element of the film's aesthetics of sensation. Elaborated in collaboration with the musician and cult underground figure Alan Vega (for *Sombre*) and the experimental group *Étant-donnés* (for *La Vie nouvelle*), the sound-track mingles music and sound-effects to endow the films with a deep, subterranean form of rhythm – a kind of breathing. The sound-effects of *Sombre* – deep breathing combined with a distant rumbling, for instance[60] – are further developed in the rich, complex audio mix of *La Vie nouvelle*; the sound of the earth recorded underground, dogs panting and barking, the crack of a whip, and many different wind sounds mingle with urgent, repetitive, high-pitched electronic chords.

In turn, the underlying editing principle is one of variations in intensity and rhythm. The sequences that compose the films are assembled as contrasted blocks of sensations and effects: the effect of vertiginous calm in the sequence of the car driving into the darkness succeeding directly to the quivering images of the children shouting at the beginning of *Sombre*; the contrast between the pale, icy light of the exterior day scenes of *La Vie nouvelle* and the engulfing darkness of its nightclub sequences.

The fluid, elliptical structure of the two films thus eschews conventional dramatic progression, and the viewers, denied the comforting

---

[60] It is the recording of the sound of a beehive that was used.

framework of narrative logic, are left to experience the powerful, per-plexing effect of the films' imagery. If anything, as in a traumatic process of involuntary memory, the repetition of certain visual motifs suggests a loosely circular structure. In *Sombre*, for instance, the images of people watching the Tour de France, shot from behind at the beginning of the film, are mirrored at the end by views of the same event shot facing the crowd, as if the whole film represented the interstice, the gap usually erased by the suture of the shot/counter-shot combination. These repe-titions also contribute to the rhythmic, associative quality of the montage. Across various parts of the film, characters can be connected by the uncanny resurgence of a gesture or a look (Boyan's demonic laughter and Seymour's horrific cry at the beginning and end of *La Vie nouvelle*). Short scenes function as enigmatic linkages – as with the images and clicking sound of the chained dog running in circles in *La Vie nouvelle* – feeding into an indefinite atmosphere of expectancy and threat. In both films, the uncertainty created by the ellipses and the apparent lack of clear action-motivation functions less as suspense, than as the source of a per-vasive feeling of anxiety or terror. There are no precise explicit motiva-tions behind the actions of *Sombre*'s main characters, and their journey does not seem to lead anywhere in particular. If *Sombre* still offers ele-ments of plot development, in *La Vie nouvelle*, however, there remain only traces, the mere fragments of a story. The film's initial locations evoke a nondescript geographical and fictional space of devastation, that vary, like *Sombre*, between any-spaces-whatever (post-conflict land-scapes) and 'originary world' (the forest), and where the characters appear in erratic, elliptical fashion, to fall victim to an obscure tale of desire and revenge.

Only the awe-struck but persistent gazes of the anonymous, wandering people that withstand the preying gaze of the camera at the beginning of the film, and appear as enigmatic inserts of faces later on, seem to carry the weight of the 'third eye' – the exile's ability to bear witness to the sur-rounding chaos.

If Grandrieux's work does indeed recall Worringer's description of modern man's desperate struggle against world chaos, the director's vision need not be understood as nihilistic. Violence, graphic or implicit, is ever-present but not aestheticised; nor does it appear as an aim in itself. Between Bataille's formless continuity and Deleuze's immanence, the creative dynamics at work in the films offset the destructive pull that threatens to annihilate the human figures who inhabit his worlds. Indeed, the director describes his own work in such terms; the shooting itself is but one aspect of the practice of cinema as sensual experience, both pleasurable and terrifying, into which the film-maker hopes spectators will also let themselves be drawn. Highly suspicious of pre-existing screenplays, Grandrieux talks of the act of filming as a momentous event, where the pro-filmic reality takes hold of the filmmaker driven by a desire to make certain images. Rejecting the use of the steady-cam which would sanitise the movement of a shot, Grandrieux insists on the importance of carrying the camera himself, and describes himself as driven by the need to shoot in the thick of things, to the point where he feels 'completely sucked into the field of the shot' (Grandrieux 1999b). Thus couched in surrealist terms, the definition of the director as author takes on an ambiguous character; he is the subject who originates the work and seeks to express a personal vision, yet is also pulled into the fluid field of the gaze, on the brink of fusing with the reality being filmed.

If sound was added to 'visual', of all the films cited in this book, Grandrieux's work probably comes closest to Artaud's definition of the ideal film as 'a film with purely visual sensations, the dramatic force of which springs from a shock on the eyes, drawn, one might say, from the very substance of the eye' (Artaud [1928] 1972: 21). However, Grandrieux's work is also a present-day response to the challenges of its epoch. Ultimately, Hal Foster argues, it is the despair about the staggering scope of continuing violence and worldwide destruction that underpins the shift in contemporary art practices, and the prevalent concern for the traumatic and the abject (Foster 1996: 166). In a similar vein, Raymond Bellour relates Grandrieux's work to the endless multiplication of images and sounds of destruction that fill our daily lives. No matter how shocking, these fragments remain distant, their impact and meaning eventually lost in the sheer mass and rapidity of the circulation of information and its transformation into mere cliché. In Grandrieux's work, these images find an echo, a space where we encounter 'the interminable suggestions that the violence of information brings to us'.

> One thing surprises me: that so few understood that the significance of this film comes from this alarming sense of an unsaid, an unseen, of the mad need to imagine all that rumour fills us with and in which the film throws us. (Bellour 2005: 16)

Grandrieux's films, Bellour stresses, capture the impossibility of the image to form with any clarity and lasting truth. Yet, they nevertheless reverberate with the vibration of the outer field, the world's inchoate hubbub, punctuating it with dazzling, fleeting apparitions that put the customary coherence of the screen image out of joint and force us to revisit these 'ellipses of real-life' that, benumbed by the overload of real horror, our recourse to expedient amnesia helps us to create.

> To forbid visual clarity, to draw it into its own impossibility: to know how to bring the camera too close or keep it too far, to shoot too slowly or too fast, to plunge the image in the shadows or blow it out in its excess of light; and then this psychical rustling can happen, between the sharp and the blurred, the fixed and the trembled, that which creates the opaque background or the transparency of all images, because it is incorporated to the image like the trace of its mental passage. (Bellour 2005: 16)

This description of the visual regime created in *La Vie nouvelle* could equally apply to many a sequence of Arnaud des Pallières' *Adieu*.

Adieu

'It is a grey twilight. The road is plunged in shadowy light.' A priest is reading a sermon at a burial. Accompanying his voiceover is a view of a mysterious landscape, the earth a dark mass, the sun hardly piercing through a thick blanket of cloud; in *Adieu*, as in *Sombre* and *La Vie Nouvelle*, the light that prevails is that of dusk, and the border between ground and sky is always tenuous. Like Grandrieux's work, des Pallières' film creates a figural field where the vulnerability of the human form emerges in the encounter with reality's matter which the film stages. Long focals crush the human silhouette into the background and transform depth into a fuzzy mass; blurring and trembled images caught in hand-held camera, superimpositions, graininess and low contrasts conjure up the changing densities of the real in which the human form is caught. In mourning clothes, the silhouettes of the country men are outlined against the low light like hollow shapes. The figure of the father in particular, incapable of grieving, caught between 'that which is alive, and that which could have stayed alive', forms a black spot embedded in the fabric of the film. At the burial of his youngest son, the world seems literally to metamorphose around him; it is as if the usually invisible movements of the matter, in its senseless, organic workings, were suddenly perceptible and audible. A striking combination of superimposed and trembled images, the sequence in the graveyard recalls the opening of Carax's *Pola X* (Chapter 3); concrete, granite and marble surfaces and the shapes of gravestones, crosses, ironwork and wreaths shake and overlap as if caught in an earthquake. The sound-track creates a similar sense of turmoil, layering the feeble echoes of organ music with the sound of wind and the hysterical, high-pitched clamour of birds. Eventually, the voice of one of the sons is heard and the vision washes out in over-exposure. As François Bégaudeau's comments encapsulate:

Adieu stands at the borders of representation, in a liminal space that flirts with abstraction (the camera oscillates on the edge of blurredness) and even within visibility, the crucible of absence where truth can be found. Anti-figurative, the strategy of *Adieu* partakes in a logic of disentanglement that aims to extract Being from the gangue of presence. In this general approach, the remarkable work on the sound-track is crucial. The mixing and the experimental-repetitive texture maintain the sound-track between noise and composition, as close as possible to the quintessential. (Bégaudeau 2004: 77)

Like Grandrieux's *La Vie nouvelle*, Arnaud des Pallières' ambitious first feature film is a reflection on world chaos. In more explicit terms than in Grandrieux's film, in *Adieu*, as in Klotz's *La Blessure*, the presence of the exiles (and their gaze or, as in *Adieu*, their voice) and their embodied experience of exclusion form the necessary counter-shot to the evocation of an ossified Western world, and the concrete testimony of the shattering effects of the Occident withdrawing into itself. But as the title[61] suggests, the conflictual engagement of the subjective body with the objective world is redoubled by another, which connects the world of Ismaël (Mohamed Rouabhi), the asylum seeker who leaves his family to try and enter the French territory illegally, with that of the French farmers who are burying a son and brother – it is the confrontation between God and matter. As Emmanuel Burdeau comments:

Why this title? Why *Adieu*? There is, of course, a thematic thread that runs through the film: dereliction on the one hand, bereavement on the other. One scene, however, suggests a more precise answer. In church, the priest rehearses his sermon – a mix of religious maxims and microphone tests: 'My brother . . . One, two, three . . . Beat your own breast . . . One, two . . . Can you hear me well enough at the back?' Is this the sign of a battle between God and matter? . . . Or a sign, on the contrary, that God has now entered the machine? (Burdeau 2004: 15)

In close-up, a hand clumsily tries to cut through an aspirin; the priest, in the throes of acute toothache, places the painkiller directly on the infected cavity. The sequence alternates between close-ups of his pathetically grimacing face and the television screen, on which a documentary on insects unravels: low-resolution images of ladybirds[62] and greenflies, accompanied by a relentless commentary that details predatory instincts as well as reproduction methods – the insertion of one breed's larva into the body of another. The sound-track, with its mix of voiceover and violin and accordion music, underlines the grotesque of the scene. For all its

---

[61] *Adieu / À Dieu*: phonetically, the title sounds like both a farewell and an address to God.
[62] Ironically, in French, ladybirds are called *'bêtes à Bon Dieu'*.

grotesque absurdity, the scene encapsulates the sense of terror that is at the heart of the film, and in which matter, organic or non-organic, seems to enfold the human figure. Indeed, here we are again reminded of Deleuze's extrapolations – based on Worringer's insights – about expressionism and the 'opacity' of the world 'lost in darkness'.

> *The non-organic life of things*, a frightful life, which is oblivious to the wisdom and limits of the organism, is the first principle . . ., valid for the whole of Nature, that is, for the unconscious spirit, lost in darkness, light which has become opaque, *lumen opacatum* . . . in all these cases, it is not the mechanical which is opposed to the organic: it is the vital as potent pre-organic germinality, common to the animate and the inanimate, to a matter that raises itself to the point of life, and to a life which spreads itself through all matter. (Deleuze 1986: 51)

Indeed, in *Adieu*, the vision of the priest suffering senselessly in front of a televised representation of Nature's laws goes together with the celebration of the God of technology that the opening credits sequence encapsulates. A powerful montage of shots turns it into a strange ceremonial: the construction of a monster of new technology, the modern leviathan that will transport Ismaël in its belly and bring him back to where he started. And montage is, indeed, the term here, as the series of shots constructs the machine visually just as it is put together on the factory's assembly line. The sequence alternates close-ups and medium close-ups of machinery, the camera moving ceaselessly along the assembly line, following the robotised trajectory of axle parts, pieces of an engine, a massive steel cabin, wheels, tyres, all of which are being fitted together through a practised ritual as smooth as a mechanical dance. The camera travels inside the body of the machine, moving through a dark tunnel of densely coiled cables, then brushes past the steel structure, taking in the gaping mouth of the petrol tank's aperture. The sequence eventually cuts into a long shot, revealing the expanse of factory floor and a huge engine being floated overhead by a crane. A series of jump cuts shows its complex assemblage of black steel, electrical parts and cables being lowered down into the body of the truck, ready to be covered with the shiny white frame of the truck's cabin; in close-up, the glazed gaze of the headlights moves forward towards the retreating camera. The sound – initially, a few electric guitar chords – crescendoes into a full uproar and, like the images, hovers at the edge of naturalism and abstraction: an electro-instrumental mix that carries in its composition the distant echoes of the factory noises (steel pounding against steel against the thunderous noise of industrial machinery). The living flesh has little place here; human silhouettes are barely glimpsed as fragments of bodies or blurred silhouettes, and the workers' bodies seem but mere additions to the complex configuration of the assembly line. Later on, as the camera follows the truck leaving the factory floor in a perfectly paced movement, and thanks to the angle of shot, the cabin appears devoid of driver, the machine moving forward blindly, its dark windscreen merely reflecting its surroundings.

Like a modern Jonah, Ismaël hides inside the truck and crosses the border, but caught in the nets of the customs police, he is brought back and brutally holstered into a plane to be sent back to Algeria. As in Denis' *L'Intrus*, the scale – the scale of things, the scale of shots – is crucial here, in the evocation of a paranoid world that confuses the existence of actual men and women forced to leave their countries and cross borders, with the senseless movement of organic matter and, in turn, crushes them in the equally senseless weight of its police control and technological order. The cruelty of the concluding sequence, shot at the airport, comes from the clichéd quality, the sense of *déjà vu* that the images elicit (indeed, the scene recalls the images shot by Klotz in Roissy for *La Blessure*), and also from its ruthless play on scale. Crushed by the high-angle long shot, next to the massive inert body of the plane, the struggling figure of Ismaël seems but a small insect.

Leçons de ténèbres

> The city is too full of prying eyes, dark streets with dead ends, the messiness of sexuality, motion masquerading as emotion, effect as affect. Like black holes, matter collapses into itself, indifferently, in violent, epiphanic stillness. (Powrie, forthcoming)

Fiction or documentary, filmed diary, imaginary journey or stream of consciousness, Vincent Dieutre's atypical work eschews all strict categorisation. Yet, through his analysis, based on genre, this evocation, by Phil Powrie, of what he calls French 'hyper-noir' cinema, seems a perfect foreword to Dieutre's *Leçons de ténèbres*. Like those of Grandrieux and des Pallières, Dieutre's films appear to function like a sensitive surface, an audio-photographic base that has been exposed to the world's hubbub and has caught and retained the echoes, distant and close, of world chaos. Dieutre adopts a more modest, more intimate format than Grandrieux or des Pallières, yet his filmmaking also entails a confrontation with the senseless pull of matter and, at first, it seems that, in the narrator's experience, all is reduced to a meaningless undifferentiated record. To Denis' melancholic yet joyful explorations of youthful sensuality, Vincent Dieutre's *Leçons de ténèbres* arguably represents the darker facet. In place of Denis' exploration of cinema's synaesthetic pleasures (but like an extension of the nostalgia that imbues her fleeting evocations of the newborn's unob-structed – pre-linguistic, pre-objective – relationship to the world), Dieutre proposes a voyage of mourning, where the link between desire, sensation and affect appears to be severed. Between autobiography and fiction, the filmmaker casts himself as the traveller and art lover on his way to Italy, in the footsteps of Caravaggio (and, cinematically, Derek Jarman). The opening sentences of the monologue that accompany the film spell it out. For the middle-aged man who is about to start on this 'lesson of dark-ness', all seems to have become relative. Art, rather than life, elicits feeling, of which live experience seems but a pale imitation; even in close human relations and physical contact, even in sex, sensation and emotion have become muted, and the noise of the world is but a distant hum, an endless stream of undifferentiated commentaries in Italian pouring out of the radio like a remote sing-song. As the journey unfolds, encounters appear to amount to little more than short-lived gusts of pleasure and illusory moments of intimacy. Ultimately, it seems that sensation as 'true' affect must belong to a different plane of existence, one that is hardly open to the narrator any more. It is in the contemplation of the petrified body of a martyr's statue that the narrator is filled with the most acute sense of being out-of-sync with the world he inhabits. The answer, then, is the journey into the dark, the ultimate desensitisation – the death-like sleep induced by hard drugs. At first, it seems that the video aesthetic that dominates the film, and is recurrently offset by the reminder of the rich textures of Renaissance painting, is but the benumbing 'gangue' from which 'Being' cannot be 'disentangled'. And yet, though the main part of the film is shot on Digital Video camera, Dieutre uses a variety of media, from HD to 16 and 35mm film. Next to the levelling greying effect of the video image, changes in the quality of the picture thus reinject the journey with difference and variation.

The film is punctuated with visions of dazzling luminous beauty. A narrow street in a popular district of an Italian city at night. The camera is set on a stand and the frame remains unchanged. The image has the lush, detailed quality and depth of field of celluloid film and, in its simplicity, the scene – a few people setting out chairs to chat on their doorsteps – creates the exquisite effect of expectancy of a theatrical setting at the start of a play. Similarly, the complexity of the sound-track, its alternation of voiceover, urban noises and radio news, creates melodic variations, and the warm tone of the voice, its *tutoiement* (the use of the informal address as a direct address to the listener) touches us in spite of its disenchanted message. And ultimately, it is the video image itself, as it emerges not as the poor relation of other media, but as a mode of visual address in its own right, that comes alive; in Naples at night, the narrator feels, at last, that the vibration of the urban hubbub resonates through him. It is then that the video film provides us with an intuition that there is another way of relating to the world, a different plane of immanence. Its images cease to appear like a greyish coating spread on reality to become a skin-like surface, where the turmoil of the city, in its multiplicity, imprints itself through the pixelation like a rustling of sensations.

As Sobchack reminds us, a 'diminution of subjectivity' need not be equalled with perceptual and epistemological atrophy (or, indeed, with a loss of a sense of ethics). The objective world returning the gaze does not merely equate with the evil eye, with the nullification of the subjective being; it reminds us that the world is not there just for us, to be transformed 'in the image of our desire', to be consumed by us. In turn, through an enhanced awareness of the world's materiality, we may also experience an opening out that provides the foundation of 'our *aesthetic* behaviour towards the world and others' (Sobchack 2004: 289–90). To open oneself to the powerful impact of Grandrieux's and des Pallières' disconcerting film work, or to let oneself be touched by the emotional longing at work in Dieutre's cinematic journeys, is to feel the abject pull of the senseless that emanates so forcefully from our godless, information- and violence-saturated world; but to be immersed in the films' sensuous and aesthetic fields, to experience the effect of the films' materiality, the multi-sensory variations of intensities, is also to delight in the distinctive capacity of film to become 'a *sensual* and *sensible* expansion' of ourselves.

CHAPTER 3

Film Bodies (Becomings and Embodiment)

What kind of strange, metamorphosing figures breed in the interstices of the cinema of sensation's fluctuating audio-visual fields? What kind of mutants does the aesthetics of chaos generate and, ultimately, what kind of monstrous film bodies? How do these various processes of filmic embodiment speak, directly or indirectly, of the most pressing issues in contemporary France, of the closely interwoven questions of identity and difference we associate with globalisation, immigration and colonial after-effects, work and exploitation, gender, desire and possession? This chapter looks at how, where cinema becomes a cinema of sensation, the questioning about identity and otherness is evoked not merely in narrative and representational terms, but through the very texture of the films; how it materialises in forms of 'becoming' and, ultimately, imprints itself in the make-up and 'in the flesh' of the filmic body itself.

From Genre to Archetype

Fuck, we don't even have a sense of the formula; we don't say the good lines at the right moment. (Manu/Raphaëlla Anderson in *Baise-moi*, 2000)

Though the filmmakers whose work is explored in these pages often draw on and subvert generic elements, the end result is neither predefined nor determined by the narrative or discursive operations of genre. Where, for instance, the term 'excess' as it is used in the context of genres (Williams 1991) is applied here, it is in a Bataillean sense, to connote the 'gratuitous' dimension of artistic choices, choices largely unjustified by, and independent from the expectations, functions and economic rationales attached to genre production. Asked about his foray into the violent thriller – the Hollywood genre par excellence – for *Demonlover*, Assayas underlines where the appeal and the limitations lay:

What I like in genre is utterly basic; it has to do with physical excitement . . . The specificity of American cinema lies with the capacity to establish this kind of physical relation with the spectator, bringing the body of the viewer into play. This happens also as far as sound is concerned: you become tense, you relax, you are on edge again, etc. All that is commonly described as cheap in film, I don't consider it cheap. Anything that produces physical effects in the spectator should be taken into account . . . On the other hand, however, I am not interested in the way genre, unhappily, reproduces already conventional situations in equally conventional ways. Where the unexpected and the excitement of discovery should rule, we find ourselves with twists that are predictable and predicted to the point where formula itself is utterly worn out. (Guilloux 2002)[1]

In effect, in many of the films this book is concerned with, genre is not so much a framework as a part of the film's make-up; the generic component, incorporated into the body of the work, contributes to making the film into a process, a superimposition of blocks of sensations and atmospheres that infiltrate each other. Describing the reworking of the generic ingredient in Denis' Gothic horror feature, *Trouble Every Day*, Jean-Sébastien Chauvin remarks:

Genre, in Claire Denis, resembles a wandering-infiltrating process. It has less to do with the perverting of cinematic modernity than with providing it with a wider horizon . . . What is striking in *Trouble Every Day*, is the freedom with which all the elements circulate, and the ability with which Denis goes from one space to another. (Chauvin 2001: 77)

Just as the presence of genre elements does not pertain – or at least not chiefly – to a play on citation, in the films considered in this book, the emergence of hybrid techniques (the painterly or sculpted qualities of the film images, but also the co-optation of other artistic techniques, from music to opera and dance in particular) does not appear primarily as the manifestation of a postmodern tendency to combine and even out references across historical periods, genres or techniques. More simply, it represents one facet of the willingness to experiment with sensory correspondences and, simultaneously, to restore film as the art that uniquely combines thinking process and sensual experience. Hence, it is an approach to filmmaking that opens itself to, and weaves together, the most

---

[1] Like de Van's *Dans ma peau*, Assayas' *Demonlover* has prompted comparisons with David Cronenberg's films (Rouyer 2002: 31; Maule 2004). If, like a number of Cronenberg's features, *Demonlover* engages convincingly with the rules of the thriller genre – or, more precisely, of the cyber-thriller – it rapidly overrules the primary postmodern play on conventions. By the same token, if Assayas' film bears unmistakably Lynchean accents and if some of its images bring to mind some of Van Sant's features, citation is not *Demonlover*'s defining characteristic. As discussed in the section entitled 'Corporate (Dis)embodiment', the film offers a complex reworking of clichés into a critique of the desensitising effect of virtual regimes of imaging.

physical with the most abstract styles and forms of expression – from body-centred performance arts to philosophy, from graphic sex and violence to essay writing.

There is, in fact, an underlying sense of resistance (conscious or unconscious) to the effects of postmodern distanciation at work; whereas the contemporary revisiting of the conventions of long-established genres is most commonly associated with the recourse to irony, kitsch and pastiche, such reflexive strategies rarely come into play here. On the contrary, the denial of parody is typical of the kind of filmmaking developed by directors like Grandrieux, Denis, Dumont, Assayas or Bonello, to name but a few, who have taken the risk of encroaching on the territories usually occupied by the cinema of the genres 'of excess' without resorting to the reflexive strategies characteristic of postmodern art practices (with which some of François Ozon's early films, for instance, are more easily associated). Commenting on the uncharacteristic shift towards horror that *Trouble Every Day* represents, Denis explains:

> Before cinema, already in literature, biting could be said to belong to the collective patrimony of the unconscious. I approached the genre without irony, because I am incapable of irony and pastiche. (Morice 2001, cited in Beugnet 2004b: 173)

Indeed, French directors interested in cinema as a cinema of sensation (even a director like Breillat, whose filmmaking generally encompasses a high degree of reflexivity) hardly resort to ironical detachment and self-conscious effects of citation as an end in themselves, even if, as the following remarks on Grandrieux's *Sombre* suggest, to adopt such an approach in contemporary film is to open oneself to accusations of being pompous and lacking in the critical, self-reflexive distance typical of the parodic mode.

> I have heard the film dismissed as 'portentous' and 'pretentious', 'silly' and 'risible' – responses partly triggered, I suspect, by the unblinking graveness and solemnity of its tone, a seriousness that allows for no 'comic relief' whatsoever, no variation in mood that lightens the exacting demand placed on the viewer. (Martin on *Sombre* 1999)

As Denis and Martin's comments imply, the rejection of the satirical is a sign of the refusal to use camera, script and *mise en scène* as means of distancing and shielding oneself and the spectator against the sensual as well as intellectual impact of the cinematic experience. The affirmation of the value of the archetypal against the appeal of pastiche and irony is one more indication of a shared disinterest for filmmaking as a formalist or narcissistic exercise. In fact, the wilful embracing of the archetypal suggests a common willingness to engage with broad collective concerns. Although he readily acknowledges the controversial nature of his films in terms of violence and stereotypical character traits, Grandrieux, for instance, denies accusations of gratuitous shock tactics by locating his filmmaking in the realm of the fairy tale, and by relating it to an archaic state of wonder and fear that recalls Bataille's elaborations on the paradoxical nature of being human: 'Fairy tales . . . contain a great deal of violence and cruelty, like the desires that pass through us. They contain and reveal that founding, archaic and animal part of us that is eventually tamed by society' (Grandrieux 1999a). Similarly, Assayas claims (with a characteristically anti-Hegelian touch) the opportunity of creating dream-like figures as a path into the exploration of that which escapes logic:

> My approach is embedded in the framework of the thriller, in its syntax as well as its stylistic system; yet, I do not seek to turn these elements into an endless reproduction of the same but, on the contrary, use them as tools for the exploration of the unconscious. Can I make a film that is a dream or, rather, a conscious nightmare about the world in which I live? A raving vision where the relation of one scene to another follows the logic of automatic writing? Art and poetry can bring together that which cannot be captured by the tools of reason. (Guilloux 2002)

For those critics who have welcomed the emergence of a cinema of sensation, films like *Sombre*, *La Vie nouvelle*, *Trouble Every Day*, *Tiresia* and *Demonlover* may indeed be understood as a foray into the unconscious, an exploration of the kind of archetypal world of repressed drives incarnated in the monstrous creations of dream-like worlds and fairy tales. Crucially, however, it is a collective unconscious that they strive to evoke (Brenez 1998: 21). The archetypal dimension thus sends us back to the crux of the matter: the attempt to create a cinematic experience that connects us, even fleetingly, with those pre-objective sensations and affects that operate before desires and drives are inscribed (defined, encoded, fixed) in the linguistic or discursive planes of organisation.

Hence, beyond the transient, interchangeable spaces, the 'any-spaces-whatever' born out of the historical realities and confusion of our contemporary world, the films also construct the kind of spaces that Deleuze describes as an 'originary world'. The originary world 'may be marked by the artificiality of the set . . . as much as by the authenticity of a preserved zone (a genuine desert, a virgin forest)', and in opposition to geographically and socially defined spaces and milieux described in a film, the originary world

> is recognisable by its formless character. It is a pure background, or rather a without-background, composed of unformed matter, sketches or fragments, crossed by

non-formal functions, acts, or energy dynamisms which do not even refer to the constituted subjects. Here the characters are like animals: the fashionable gentleman a
bird of prey, the lover a goat, the poor man a hyena. This is not because they have
their form or behaviour, but because their acts are prior to all differentiation between
the human and the animal. These are human animals . . . It is thus a world of a very
special kind of violence (in certain respects, it is the radical evil); but it has the merit
of causing an originary image of time to rise, with the beginning, the end, and the
slope, all the cruelty of Chronos. (Deleuze 1986: 123–4)

Moving through the porous borders between these originary worlds[2] and
the films' any-spaces-whatever, figures of becoming populate the images of
the cinema of sensation; growing on the instability of the filmic matter,
they are the very incarnation of an endless process of mutation that radically challenges our way of thinking about difference and otherness.

Becomings

Film is, by definition, the medium of being as change. From one image to
the next, space and figure, composition and texture, volume, colours and
light will vary, and as we know from the mainstream models of film production, to reinscribe these alterations into a pre-existing spatial and narrative logic and, by extension, into a specific discursive regime (to which,
in turn, the viewer's perception will be subjected) is to set out a whole array
of tricks, rules and prescriptions – a continuity system – that ensures a sense
of linear stability to the end result. Though notoriously problematic in
some of its political implications,[3] the Deleuzean notion of 'becoming'
(*devenir*, both a noun and a verb) is key here; the endless process of metamorphosis through contagion/proximity that 'becoming' entails accounts
remarkably well for the inherently changeful nature of cinematic images.
Indeed, envisaged specifically in the context of cinematic practices, the kind
of undermining of the concept of fixed identities that 'becoming' implies
offers a radical reworking of binary models that goes beyond the level of
representation to connect with the operations of film as material entity.

All becomings are already molecular. That is because becoming is not to imitate or
identify with something or someone. Nor is it to proportion formal relations. Neither

[2] The originary world takes two or three main aspects in the films discussed here: the desert
(*Beau Travail, Twentynine Palms, Flandres*), the sea (*Beau Travail, La Captive*) and the forest
(*Pola X, Sombre, La Vie nouvelle, L'Intrus* . . .). In *Adieu*, it could be the farmland with the
concentrationary vision conjured up by the nightmarish sight of the estate's industrial pig-
farming buildings.
[3] For a discussion of becoming-woman and feminism, see Kennedy 2000: 93–4, and Braidotti
2002: 79.

of these two figures of analogy is applicable to becoming: from the forms one has, the subject one is, the organs one has, or the function one fulfils, becoming is to extract particles between which one establishes the relations of movement and rest, speed and slowness that are *closest* to what one is becoming, and through which one becomes. (Deleuze and Guattari 1987: 272)

As Barbara Kennedy reminds us, Deleuze and Guattari's elaboration of the concept of becoming is grounded in the Nietzschean critique of transcendence. To the illusory belief in a transcendent order, Nietzsche typically opposes the inescapable unpredictability of the real, the transience of time and the fluctuation of natural energies. For Nietzsche, Kennedy summarises:

There is no other 'place' to which we can aspire. Belief in such metaphysical Being has only served to prevent humankind from accepting the sheer brutality, pain and transience of the 'real' . . . The concept of 'becoming' is what exists as the 'real' for Nietzsche: sometimes referred to as multiplicity, change, world, life or flux, 'becoming' exemplifies a continuum, a constant process of movement and changing volatilities and dynamisms. (Kennedy 2000: 1987)

The critique of transcendence that founds the theory of becoming is inseparable from that of language; with its inherent tendency to structure, define and fixate, language cannot adequately express 'the sheer flux, instability and profundity of life's ineluctable chaos'. Coming into effect in the form of pre-linguistic insights, it is via intuition and sensation that this process is felt:

This world of 'becoming' is predicated upon the sensual, through the body . . . This body, however, is not fixed into any singular identity. There is, according to Nietzsche, no fixed identity or form to the concept of 'body'. All we are is body, a multiplicity of changing desires, sensations, instincts, some purely physical, some sublimated . . . Rather than transcendence, 'becoming' is expressed through a sense of '*immanence*' or a processual continuum of movement and flux. (Kennedy 2000: 87)

Yet, the world we live in is inevitably structured by language, and subjectivity is thus always 'a process of negotiation between material and semiotic conditions that affect one's embodied, situated self' (Braidotti 2002: 79). This is where film, within its unmatched blend of encoded/'molar' expression and sensation or pre-linguistic/'molecular' experience, offers a remarkable actualisation of the subject as a historical formation. Film worlds are, intrinsically, worlds of 'becoming'. Deleuze's insistence on the notion of proximity ('Becoming is to emit particles that take on certain relations of movement and rest because they enter into a particular zone of proximity,' Deleuze and Guattari 1987: 272) describes very well the processuality at work in the film event, in the decomposition-recomposition that takes place from one frame to the next (film) or through the variations in the grain of the image (digital imaging as well as film). But whereas in the majority of film works this instability is, as much as possible, denied, in the cinema of sensation, it is emphasised not only at the formal level, but also at the level of representation; the process of 'becoming' permeates both planes and thus also works to destabilise 'molar' identities.

With its emphasis on filmic corporeality, the cinema of sensation allows even for those elements that are conventionally reduced to a fixed, representational or generic/narrative function to become a part again of a material process of 'becoming'. Beyond the rule of continuity that dictates that a character must be endowed with fixed, consistent and recognisable traits, for instance (in terms of physical aspect and social representation as well as narrative function), the human figure is caught again in the material event of the film.[4] As such, it partakes in and alters with the film's variations in movement, light and sound, through its 'relations of movement and rest, speed and slowness'. Hence the importance of wandering (often contrasted to enforced stasis) in the cinema of sensation and the multiplicity of nomadic characters who drift through films, caught in a process of becoming that affects them like chemical components thrown in a solution that alters their make-up.[5]

Certain generic features – technically, a limited array of pre-set narrative structures, moods and character identities – even facilitate the emergence of cinematic becomings. As Powell underlines, the archetypal worlds of the fairy tale and folk tale 'as well as their modern horror film equivalents, suggest that the boundaries of humans and other life-forms are not fixed, but that molecular flows conjoin singularities' (Powell 2005: 67). These are territories explored in many of the films discussed in this book, works where the evocation of the darker side of the human psyche encroaches on the universe of the dream-like, to include fairy-tale or mythological figures of becoming that detach the subjective body from fixed gender identities – the hermaphrodite (*Tiresia*, *Wild Side*) – and stress the kinship of the human figure with beasts, plants and minerals: the half-human/half-beast (*Trouble Every Day*; *Sombre*; *La Vie nouvelle*; *À ma sœur*; *L'Intrus*); the mermaid (*La Captive*); the human becoming plant or mineral (*Twentynine Palms*; *Beau Travail*).

---

[4] For an alternative approach and taxonomy of the figure in film, see Brenez's impressive study (Brenez 1998).

[5] Indeed, certain images, like discreet, reflexive encapsulations of this process, echo from one film to another: the body of actor Laurent Lucas immersed in bath water, emerging to catch his breath then plunging again in *Adieu* (2003), and resurfacing in *Les Invisibles* (2005).

Crucially, as Deleuze and Guattari, quoting Duvignaud's work on anomy, point out, however, 'becoming' is neither contained nor reducible to mythical constructs. Rather, myths tend to recuperate some of the forms generated by the dynamic forces of 'becoming' and integrate them to their specific framework; whereas figures of 'becoming' belong to lines of flight, myth is immobilisation, it recuperates aberrant phenomena and attempts to integrate and fixate them (Duvignaud 1970; Deleuze and Guattari 1987: 291).

Both Chantal Akerman's *La Captive* and Claire Denis' *Beau Travail* probe into the relationship between myth and 'becoming'.[6] In *La Captive*, the poetic force of 'becoming', crystallising around the figures of the mermaids, reintroduces uncertainty and lines of flight in a universe ossified by the sterile fixating effect of jealousy and gender stereotyping. Gender is also part of the mythical construct that *Beau Travail* debunks, the process of 'becoming' a part of film's thinking through the issue of 'being' in a shifting historical reality. The films thus offer a stunning denunciation and subversion of myth as a principle of stasis via a vivid evocation of 'becoming' as the principle of being as change.

In Praise of 8mm (Becoming Mermaid/*La Captive*)

We hear the sound of the rolling waves before we distinguish them, a succession of coiling ribbons of foam lining the dark fabric of the screen. As the spectator realises after a first viewing, the opening images of Chantal Akerman's *La Captive* (2000) follow on from its closing sequence. The ominous presence of the ocean's mass at the beginning of the film appears to echo the final images, where, as the silhouette of the main character, carried by a small boat, exits the frame via its lower border, the surface of the screen merges with that of the sea at night. A free adaptation of Marcel Proust's *La Prisonnière*,[7] *La Captive*'s tragic tale is that of a young woman irremediably trapped in a claustrophobic relation with a morbidly possessive lover. In harmony with the unending movement of the water, the film thus espouses a circular form and rhythm that simultaneously mirrors the repetitive quality of obsession and evokes the effect of a recommencing film loop. Though a part of this movement, the 8mm sequence that comes directly after the opening credits will not only remain difficult to situate

---

[6] For detailed discussions of the films as a whole, including factual details and a description of the conditions of production, see Beugnet 2004b, and Beugnet and Schmid 2005b.

[7] *La Prisonnière* is part of volume III of Marcel Proust's *À la recherche du temps perdu*, Jean-Yves Tadié (ed.) (1987–9), 4 vols, Paris: Gallimard, 'Pléiade'. For a detailed study of Proustian adaptations for the screen, see Beugnet, Martine, Marion Schmid (2005), *Proust at the Movies*, Aldershot: Ashgate.

within the internal chronology of the whole, but it also initiates a series of lines of flight that pierce through the cyclical format of the body of the film. Unfolding like a temporal parenthesis, a smaller reel within the larger cycle of the film in its entirety, this new sequence is in stark contrast to the atmosphere created by the dark, foreboding images that precede it. It also depicts the seaside, but this time the 8mm images fill the screen with a luminous glow. They show a group of young women playing in the sea and on the beach (an evocation of the *Jeunes filles en fleurs*). If the mere mention of this visual theme immediately conjures up the most trite of clichés, its treatment here belongs to a wholly different imagery to, say, that of tourism, advertisement or commercial film and TV. Even before we see, in counter-shot, the young man who is operating the projector, the quality of these mute images, accompanied by the characteristic sound of the unfolding reels of film, imbues them with an oddly familiar and old-fashioned feel. In spite of the fact that what we see is but the picture of a film within a film, the grainy surface, animated by the erratic appearance of small scoria and the jumpy movement of the projection, is instantly recognisable. Together with the crystalline aspect of the outlines and colours – as if the images were lit from within – and the unrivalled sensitivity to the changes in luminosity, the physical qualities of the images all designate the characteristic world of 8mm film. It is neither the placement of the sequence (since it occurs at the beginning of the film) nor its figurative content that initially suggests that these images come from the past. (If the sequence was a celebration of one's lost youth and lightness of being, would its diegetic spectator be a young man, rather than an older observer reminiscing over his or her past, for instance?) At first, it is the very material qualities of the medium itself that account for the nostalgic nature of the vision. (The narrative eventually suggests – only in retrospect – surmise that at this point, the young woman who is eventually singled out by the super-8 camera and closely observed by the projectionist of the film has, in fact, already disappeared, in which case the rest of the film becomes one long flashback). If memory as the kind of sensual experience described by Proust seems best encapsulated in these images, it is not merely because super-8 is associated with film as home movie and family memories, and, by extension, with the emotional pitch triggered by such feelings of intimacy. Beyond its economic and socio-cultural status, it is the material and aesthetic characteristics of the medium itself that endow its images with a specific corporeal and synaesthetic appeal.

The brevity of the 8mm reel connects its use with the recording of the episodic and contemplative rather than the construction of elaborated narrative structures; the aim is simply to document a moment, the memory of an instant or a particular atmosphere. Moreover, the footage often shows the marks of repeated manipulation – scratches that are, to paraphrase the title of Marks' book, like scars on the 'skin of the film'. Regardless of what is being filmed, whether landscape in long shot or face in close-up, the uneven, grainy and pulsating quality of the images renders them particularly tactile in appearance, inviting, in the first instance, a haptic form of vision. Like the texture of the images that foreground their tactile character before their narrative-figurative content, other effects, such as changes in framing or light, trigger sensations and feelings beyond the visual. In this case, when the young women are filmed playing a ball game on the sand, for instance, the sun comes from behind the clouds to illuminate the scene. The image fills with a warm glow and its tones take on the transparent vibrancy of watercolours, vividly evoking the feelings of enveloping warmth bestowed by the sudden apparition of bright sun rays. The poignant effect that super-8 film seems to yield also comes from the specific quality of its projected images, fluttering as if they were animated by an inner pulsation. The silent scenes and bodies that appear on the screen, as well as the body of the film itself, thus convey a strange and affecting sense of vulnerability; like that of the slightly quivering silhouettes that fleetingly appear on the screen, the fragility of the super-8 film is always perceptible.

Interestingly, *La Captive*'s opening sequence simultaneously celebrates the affective power of the cinematic image and points to its limitations. On the one hand, what could be described as the vivid expression of an art of the sensation calls for a participatory, rather than a distanced, analytical gaze. On the other, however, Simon, the key male character of Akerman's film (Stanislas Merhar as a young version of the Proustian narrator), trapped in the obsessive mode of the jealous, possessive observer, remains incapable of engaging with the reality around him as it manifests itself in its sensual ambiguity. Whereas Simon seeks to find evidence and certainty, the physical presence of the images he faces (and that he supposedly shot himself) is engaging because of their ability to appropriate the pro-filmic and transform it into a material event in itself; that is, they derive their appeal from their very limitations in terms of the transparent and 'purely' faithful recording of live reality. In the end, drawn by the images, the young man, who had been standing next to the projector, comes and squats down close to the screen, now filled with a shot of his lover (Sylvie Testud as Ariane, Akerman's version of Proust's Albertine). Yet, his own body, placed between projector and screen, casts a dark shadow – a black hole that threatens to engulf Ariane's silhouette. The young woman is then seen turning her back to the camera and running away towards the sea.

Simon searches the image for certitudes, for the signs that will solve the mystery of his lover's personality, of the elusive nature of her sexuality, and elucidate the bond that connects her to the other young women. The significance of the film images, however, lies elsewhere. Ariane's body relives only as a trace on the skin of the film, highly recognisable, yet hardly enough of a representation to create an imperfect illusion of actual co-presence with the viewer. At the same time, the figure that inhabits the film world forms a series of marks sufficiently imprecise, yet sufficiently rich to elicit a seductive and vividly evocative multi-sensory perception; in the end, because the moving image appears as a material entity on its own, its relation to an external referent – in this case, the actual body and face of the young man's lover – remains fluid and transient. The value of the image, and its suggestive power, thus rests less in its representative capacity as such, in relation to another reality that it documents, than *in itself*, as a material entity, before it becomes part of a narrative or the subject of an interpretative discourse. Here, as with the enigma of the photograph that consumes the hero of Michelangelo Antonioni's *Blow-up* (1966), the image will not yield any truth and no revelation other than the precious sensual and emotional experience offered by pictures in movement; but Simon, as a young version of the Proustian narrator, still too imprisoned by the need for possessive certitudes, does not yet appear able to abandon himself to this experience.

In contrast with his endless investigations and jealous, fixating gaze, the inherently transgressive nature of the images where his lover first appears in the company of her female friends emerges more strongly. By transgressive here, I mean, in the first place, the disregard for pre-established or dominant rules of representation that, in turn, encompasses a disregard for the heterosexual norm (and Steven Shaviro dedicates long passages to the fundamentally transgressive nature of the Proustian project in relation to representation and sexuality (Shaviro 2004: 70–80)). By remaining close to the order of the figural (as opposed to fully embracing the merely figurative and representational), while also imposing its own trembling pulse on the film event, the sequence in 8mm film espouses the cinematographic ability to evoke the existence of the beings and inanimate objects that appear on screen as a process – a 'becoming' or a flux – rather than as pre-existing, fixed identities. If, in spite of its ephemeral quality, this initial vision proves to be the most enduring evocation of the young woman, it is because it conveys her Proustian character's resistance to being reduced to a precise sexual and social identity. No matter how many times Simon replays the same few images, trying to put words on the silently moving lips of Ariane and her friend Andrée, the actual nature of their relationship will remain unspoken.

In the following sequence, the female figures are transposed from one world to the other, from the arcadian free-floating parenthesis of the 8mm sequence to a defined world of social respectability, heterosexual norm and photographic precision. Painfully perched on stiletto heels, Ariane's silhouette resembles that of a mermaid in exile. Yet she walks, legs cutting through space like scissors, heels clicking; followed by Simon's relentless, obsessive gaze, yet forever eluding it, she traverses the film and manages to weave her way through the controlled and claustrophobic spaces where he hopes to keep her captive. Even the confines of Simon's sombre apartments cannot detain her completely; hence, to the rustling silence of the 8mm images of the beach corresponds the eloquent duet which Ariane performs, from her balcony, with a mysterious woman standing at the window opposite. The two women are physically separated yet by intertwining their voices they seem to touch each other. Simon can only look on haplessly and listen to their singing – 'a nostalgic lament to their separation, yet also an affirmation of their bond' (Beugnet and Schmid 2001).[8] Ultimately, Ariane chooses freedom over her attachment to the young man. At the end of the film, in a sudden movement of flight that echoes that of the final images of the 8mm sequence, she runs across the beach and goes back to the sea.

The whole film is imbued with the tension between the material and transgressive presence of the filmic reality, with its fluidity and lines of flight on the one hand, and the need to appropriate and interpret that translates in the exercise, by the male figure, of an objectifying, omniscient gaze on the other. It becomes most tangible in the contrast between a sensual cinematographic understanding and a distant objectified vision of the same environments. The film, thus, places in parallel contrasting universes. The secluded space of the cars, behind whose windscreens the lonely Simon observes Ariane, and the dark, maze-like flat where the young man would like to keep her materialise as a visualisation of his obsessive, closed mind and allergic (literally – like the Proustian character, Simon is allergic to flowers), distanced relation to the world. Conversely, the young woman's presence, and that of her friends, seem to generate a sensual richness through an abundance and diversity of places, voices, musics and gestures, fabrics, colours, textures and perfumes that culminates in the delicate palpitation and crystalline corporeality of the 8mm image.[9]

---

[8] For a full discussion of the role of music and, in particular, the use of Mozart's *Così Fan Tutte* and Rachmaninov's *The Isle of the Dead*, see Beugnet and Schmid (2001), pp. 195–8.

[9] Ultimately, this tension also works as a kind of *mise en abyme* of Akerman's project in itself: to start with the task of adapting an existing work but escape the constraints of representing or illustrating its source text in order to create an independent art work and an autonomous cinematographic universe.

Today, the distinctiveness of the affective power that I tentatively evoked above in my description of *La Captive*'s opening sequences might feel even more precious and vulnerable as Kodak announces its decision to close its last super-8 factory and laboratory.[10] Paradoxically, a crucial filmmaking tool may thus vanish or be restricted to the status of archive at the time where, as part of a wider shift that involves most artistic, philosophical and literary domains, a fraction of today's filmmakers and film theorists seek to explore anew that sensual interweaving of affect and thought process created by film, and that, amongst other filmmaking techniques, the choice of shooting in super-8 encapsulates so well.

Becoming Mineral (*Beau Travail*)

We are not in the world but we become with the world, we become by contemplating it. Everything is vision, becoming. We become universes. Becoming plant, animal, becoming zero. (Deleuze and Guattari 1987: 263)

The sound of wind and a long shot of a desert plane delineated by the hazy, layered horizon of a mountain range. Cut: the rustle of rusting metal mixes with the sound of wind. A medium long shot of an abandoned tank, cannon aimlessly pointed towards the sky. Cut: long shot of the tank's forlorn silhouette in the midst of the barren expanse. Cut: close-up on tufts of dry weeds quivering in the breeze. Cut: the sound-track fills with a choir of male voices starting a litany.[11] An elongated shadow on the dry sandy ground. The camera pans slowly, follows its outline, then reveals more shadows and, eventually, encounters the body of a man standing. Gradually, the frame fills with the silhouettes of a group of soldiers facing each other, eyes closed, arms raised, hovering slightly, as if in a trance.

Set in Djibouti, *Beau Travail* (1999), Denis' remarkable opus about the French Foreign Legion, offers a highly atypical exploration of this great (masculine and cinematic) myth. The film's title, like the lushness of its photography, the magnificence of the natural setting and the beauty of the soldiers' bodies, outlines the enduring force and seductiveness of the legion's appeal; beyond the exoticism, it is the illusory ideal of integration and fusion within a *corps d'élite* that creates its attraction.[12] Denis' film,

---

[10] See Renaud, Nicolas (July 2005), 'Disparition du Kodachrome: La Fin d'une image hors du temps', www.horschamp.qc.ca/article.php3?id_article=193.

[11] From the choir comes part of Benjamin Britten's opera, 'Billy Budd', inspired, like the film, by Herman Melville's eponymous novella.

[12] Here, the notion of military fusion goes beyond the reshaping of bodies through identical training and uniforms. The legion is famous for its unusual mode of recruitment; those who

however, explores the myth and simultaneously reveals it as a destructive chimera, part of a colonial relic. As Susan Hayward reminds us, 'the colonial is not after all dead, but lives in its after-effects.' Denis' films, she adds, thus accounts for its ravages in their staging of the 'post-colonial-body-as-the-after-effect-of-colonialism' (Hayward 2001: 159, 161). Through its stylised aesthetics, the film emphasises the archaism of both the military structure and of the concept of time and history it implies. The legion is a body that has outlived the imperialistic ideal that founded it and its survival rests on a double denial: on the one hand, the denial of historical change that is inscribed in its system, in the rituals and routines that form the basis of military life, and on the very bodies of the soldiers that belong to it; on the other, the denial and exclusion of the 'other', whatever he or she may be – those who cannot abide completely by the rule, whose difference cannot be effaced, the people of Djibouti and in particular the women. In the dance sequence entitled the 'dance of the weeds', differences (the variety of ethnic backgrounds) seem to be transcended into an ideal of self-sameness and the fusion into a unique, collective body. Yet the scene is imbued less with a sense of timelessness than with one of desuetude – the approaching dissolution of a body threatened by the very logic that founds it. Like the disused machinery already colonised by the sand, the men, caught in the breathing rhythm of the desert, move with the plants and the wind as if they were on the brink of merging with their surroundings. If this process of 'becoming desert' evokes the fearsome pull of the organic, the attraction of the formless, it also reveals the impossibility of the model of invariability and homogeneity imposed by an obsolete military order.

Towards the end of the film, the soldier Sentain (Grégoire Colin), punished for disobedience, is condemned to walk alone through the desert. His compass broken, he gets lost and ends up on the edge of the sea, in the midst of an immense saline field. A long shot shows a coastline so saturated with salt that it has paled into a near-white expanse where water and ground merge seamlessly. On the far side of the frame, the tiny silhouette of Sentain, dwarfed by the ominous landscape, seems but a speck of dust. The shot then cuts to a close-up of the surface of the ground, covered in salt crystals. The sound-track conveys the strange combination of liquidity (the waves that beat feebly against the salt-ridden beach) and solidity (the crackling sound of Sentain's feet crushing the saline earth). Cut: a medium close-up of Sentain lying down on the ground, exhausted, his face

Footnote 12 (*cont.*)

   join acquire a new identity and leave their past behind. Any young man can join, regardless of ethnicity, religion or nationality. The price to give is unquestioning obedience to the legion's rules and set of values.

and shoulders covered with specks of salt. In slow, feeble movements, he reaches for his jacket and pulls it up next to his head to protect himself against the sun. The fabric, however, colonised by salt, has changed into a hardened shape that bristles like sand paper. Cut: a long shot of the landscape – an endless, dazzling white expanse that extends towards the silhouettes of the mountains in the faraway background. Here again, in its vivid evocation of a process of 'becoming-earth', the sequence works as a metaphor for the legion's anachronistic ideal of self-effacement and timelessness – the subject trapped and 'fossilised' in the static space of myth. At the same time, the poignancy of the embodied process of metamorphosis counterbalances the abstracting effect of the metaphor and reinjects timelessness with change, even if it is the slow, inexorable rhythm of organic alteration. In the end, Sentain is discovered and saved by the nomads of a salt caravan.

All the way through, the body of the film is punctured with images of passing trains. The constant reminder of time and change, they cut through sequences as through the cyclical and repetitive space created by the legion's presence. It is by train that the rescued Sentain is eventually transported away. Caught back into the shifting reality of time as change, he will face again what Kristeva calls the 'cosmopolitanism of the excoriated': the reality of non-belonging and foreignness with its endless possibilities for becoming (Kristeva 1994: 25, quoted in Beugnet 2004b: 123).

As *Beau Travail*'s bewitching evocation of the obsolescence of the colonial project demonstrates, there is something both exhilarating and deeply unsettling in the way 'becoming' brings back transience to the heart of the illusory work of transcendence. It is because the profound, ineluctable alteration brought about in the process radically threatens traditional definitions of subjectivity, because '[becoming] undoes one of the major borders of the metaphysics of the self, scrambling the distinction between human and non-human'. On the one hand, the inherently anti-anthropomorphic, anti-humanising drive at the heart of the theory raises 'ethical questions about how far to go in pursuing changes and stretching the boundaries of subjectivity' (Braidotti 2002: 145). At the same time, it points to alternative ways of approaching the transformations (decolonisation, globalisation, transnationalism, technological and genetic mutations) that affect our world, or at least, to the ambivalence (the expectations and the fear) with which we face these changes. It is this incertitude that opens the door for the cinematic figure of 'becoming' par excellence, the vampire, to come back and haunt the worlds of contemporary films.

Vampires and Werewolves

Man does not become wolf or vampire, as if he changed molar species; the vampire
and the werewolf are becomings of man, in other words, proximities between mole-
cules in composition, relations of movement and rest, speed and slowness between
emitted particles. (Deleuze and Guattari 1984: 107)

Cinema, and, for that matter, all the media born out of the industrial revolution, is ceaselessly suspect for its ability seemingly to 'vampirise' physical reality.[13] In two of Olivier Assayas' films, the protagonist becomes
increasingly wrapped up in a shifting matrix of global media representations to the point where her persona is at risk of being completely absorbed
by the characters she is merely supposed to incarnate. In *Irma Vep* (1995)
and *Demonlover* (2002), star actresses Maggie Cheung (asked to play the
eponymous French vamp in a Louis Feuillade remake)[14] and Connie
Nielsen (who plays the American executive of a French-based company –
a communication corporation aptly called 'Volf') don the characteristic
tight, sleek black costume first sported by the mistress of the 'Grand
Vampire'. The outfits cling to their bodies like a film as they slip through
the window into the night; 'becoming-vampire' is also 'becoming-image',
'becoming-film'. Characteristic of the film's unusual combination of
melancholy and humorous reflexivity, the end of *Irma Vep* offers a striking
collage of footage that recalls the experiments of the early avant-gardes
(from Man Ray's *rayographes* to the German abstract films of the 1920s),
and inscribes the marriage of vampirism and film into the material make-
up of the images. The sequence mixes shots of the female 'vamp' excerpted
from two films: the original Feuillade serial and the unfinished remake with
Cheung as the new Irma. In addition, the highly contrasted black-and-
white images are heavily scratched and marked as if alternatively to celebrate or attack the female forms that appear on their surface, or, indeed,
scar the 'skin' of the film itself. In a nutshell, the sequence seems to evoke
the sum of ambiguities and contradictions borne by the cinematic vampire:
the weaving together of a transnational intertext; the interpenetration of
past and present, of the modern and the old (or, in this case, the modern

---

[13] See article in *Modern and Contemporary France* (Beugnet 2007a). Not only does film appropriate and reproduce endlessly life-like simulacra of the human form, but, to borrow André
Bazin's well-known expression, film 'embalms' the present, and can conjure up at will that
which has long disappeared from material realities, if not from memories (Bazin 1967: 9, 14).
Like Philippe Arnaud, other theorists have since turned to television (using the example of
reality shows) as the medium most prone to the vampirism of reality (Arnaud 1995: 306).

[14] The term *Vamp* was first applied to Musidora, the actress who played the seductive criminal
in the 1915 *Vampires* serial. (*Irma Vep* is an anagram of vampire.)

as old), and, as an aesthetic phenomenon, the alliance of the destructive and the creative. Paradoxically, the more altered or 'damaged' the images and sounds, the better the corporeality of film is affirmed.

The vampire came to haunt the screens very early on in the life of the cinema. The two phenomena belong to the same elusive realm, at the fragile border between sleeping and waking. Like the film image, the vampire appears when the lights go down and vanishes before they come on again, the unnatural quality of its kinetic deftness a reminder of its monstrosity as well as of the mechanistic quality of all filmic bodies as they circulate through shots, inhabiting the body of the film itself for the duration of the screening. Hence, the seemingly unlikely attraction that drew together an ancient figure, commonly associated with obscurantism, and a new medium, often hailed as the artistic and technological epitome of the advent of modernity, is, paradoxically, easily fathomed: ubiquity and 'becoming'. Seductive and repellent, hovering at the border of the real and the virtual, the figure of the vampire typifies the inhuman capacity to materialise and disseminate itself seamlessly through time and space (also the privileged ability of the cinematic image, even before the advent of digital technologies and the internet). Neither alive nor dead, neither human nor animal or mineral, the vampire reinvents itself endlessly through proximity and con-tamination, epitomising the 'becoming' at work in all figures created by film.

At the same time, against a backdrop of conflicting local, national and global values, the vampire draws renewed fascination from its paradoxical status as a mythical yet constantly actualised figure. The vampire harbours the shadow of a near-forgotten world of superstitions and archaic fears. It appears the very opposite of French modernity's tradition of enlightened rationalism; yet, with its endless powers of metamorphosis, it also appears destined to thrive within the new era ruled by global circulation and the seemingly irresistible law of universal, deregulated greed.

Thus, it seems uncannily fitting that, at the junction between the twentieth and twenty-first centuries, as the borders of the 'old' Europe become more porous and expand to reflect the emergence of a richer but also more unstable concept of European identity, the figure of the vampire should make a discreet reappearance, returning to haunt the film worlds of a number of contemporary French directors. Indeed, the vampire acquires an unusually potent aura at a time when Western European nations are beset by the fear of hidden colonisation and the paranoid desire to control movement across borders, be it of people, capital,[15] information or images.

---

[15] The vampire's ubiquitous presence is readily associated with capital and has long been part of its metaphorical discourse. In their Gothic literary guises in particular, the ability of vam

Hence, the vampire arguably comes to typify the anxieties conjured up by the emergence of a global era.

Contemporary Transylvanias are shifting sites, and vampirism a discreet yet ubiquitous phenomenon that feeds on the increasing circulation of bodies and images, thriving on the internet, through international networks and new forms of human slavery, sexual exploitation and organ traffic. The vampire returns in an era marked by the dissolution of national, localised markers at a 'systemic level' and imbued with the fear of the absorption or subjugation of individual, *incarnated* realities in/to a matrix of virtual, '*disembodied flux*' – a process that 'traditionally told stories focused on individuals in concrete spatial locations are increasingly inadequate to deal with' (O'Shaughnessy 2005, italics mine).

In its present-day guises, however, the vampire exceeds and, indeed, contradicts its original role in the stigmatisation of a fantasised (Eastern) other. It does not merely typify the force of anomy menacing the order from the outside any more; contemporary vampirism is attuned to transnational fluxes.[16] On the one hand, 'becoming-vampire' thus epitomises the condition of those who live in a global system where only those who are powerful and in the position of the exploiter can thrive and circulate freely. On the other hand, in its defiance of traditional notions of collective identity, it suggests the possibility of new assemblages, becomings that deny the old dichotomy that opposes self to the other, the foreigner. 'Becoming', as Deleuze and Guattari stress, is not 'to imitate or to identify with something or someone' (1984: 272); it is a process of metamorphosis that works like vampirism, through contiguity and dissemination. In the films concerned

Footnote 15 (*cont.*)

 pires to travel invisibly, establish themselves anywhere at will, and multiply and breed corruption, extends to the wealth they hoard and the capital they control. In their reading of the vampire, both Ken Gelder and Franco Moretti comment on the early connection between vampirism, capitalism and the fear of the corruption of national identities. Both authors quote Marx's famous description of capitalism as vampirism – 'dead labour which, vampire-like, lives by sucking living labour' – and note how, in spite of his own origins, Marx further associated capitalism with the then epitome of the transnational figure, the Jew (Moretti 1988: 92; Gelder 1994: 17).

[16] It is tempting, initially, to claim that today's vampiric figures are but a continuation of the metaphor associated with early tales of vampirism and, in particular, that they stand for what Stephen Arata calls the 'anxiety of reverse colonisation' (Arata 1990: 622). They could also be related to the contemporary phenomenon identified by Max Silverman as 'new racisms' (Silverman 1999: 40): that is, a fear of the Eastern European incomer, the white migrant, who is more difficult for Western Europeans to single out than settlers from other ethnic backgrounds. For this corpus of films, however, these explanations are not fully satisfactory. Here, the figure of the vampire is a fluctuating one; alternatively male or female, it takes on the appearance of a foreigner or a national figure, a victim or an exploiter.

here, the vampire lends its features to the Westerner as well as the Eastern other, to the insider as well as the foreigner, to both exploiter and exploited. The trajectories and histories of both the victims and the guilty are thus woven together so that, ultimately, 'becoming-vampire' typifies the impossibility to disconnect, to bury the past and keep but one consistent facet of the (hi)story.

Although as a discreet or ominous presence, the vampire manifests itself in many recent French films,[17] it is when cinema becomes a cinema of sensation that film opens a space where 'becoming-vampire' is also a cinematographic becoming. Working through the content as well as the structure and material appearance of the films themselves, it then inscribes the uncertainties and mutations of the global age into the body of the film itself.

'Becoming-vampire' escapes genre expectation to permeate the films in a diffuse, polysemic manner, yet the tell-tale signs are still there: in the spectral beauty and emphasised accent of Lithuanian-born actress Katia Golubeva (*Pola X*, *L'Intrus*); in the way the smuggler conceals his face under his hood in *Adieu*; in the masks and costumes that the puppeteer Jean (Marc Barbé) uses to scare and captivate children (*Sombre*); in the werewolf-like looks of Béatrice Dalle (*L'Intrus*, *Trouble Every Day*) and Vincent Gallo (*Trouble Every Day*); in the playful yet predatory pose of Dalle as killer Coré, as she briefly appears, walking along the Parisian *périphérique* at sunset, arms extended behind her under her coat as if they were the wings of a bat (*Trouble Every Day*); in the osmosis that typifies the relation of humans and dogs in the dark forest kingdom that the characters of *L'Intrus* share . . . . And there is the kiss: Melania (Anna Mouglalis) appearing at the nightclub, furtive and dream-like, and bending over Seymour to kiss him, then vanishing in a maze of shimmering artificial lights in *La Vie nouvelle*; Pierre offering his neck to Isabelle's avid lips in the corridor of the dingy hotel where brother and sister have sought refuge in *Pola X*; the kissing couple of the long, anxiety-ridden sequence that opens *Trouble Every Day* . . . .

The characters of these films inhabit hybrid, ambivalent spaces – border-zones made up of dense forests, but also urban 'any-spaces-whatever' made up of post-industrial sites, defamiliarised city centres, no-man's-lands and soulless suburbs; theirs is a Transylvania operating 'as a transferable sign, which carries its meaning to other places' (Gelder 1994: 1).[18]

---

[17] See Beugnet (2007a).

[18] In *Reading the Vampire*, Ken Gelder repeatedly stresses the impossibility, ever since its appropriation by travelogues and Gothic fiction, for Westerners to describe a place designated as 'Transylvania' objectively: 'One of the peculiarities of vampire fiction is that it has – with great success – turned a real place into a fantasy' (Gelder 1994: 1). Most historical studies on

In *Demonlover*, a transnational corporate world of customised global architecture extends into the simulated spaces of interactive computer games further connected to sinister subterranean mazes. Here, at the crossover between the actual and the virtual, Transylvania becomes a truly global concept. In the sinister world of global media vampirism portrayed in Assayas' film, all human relations are prone to be infused and altered by the toxic effect of an economy of manufactured desire, and shifts of identity and loyalties become inherently unfathomable. Hence, even the predatory businesswoman, the appropriately named Diane de Monx, ends up caught in a web of internet sexploitation that knows no boundaries. In *Demonlover*, time itself is enslaved to the profit-bound logic of virtual games, where human life is but a pawn in the service of global economic interests and internet players' paid-for fantasies.

The power of the vampiric figure lies in its ability to navigate through these temporal and geographic spaces just as it crosses from one diegetic world to the next, moving through conceptual and historical categories to inhabit changing human forms. Indeed, its symbolic or actual presence permeates the films' space, where living beings and dead bodies, individuals and groups, hunted, bought and sold, cross official and virtual borders, legally and illegally. In one form or another, the films, thus, involve actual or virtual journeys, through a global world of international trade as well as the furtive flights of migrants chased by police and herded like cattle by modern slave traders. It is not merely the integrity of the human body that is at stake here, but that of a nation circumscribed by its frontiers and, ultimately, the body of the film itself. Infiltration, circulation and rupture become determining elements of the texture of image and sound-track, as well as of the structuring of the narrative space; they inform the discontinuous editing modes and kaleidoscopic narratives that interweave the characters' trajectories as they wander through the loose plots and contrasting blocks of space and time that make up the films.

In *L'Intrus*, the deep scar that runs across the body of the main character finds its visual equivalent in the duplication of man-made borders that deny the openness of even the wildest of landscapes and in the frames that similarly limit and fragment the film's images: frontiers and customs, walls, blinds, doors, windows; scars (as incongruous and rectilinear as the human borders that divide the surface of the earth). The film speaks of a

---

Gothic fiction underline the process whereby the existence of those mysterious legendary lands that lie 'beyond, or to the other side of the forest', 'between Western Europe and the far East' (Gelder 1994: 1, 4), has progressively been forsaken to the Western imaginary and become little more than the 'expression of Europe's unconscious' (Wall 1984: 20).

world of violent and paranoid ownership, fixated on the delimitation and defence of a territory where the foreign body is always the intruder, always reducible to a threat, to be hunted, driven away or destroyed.

Yet, the film also shows enclosures, boundaries and partitions as porous, vulnerable to the intrusion of the gaze, the movement of bodies, the impact of a weapon, and to the effect of time. At first, the main character, Trébor, seems immune to change; he is a predatory man, able to live in harmony with his dogs as well as being a part of the world of international business. Yet, in order to gain a new lease of life – a heart transplant – Trébor has to make a Faustian pact. From then on, like the blood that circulates through his body, pumped by a strange heart via artificial arteries, Trébor travels, trying to recapture a lost past. In the course of the journey that takes him across the globe by car, plane and boat, he undergoes a discreet metamorphosis that transforms him from hunter to hunted, from observer to observed, from being the guardian of his own realm, to being the foreigner, the intruder. And, ultimately, it is the body of the film itself that appears pieced together, through its alternation of close-ups and long shots and its blocks of sequences of conflicting tonalities and moods assembled like the constituents of a monstrous creature.

As *L'Intrus*' elliptical tale suggests, vampirism thrives through uncanny overlaps of space and time which enable ghosts of a conveniently forgotten history to return to haunt the present. Indeed, as the past comes back to reveal the soiled foundations on which the present is built, vampirism starts to infuse the cinematic form itself.

Like Denis' *Beau Travail*, Leos Carax's *Pola X* is a loose adaptation of one Herman Melville's novels, *Pierre or the Ambiguities*, and, like *L'Intrus*, it has been dismissed by many critics on the grounds of its *informe* structure – an impressive and perplexing sum of uneven generic and mood-contrasting blocks. The film opens on a spellbinding montage of World War II newsreels, images that unfold to a punk-rock track (by Scott Walker). Grainy, black-and-white footage of Luftwaffe operations shows planes flying over graveyards, speed-diving and dropping bombs. The sequence alternates shots of the planes, aerial views and images of tombstones exploding, a vision of mayhem that fills the frame till clouds of dust obscure the screen completely: startling images of the dead being awoken through the desecration of death itself.

The archive footage, thus, initially serves as a shrine for a forgotten past about to resurface – a form of cinematic vampirism that lends an outlandish, melancholic quality to the evocation of obliterated areas of official history. It also foretells the appearance, in the comfortable life of the film's eponymous hero, Pierre, of a half-sister who was raised in Bosnia, and whose existence he never knew about. Carax describes the character of

Isabelle as an apparition; born out of the sequence of the bombarded tombs, she marks the unavoidable return of (hi)story, a ghostly reality, yet one that is as irreducible as the Bataillean's 'accursed share'.

> It was something I had [in me], something that happened in Bosnia . . . you could think Isabelle comes out of one of these bombed tombs, and walks towards us like in Abel Gance's film *J'accuse*, where the dead of the First World War walk towards the camera, towards us . . . She is this kind of ghost . . . The accursed share. (cited in Daly and Dowd 1999)

In the first proper encounter between Pierre and Isabelle, this spectral dimension is played up to unusual effect. Pierre first spots Isabelle walking on the edge of a forest at night, and when she flees from him, he runs after her, moving deeper into the woods. The images that follow look almost as if they were printed on to a negative: extremely dark and contrasted, with a bluish hue that recalls early expressionist movies, endowing the flesh with a cadaverous quality. Combining lateral travelling and scope with the effect of distance, the first shot creates a striking fairy-tale-like scene, with the two tiny silhouettes running through the crepuscular forest, dwarfed by the tall trees. As the camera gets closer and follows the characters through increasingly dense undergrowth, the bodies almost seem to fuse with their surroundings. Face half-concealed by her mane of dark hair, Isabelle walks and tells her tale, her eye sockets like two dark hollows. Daly and Dowd describe the character as a figure of 'becoming' – 'She exists as an amalgam of speeds and slownesses' – whose 'rapid logorrhoea and mute catalepsy vie for position' (Daly and Dowd 1999: 153). But it is in the way the character-as-figure, as if undergoing 'an exchange of particles', appears drawn into the background created by the film's diegetic world (the forest, with its dense, obscure mesh of vegetation) and of that of the image itself (with its almost opaque texture) that her 'becoming' manifests itself and, in turn, starts to affect the other human figure. Indeed, in the scenes where Pierre and Isabelle grow progressively closer, the light continues to be sucked away from the images to the extent that human forms, naked pallid flesh or darkly clothed silhouettes, often seem to merge together. It is thanks to this discovery of being-as-becoming that Pierre literally gets in touch with a different historical reality. Considered from the point of view of the representation and characterisation of the 'other', *Pola X* raises obvious issues.[19] Experienced

---

[19] And, indeed, the casting of Golubeva in this type of role raises further questions. In Bruno Dumont's *Twentynine Palms*, she is again a figure caught in a process of becoming that manifests itself, this time in the 'originary world' of a desert. See also the following footnote on the female character of *La Vie nouvelle*.

as a locus of becomings, however, the film offers a vivid visual evocation of the metamorphosis and re-emergence of that which has been granted little or no space at the level of organised (historical; cinematographic) discourses.

Released the same year as *Pola X*, Philippe Grandrieux's *Sombre* offers an intriguingly similar evocation of becoming-as-the-pull-of-formlessness. The filmmaker compares the character of Jean, the murderer, to a 'block of night, blinded by sensation' (Grandrieux 1999b) and further describes him as a figure that 'incarnates mythology, a kind of chimera, half-man half-beast, walking slouched . . . a homage to the films that I was brought up on: Dreyer's *Vampyr*, with the stooping man who carries visions on his body' (Grandrieux 1999c: 43). Like the *Pola X* character, Jean is a figure born out of the originary world; he appears to belong to a different plane of intensities than other characters and the commonly perceived reality; his relation to the world is one of fusion and becoming rather than differentiation. Discussing his choice of location for the film (the densely wooded Haute-Loire countryside), the director stressed how small the variations in light and colour were between the ground and what lies above it, the forest trees and the sky (Grandrieux 1999b). The choice to shoot with the sun just above the horizon, and to enhance the images' under-exposure by lowering the diaphragm, creates an atmosphere of opacity where ground and background, and the human figure itself, often seem at risk of fusing. In the end, in the forest, like Isabelle, Jean appears to give in to the pull of the formless; in the film's closing sequence, we follow him as he moves deeper into a dense wood, till he eventually lies down and lets his body be absorbed into the organic mesh that covers the ground. As we have seen, Grandrieux's second feature, *La Vie nouvelle*, is, like *Sombre*, an exploration of 'radical evil'; like *Pola X*, however, it is haunted by the shadow of the recent Balkan conflict.

A chilling but beguiling feel: two tiny silhouettes lost in the midst of a desolate no-man's-land, quivering in the low morning light, the cold palpable . . . . Like Grandrieux's first feature, *La Vie nouvelle* is shot under a low sun – at dawn or dusk (in French, the '*chien-loup*', literally, that time of day when dog cannot be distinguished from wolf) – the washed-out light of its exterior day sequences contrasting with the dense darkness and ochre and golden tones of the film's interior and nocturnal shots. *La Vie nouvelle* takes place in and around an unnamed city of Eastern Europe. In its soulless suburbs and the no-man's-land that surrounds them, bodies tend to be reduced to mere flickering shadows haunting bleak, post-conflict 'any-spaces-whatever'.

The film's protagonists, the French dealer Roscoe and his American friend Seymour, first appear as two small figures outlined against a reddish horizon, as they progress through a vast barren expanse towards a set of semi-derelict buildings. As they move nearer, their silhouettes recall those of medieval figures: Seymour's face hidden inside a hood; Roscoe's sharp profile showing below his old-fashioned, heavy fur hat. But if some of Roscoe's features evoke the vampire, Boyan, the local slave trader, whom we first see with his back to the camera, is the most ominous presence of all, clad in a black leather coat and bearing with contemporary ease the shaven skull and unfathomable expression of a modern Dracula. Boyan's realm unravels at the frontier between the human and the animal. His presence is constantly associated with the furious movements of the dogs who will eventually hunt and tear Roscoe to pieces. He also rules over a subterranean world of monstrous beings, where the beautiful Melania metamorphoses into a half-woman half-beast.[20]

In one of the film's early scenes, Boyan is seen appraising, as if they were cattle, a group of people who are lined up naked in front of him; the fictional then feeds into the fearsome evocation of a terrifyingly factual horror – contemporary human traffic. It is here, where the border between fiction and outer reality is most visibly porous, that the film is at its most unsettling: hence, the powerful effect of the opening sequence – a striking, sensation-filled viewing experience and a forceful evocation of a post-conflict world of displaced populations where attraction, preying and exploitation are rife.

The film opens on an almost completely dark screen where a cluster of lighter dots emerges; the shot progressively reveals a group of people standing close together in the night. The sound is inchoate and threatening, like the muffled rumbling of a storm. In repeated tracking movements, the camera travels forward at great speed, launching itself into the group like a vampiric force, a bird of prey or a missile, before it eventually rests on individual faces. Though the presence of these people will never be directly explained, the sequence appears emblematic of the uncertainties of our transnational age. The silhouettes are evocative of those of a group of exiles: lost in a post-conflict no-man's-land, surrounded by the opacity of an in-between zone, between two planes of different intensities, they could be the Deleuzean 'seers' in search of the 'new life' of the title. Shot in close-up, their faces gaze intensely forward, eyes wide open: entranced by the light reflected in their pupils, or resisting it, seeing the horrors and the scars through the illusory facade of the 'new life'?

Throughout the opening shots, the image literally vibrates; the effect comes from the speed of the recording – 8 to 6 images per second instead of the customary 24. During these sequences, it is as if the body of the film

---

[20] There are distant echoes of the destiny of the heroine of *Cat People* (Jacques Tourneur, 1942) here; like Melania, the heroine of Tourneur's film, Irina Dubrovna, was from Eastern Europe.

itself had been drained, 'vampirised', its images and its light sucked away into the outer field.

Film Bodies

Between the cinema of 'psychological situations' and that of pure abstraction, the cinema of sensation opens a space of becoming, a space where the human form is less character and more figure, a figure caught again in the material reality of the film as event. In turn, 'becomings' also appear embedded in the film form itself: in the hybrid quality of the filmmaking, the impure combination of diverse genre elements, the superimposition of the hyper-realistic with the expressionist and dream-like, as well as in the variations in the material appearance of the images and sounds and the fluctuations in speed and intensities effected by the editing.

In an interview following the ambivalent reception of her last feature at the Toronto Film Festival, Claire Denis humbly admitted: 'My films, sadly enough, are sometimes unbalanced. They have a limp, or one arm shorter, or a big nose, but even in the editing room when we try to change that, it usually doesn't work' (Denis 2004).

This humorous apology may sound insignificant, yet the choice of terms is noteworthy. Some films are possibly best understood when described in the kind of corporeal terms that Denis uses: as monstrous, misshapen creatures (*L'Intrus*); as intoxicated organisms, drained of light as if of their blood (*La Vie nouvelle* or *Pola X*), or colonised and poisoned by virus-like images (*Demonlover*); as a brain-like construct, a luminous memory cell embedded in its dark maze (*La Captive*).

Most importantly, it points to the need to adopt a different approach when considering filmmaking practices that, rather than merely addressing reality in the representational or metaphorical mode, develop into an actual process of embodiment. The works explored here do not only set out to evoke the mark imprinted by humans on their environment through a documentary gaze, or to depict the vulnerability of modern man's identity through the vulnerability of his/her body. They themselves are constructed like bodies of sensations, material assemblages – or 'bodies-without-organs', where the phenomenological and 'molecular' interplay with the social, the cultural and the technological.

> The filmic experience has evolved through a whole new idea of the processuality, the rhythm of the film as a set of bodies, in motion, producing a new cartography of the visual. The film does not record images, or convey representation. It acts, it performs, as a 'body' with other bodies, in a constituted body, a molecular body, through the affective. (Kennedy 2000: 103)

In the following pages, I will thus attempt to describe how certain films function in context – not only how, as sensory entities in themselves, they
'perform' and 'think' through issues relating to the construction of contemporary identities, but also how they perform as a 'body with other bodies,
in a constituted body': in relation to other films, to works born out of other
filmmaking practices; as 'molecular' assemblages, connecting and interact-
ing with the outer field; and, ultimately, as a film–spectator assemblage.

Corporate (Dis)embodiment

at the very heart of the period in which the subject emerged and geometrical optics was
an object of research, Holbein makes visible for us . . . the subject as annihilated . . .
the geometral dimension enables us to glimpse how the subject who concerns us is
caught, manipulated, captured, in the field of vision. (Jacques Lacan [1977], *Four
Fundamental Concepts*, quoted in Armstrong 2000: 147)

'Capitalist globalisation defies representation.' (O'Shaughnessy 2005: 75)

In 'Eloquent Fragments – French Fiction Film and Globalisation', Martin
O'Shaughnessy points to the contradiction faced by the French directors
who first sought to address such issues in their work: 'neoliberal globalisation is deeply resistant to representation within the framework of conventional fiction [yet] following its much trumpeted return to the real in the
1990s, French cinema could not avoid figuring the consequences of that
same capitalist globalisation' (O'Shaughnessy 2005: 75). Because the corporate world derives its power to sustain and replicate itself from its ability
to feed on and replace concrete, embodied experience with its own
abstract, universalising rule (hence its connection with vampirism), it represents a fascinating challenge in terms of cinematic practices. While part
of the production that seeks to present a critical vision reproduces the corporate discourse in order to expose it, some filmmakers oppose the corporeality of the medium to the abstracting effect of corporate discourse.
Hence, if the French cinema production of the 1990s arguably witnessed
a 'return to the real' in terms of themes, social concerns and realist aesthetics, the alternative visions offered in works that endorse the materiality of film seem less of an unrelated departure than an indicator of a
'further' move. It suggests a need to puncture the screens established by
discourses and clichés, to 'probe the wound', so as to access and evoke a
'real' of a different nature, concerned with that part of the human experience that cannot be harnessed to the logic of profit.

The closing sequence of Laurent Cantet's *L'Emploi du temps* (2001)
creates a remarkably understated yet chilling moment of existential terror.

The scene takes place in a nondescript office space. Sitting on either side of a desk, two men face each other, and in this classical *mise en scène* of power, the predictable shot-counter-shot alternation and the soft conversational tones of the exchange underline a false impression of parity; the context is that of a job interview, a game of simulation where one of the proponents at least must deny the sense of dreadful absurdity and meaninglessness that constantly threatens to overwhelm him. Through the windows, behind the recruiter, blurred shapes and blotted colours barely suggest a dull expanse of greenery. Within the closed space of the confrontation, contained and refracted by the insipidness of the interchangeable décor, the composed, synthetic discourse of the professional world rules, with the company as its ominous subject and enunciator. Through the voice of the interviewer is thus established 'ce que l'entreprise attend de vous, ce que vous pouvez lui donner' ('what the company expects from you, what you can offer to the company'). The expression sums up the fundamentals of a system that stands for all that Bataille, well before there was talk of 'late capitalism' and 'globalisation', condemned and berated: the reign of a disembodied, transcending logic that progressively comes to pervade our daily reality and control our desires. For the surrealist thinker, only the deep archaic sense of chaos inherited from the origins of humanity but denied by the civilising process could effectively strive to challenge or disintegrate the normative effect of the rational productive order (Bataille [1949] 1988–91).

Vincent (Aurélien Recoing), the job-seeker of *L'Emploi du temps*, has been unemployed for over eight months and has undergone an identity crisis that has brought him close to self-dissolution yet also back in touch with a form of reality he had lost. The return to the universe of socio-professional normality, encapsulated by the apparently innocuous event of this job interview, is in fact an intensely terrifying moment of abdication. The reintegration within the social net is at the cost of endorsing a dreadful game of constant pretence – a process of vampirism that this man can only bear *à son corps défendant* ('reluctantly' – literally: 'against his own body'). As the recruiter lists the functions, duties and responsibilities of the post, a slow forward travelling shot, 'd'une précision diabolique' ('of diabolical precision'), brings the gaze closer to Vincent's face, inexorably closing in while his features gradually decompose under the effect of a visceral fear. Simultaneously, the haunting tones of the music (composed by Jocelyn Spook)[21] that raises and progressively drowns the voices, echo the inner chaos that fills Vincent. At this point of the film, more than ever, the

---

[21] Spook previously composed the music for Stanley Kubrick's *Eyes Wide Shut*.

152   CINEMA AND SENSATION

filming itself becomes the perfect relay of the discourse voiced by the
recruiter; the unwavering forward movement of the camera effectively
recreates the disembodied gaze of the 'spécularité, sociale et existentielle'
('the social and existential gaze'; Tesson 2001: 72) relentlessly put upon the
ordinary man. Vincent's last utterance is thus the ultimate expression of
denial; asked whether the challenge represented by the post under discussion does not seem too daunting, he confirms, 'Mais ça ne me fait pas peur'
('But it does not frighten me'). Yet, his body language contradicts his
answer; although he faces the camera, he looks sideways, his body pulled
back slightly, as if his gaze were trying to avoid that of the camera and,
through it, the inexorable surfacing of the void. To the spectator, this last
image of Vincent may stand as the film's ultimate glimpse of the 'real',
while in a mirroring effect, Vincent's now too-conscious gaze appears to
acknowledge the same thing – like the glance of the anamorphic skull in
the Holbein painting, the senselessness of the real seems to seep through
the screen, opening a crack in the image of professional success and power.

L'Emploi du temps is, in Charles Tesson's words, 'a film that looked
at you' – a film made in the image of the modern corporation's buildings
with their reflecting glass facades. Hence, talking about the fear oozed by
the film, Tesson concludes: 'how can one accept the unacceptable, face the
abyss [behind] the screen that binds together our reason for living over
the theatre of existence?' (Tesson 2001: 74).

Cantet's fiction, like most of the films released in the late 1990s and early
twenty-first century that explore the condition of the present-day 'homo
professionalis', evokes a world where economic discourses progressively
nullify or normalise perception and affects, thus eventually taking the place
of reality as experience. The experience of being human in an economi-
cally 'developed' society appears irremediably reduced to the participation
in an almost entirely controlled and rationalised mode of existence shaped
into a profitable, productive form of trade, where gratuity, unprompted
desire, chance and excess are effectively reprocessed or siphoned out. In
effect, in French, the word used to designate a business or a 'company' is
the same as is used for 'society': société. This dual use of the term endows
a remark by Pierre Legendre, cited by Charles Tesson in relation to
Cantet's film, with a particular resonance. Legendre's interrogations have
an unmistakably Baudrillardian accent:

Can we go as far as stating that our society is a fiction? What we find is the symbol-
isation of the Void, the need to provide a status to Nothingness. . . . Society establishes discourse as a screen between man and his image, between man and the world;
society itself becomes man's image and world. (Legendre 1998: 8; quoted by Tesson
2001: 74)

Three films amongst a series of French features released in the same years and concerned with corporate environments, *L'Emploi du temps*, *La Violence des échanges en milieu tempéré* (Jean-Marc Moutout, 2004) and *Elle est des nôtres* (Siegrid Alnoy, 2003), recount the socio-economic integration of ordinary individuals, through employment, as a ruthless process of normalisation – a form of gradual anaesthesia. The company/*société* functions as a microcosm with infinite ramifications, where the virtual, in the form of a specialised discourse, language and set of behaviours, has drained away life and replaced it. The perception of reality in its diversity and ambiguity is thus almost completely expunged by a self-reproducing system that generates its own legitimising ideology, cannibalising the language of everyday life (hence the 'good', the 'health' or the 'needs' of the economy or *société*) to cover up the void that lies at its heart.[22] In these dystopian visions, the socio-economic process of normalisation, steeped in a banal inevitability, offers none of the heroic relief of its Hollywood counterparts. If, quoting Charles Tesson's term (Tesson 2001: 74), these films are true films 'of terror', it is precisely because of the alarming sense of ordinariness they convey.

The environments that the characters inhabit, as well as the ways they are filmed, are but an extension of the same principles. The traditional professional surroundings – factories and workshops with their noise and dirt, places of tangible, physical confrontation of the human body to the machine – have been replaced by the now-familiar battery of clean manufactured expanses and discreet borders that define the contemporary space of 'working life': automatic glass doors, escalators and lifts, closed windows, endless corridors with right-angle bends, artificial lights and air-conditioning systems, functional standardised interiors, external and internal areas dominated by accumulations of signs addressed to all and no one and awash with bold primary colours and soft combinations of beige tones respectively. Here, the human body as flesh (with its distinctive physical signs, its smell, its volumes, its fluids . . .) is banned and replaced by the interchangeable figures traded by temp agencies. In *Elle est des nôtres*, the human figure is often beheaded or truncated, caught as it is in the stylised *mise en scène* of both the corporate architecture, with its geometrical logic, and of the filmmaking, with its alternation of clean tracking shots and static

---

[22] Commenting on the importance of dialogue and language in his film, Jean-Marc Moutout, the director of *Violence des échanges*, remarks:

> Language is certainly the main tool for the relations of domination and power that the economic rule and economic education and conditioning establish . . . economic discourse operates on two levels: it is doctrinal, ideologic, and socially omnipresent; on the other hand, it is theorised or 'scientified'. (Moutout 2004: 13)

framing. One of the signs of the alienation of Christine (Sasha Andres), the main character, is the sound of breathing that accompanies her throughout the first part of the film – a persistent noise, incongruous and vaguely obscene in the workplace's sterile environment where her physical presence always seems both out of place and superfluous. In a later sequence, however, after her successful 'integration' into the professional world, the camera tracks through the empty office spaces where she is now a proper employee; it seemingly follows the sound of purposeful footsteps through deserted corridors till it reaches the building's main door which automatically opens to let the disembodied presence walk out.

The professional environment spells order and transparence; it embraces the principles of the optical regime of vision: Renaissance perspective and functional modern design seemingly denying the possibility of the Baroque 'fold', the existence of the interstices through which the irrational and uncontrolled, the mark of time passing, the signs of decomposition and death may seep in. Contained by the strict axis of linear perspectives and defined by the shadowless light that illuminates them, the movements of the camera follow the pre-existing tracks that such spaces establish, or pan over their display of reflecting facades and surfaces. Like the other filmmakers of the so-called 'New Realist' strand (Beugnet 2000; O'Shaughnessy 2005) who tend to focus on the condition of contemporary man in his or her everyday environment, Cantet's and Moutout's and, to a large extent, even Alnoy's more surreal work thus participate in a specific approach to filmmaking. The *mise en scène* does not merely seek to represent a system where, as Legendre remarks, a discourse is established 'as a screen between man and his image', but it actually reproduces and outlines its effects in order to criticise its impact. Adopting the very strategy that founds the ideology it seeks to denounce, the stylised *mise en scène* and camerawork thus emphasise the presence of a virtual screen that alienates a character and bars him or her from understanding the world in different ways, and, in turn, maintains the distant relationship of the spectator to the reality being portrayed on the cinema screen. In *L'Emploi du temps*, reality as change (the world outside the corporate sphere) appears doubly removed, observed by the character and the camera through a multiplicity of doors, glass partitions and reflecting windows which also undermine the possibility of the spectator in the cinema experiencing a form of subjective or tactile relationship with the image itself. Similarly, in *Elle est des nôtres*, the camera records the reality presented in the film in clear, apparently untampered-with images, often shot from a slightly higher angle than that of the human eye, as if applying the detached, disembodied gaze of the entomologist to the environment it surveys.

At first sight, the techniques just described could not be further from the aesthetic of sensation elaborated, in the same period, by those film-makers who chose to explore the territories of the irrational and sensual and follow the path of the cinema of sensation; indeed, they appear like its perfect antithesis. There seems to be an irreducible incompatibility between techniques that encourage a sensual relation to images, sounds and movement, and the description of the anaesthetised environment of the corporate world that implies a functional, detached economy of the gaze. The above-mentioned sequence of the unattached sound of footsteps in *Elle est des nôtres*, for example, offers a striking contrast with the use of a similar technique in Thierry Jousse's *Les Invisibles* (2005) discussed in Chapter 3. In one of the sequences in Jousse's film, sound also serves to track an invisible presence, but in *Les Invisibles*, the audio-visual combination creates an actual 'sound figure'; the presence of a lover is literally embodied through the rich, textured quality of the sound of her movements and voice, further conveying the hero's intense yearning for her return. Similarly, one could contrast Akerman's prelude in super-8 for *La Captive*, to the brief beginning and end sequences of *Violence des échanges*. Both depict scenes at the beach, but in comparison to the poetic and vibrantly sensual quality of *La Captive*'s sequence, the images captured in classic 35mm by the coolly observing gaze of Moutout's camera evoke a busy car park.

Yet, even in the highly defined world of these 'realist' films, the existence of a different, less coded level of reality is always suggested and, with it, the possibility of an alternative, more immediate and tactile understanding of the visible. Beyond the corporate world's any-spaces-whatever, the presence of originary worlds incarnates the persistence of a realm of essentially non-utilitarian drives. Alnoy in particular insists on the 'the most diabolical of contrasts' of the close presence of the nature that surrounds (and is refracted by the shiny facades of the modern buildings of) what she describes as the 'hyper-urban', 'hyper-industrial' environment of the modern suburban town (Alnoy 2004, interview, supplement to the DVD issue).[23] Like Cantet's, Alnoy's film is shot in and around Grenoble, with its urban 'techno poles', housing estates and commercial centres situated in the midst of the Alps. In both films, once the characters venture into

---

[23] The vocabulary used by Alnoy to describe both the natural environment that lies beyond the techno-poles and to evoke the significance of Christine's crime is strongly resonant of Bataille's writings on the persistence of human nature's archaic drives. Just as she talks of 'a nature close to the origins; a millenary-old geology', she insists on 'the archaic and sacred nature' of Christine's crime, a murderous gesture 'that will elicit terror and compassion' (Alnoy 2004).

natural spaces, the geology establishes unruly angles and points of view, and contours start to lose their definition. It is not by chance that, for such sequences, the two filmmakers favour the indistinct moments of dawn and sunset, when a foggy mist tends to linger on the landscape, defeating the rule of perspective. A different kind of image then surfaces, less defined, with a textured, material appearance that seems to invite the spectator's gaze to immerse and lose itself in its nebulous space like the silhouettes of the characters.

In effect, as the title of Jean-Marc Moutout's film indicates (literally: *Violent Turbulences in Temperate Environment*: an expression borrowed from meteorological terminology), even behind the smooth facades of the corporate buildings, and between the lines of the neutral, would-be scientific terminology of the professional world, simmers the expressive and emotional excess only superficially suppressed by the implicit violence of the discourses of economic requirements and social norms. In Alnoy's *Elle est des nôtres*, irrational violence briefly bursts through the soft envelope of invisible aggression that suffuses everyday life when Christine unwittingly wounds, then kills off, a young woman who was trying to befriend her. At first, the corporate world absorbs even this expression of radical evil; the murderous gesture Christine commits also signals the beginning of her acceptance in the world of normality that has so far rejected her (she obtains a secure responsible job, finds a boyfriend, gets her driving licence . . .).

The corporate world arguably offers the most elaborate examples of strategies aimed at resolving or erasing that which Silverman designates as 'modernity's fundamental ambivalence'; indeed, the discourse that prevails here is entirely geared to denying what Silverman calls the 'whole panoply of dark forces and processes which constituted the otherness of rational order' (Silverman 1999: 4), suppressing them with acceptable, functional forms of violence. It is not surprising, then, that this now-dominant facet of present-day life should provide a favoured topic for the cinema that focuses on the contemporary French *malaise*. That French society is shaped by its profound attachment to traditional values is one common explanation for its resistance to the socio-economic and cultural requirements of the late-capitalist system. In addition, however, as underlined by Silverman, there is undeniably a continuing and particularly vivid French tradition – cultural, popular, literary and artistic – where the late-capitalistic or postmodern ethos is looked at suspiciously and characteristically equated with standardisation and globalisation.

This same tradition is upheld by Varda in her documentary-cum-self-portrait *Les Glaneurs et la glaneuse* (2000), where she offers a brilliant cinematic demonstration of the tensions at work between artistic practices and the determinants of a dominant economy of production, standardisation and waste. In the falsely naïve style that has become familiar to her audiences, she opposes the hegemonic hierarchy of values imposed by the current consumerist ethos with the kind of techniques and topics that are almost systematically banned from the screens. Under the guise of investigating the gleaner's age-old activities and status, poverty, marginality and ageing are thus evoked through the free montage of documentary sequences and series of images that are literally 'gleaned' along the way. The practice of gleaning on film is akin to that of the found object so precious to the surrealists; whether they are recorded on 35mm or with a hand-held DV camera, the images and sounds retained are of those generally left-out fractions of the visible, bits and pieces of the pro-filmic reality that are usually scorned or ignored, and that Varda catches seemingly by chance, on the spur of the moment, or as the result of an irresistible urge to document. Through combinations of the diverse material thus collected – interviews, monologues, driving sequences, close-ups on paintings and postcards and other leftover fragments (misshapen potatoes, clocks without hands, bouquets of single plastic gloves) – emerge discarded, objectionable and thought-provoking evocations of our contemporary world (Beugnet 2004a). To the dominance of the virtual, the colonising of human experience by the pre-formatted and ever-more refined discourses of productive logic, and the imposition on the body, and on the images of the body, of precise standards of appearance and rational behaviour is, thus, opposed the shock of inarticulate sensual affects: the messiness of the ageing flesh in its process of decomposition; the non–utilitarianism of alternative classifying practices; the disorderly superimposition of diverse compositions, textures and shapes; the dirty, hazardous quality of images shot with hand–held and DV cameras . . . . Again, the shadow of Bataille looms as, gleaning images at the foot of the Montparnasse Tower with its fifty-nine floors' worth of office space, Varda ignores the 200 metres of glass facade that dwarf the surrounding Parisian district to turn her camera resolutely towards the ground, and mingles with the homeless and underprivileged as they scavenge for food underneath the abandoned stalls at the end of the local market.

Next to the playfully anarchistic tone of Varda's documentary-rummaging through the leftovers of the pro-filmic reality, the fictional worlds that probe the underbelly of the corporate world offer darker and more ambivalent visions. Whereas in Cantet, Moutout and Alnoy's films the screen established by the discourse that rules over the diegetic world, and duplicated by the detached gaze of the camera, only occasionally reveals the fractures woven into its apparently faultless surface, in Marina de Van's aptly titled *Dans ma peau* (2002), as in Olivier Assayas' *Demonlover* (2002), the fiction dives in, and the exploration of the cracks becomes the thematic and formal focus of the film. Theirs is a filmmaking that digs under the smooth shell of ordinary life's implicit daily brutality, searching through the often perverted violence that hides behind the most polished of facades and discourses, seeking the shock of aesthetic techniques and fictional creations that can pierce through and reconnect with other planes of reality/intensities that teem under the surface of the global norm.

> After a brief prologue, imbued with a sense of flawless normality . . . *Dans ma peau* never stops rummaging through irrationality and transgression, poles apart from the direction where the film initially seemed to head. (de Bruyn 2002: 26)

At first glance, Esther, the heroine of de Van's film, is the epitome of the unexceptional but successful modern young woman. Like her remote fictional parents, the characters of Georges Perec's *Les Choses*, Esther works for a company specialising in consumer surveys. Competent and ambitious, perfectly versed in the jargon of the professional world, she is about to obtain the promotion that will help her buy a flat where she can move in with her boyfriend. However, her existence literally splits into a schizophrenic experience when, after what seems like an insignificant accident, she damages one of her legs and fails to register the pain. Esther becomes obsessed with her own flesh and embarks on an ever-more extreme process of self-mutilation that increasingly endangers her ability to perform in the other aspects of her life. Crucially, the slit thus affects the body of the film, in its narrative as well as formal constitution, just as it affects the body of the character ('incarnated' rather than performed by the director herself, Nicolas Azalbert stresses), to the point where, as Azalbert underlines, in the second part of the film, 'the body of the character and that of the film . . . become one' (Azalbert 2002a: 82). In other words, as Olivier de Bruyn remarks, it is the film itself that, like the skin and the life of its main character, splits open and falls into the exploration of the unnameable part of reality:

> The beauty of *Dans ma peau* also lies in the way its tale of the violence of social relations in the modern working environment is embedded in the film [and it belongs] to the filiation of those unclassifiable directors (from Georges Franju to Roman Polanski), for whom deviancy is first and foremost a poetic and aesthetic experience. The mutilation, the fragmentation that is the topic of the film affects the form of the film itself. (de Bruyn 2002: 27)

Indeed, in de Van's work, the 'skin of the film' bears the mark of the character's physical experience from the very beginning. The opening credits roll on a series of split screens, presenting two versions of the same still image. The effect might feel, at first, oddly familiar. Strangely, the first split screens, with their images of skyscrapers, ring roads and large escalators, bring to mind the credit sequences of 1970s and 1980s American series, designed to evoke and celebrate the buzz of the modern city. In effect, the sequence almost functions like the standard opening in classic American film, with its wide-angle establishing shots progressing towards a closer view of the main characters and their direct environment (in this case, details of office furnishings, a computer keyboard and screen, a pile of papers, a close-up on a ruler then on a paper-clip). However, beyond its eerie insistence on focusing on trivial inanimate objects in ever more minute detail, there is already something peculiar and uncomfortable at play in de Van's treatment of the images. To the positive colour version on the left-hand side of the screen is opposed a negative, sometimes inverted, version, over-exposed and tinted in light tones of beige, on which, when the title of the film appears, the word *peau* inscribes itself.

The buildings of the credit sequence are part of the Parisian business quarter of La Défense, where Esther works, as do the characters of Moutout's *Violence des échanges en milieu tempéré*. La Défense is certainly one of the most visible illustrations of the ambiguous status given to spatial expressions of late-capitalist modernity in France. Depending on the point of view, this futuristic or monstrous accumulation of high-rise towers and ruthless celebration of global architecture, elevated in the axis of the Champs Élysées yet located on the other side of the *périphérique*, remains a marginal statement, an anomalous prosthesis to the core body of a city saturated with history. Between the series of stills of La Défense and the close-ups on the computer and desk items, de Van inserts a brief sequence which introduces Esther and her boyfriend Vincent. The young woman is sitting at her computer, looking intently at the screen, and when her boyfriend appears behind her, they both look at the screen. (As the film unravels, and she becomes engrossed with the (re)discovery of her own body with increasing urgency, Esther's gaze will turn more and more towards the camera and, in the final montage of shots, she faces it and stares back at us.) The film cuts to a close-up shot that travels upwards along the frame of the chair and the young woman's bare leg, then back to the desk, presenting her body as if it was but an extension of her laptop. In this case, the body-machine combination seems to have more to do with immobilisation than creative metamorphosis, however: less a 'becoming-computer' than a process of physical and identity formatting. Evoking the contemporary process of taming of the body – in *Dans ma peau*'s case a body shaped to become the valuable property and tool of a specific working environment – Azalbert compares de Van's film to Michel Foucault's speculation in *Surveiller et punir*, and underlines how *Dans ma peau* makes visible 'the abstract stage of a *bio-power* that does not aim to punish the bodies, but to turn them into docile entities through processes of subjection (social, sexual or aesthetic) that individuals integrate unwillingly (*à leur corps défendant*)' (Azalbert 2002a: 82).[24] The form taken by Esther's rebellion appears extreme and wanton, and, in its solitary, aimless process, profoundly nihilistic. Yet, in the way the experience of the character is portrayed and the way the viewer is, in turn, invited to experience the film, the mix of fascination with revulsion effectively works as a spontaneous reaction against the mundane horror of 'normal life'.

In one surreal sequence, having been invited along to a dinner with important potential clients, Esther fights against the irrepressible need to slash her skin by trying to keep her hands underneath the table and then sees her own arm detach itself from the rest of her body. Even then, the freakish character of this hallucination cannot compete with the grotesque nature of what goes on on the surface (above the table), in the contrast between the predictable conversation and artificial conviviality of the future business partners and the bestiality inherent in the ingurgitation of food which no table manners can successfully hide. In effect, the initial anaesthesia of the senses brought about by the professional and domestic settings of Esther's life progressively develops into a sensory overload that can only be matched by the relentlessness of the treatment she inflicts on her own body in order to reappropriate it. Her visit to a supermarket towards the end of the film initiates a comprehensive attack on the senses that will lead the young woman to take refuge in the solitude of a hotel room nearby. As she first enters the shopping centre, a succession of disorienting visuals appear on the screen. Blurred close-ups on ceiling spotlights alternate with close-up images of litter on the floor; bathed in an aggressive neon glare and deafening inchoate noise, the blurred silhouettes of shoppers pass by in accelerated motion while the camera pans wantonly right and left. Against the blinding light that seeps through the shop's main door, the silhouettes become moving black blots, almost abstract shapes, till the screen fills completely with white. The next sequence superimposes close-ups of Esther's hand holding her credit card with shots of shopping bags being packed and presented at checkouts. Amongst the eclectic collection of items purchased by the young woman are a knife and a camera.

The passage from full screen to split screen occurs through an almost invisible cut; as Esther leaves the supermarket, the door's reflecting panels,

---

[24] For an alternative evocation of a 'becoming-machine', see Émilie Deleuze's *Peau neuve* (1998), the story of a man who abandons his career as computer designer to train as a machine operator.

half-blank, half-filled with a colourful reflection of the shop, already create this divided effect. Although the noise of the street 'bleeds over' the subsequent series of images, it will now serve as a backdrop to the split-screen montage of sequences that starts to unravel with Esther undressing in a hotel room, getting ready to work on her own body. The actual mutilations are then suggested rather than shown (close-ups of a cutter followed by images of blood dripping; blood-soaked fabric; a series of imprints left on the floor by bloodied feet . . .). De Bruyn compares de Van's approach to a 'poetics of suffering', where the screen offers 'different sensory points of view on the body of the heroine turned into an object of aesthetic study' (de Bruyn 2002: 27). In place of the conventional effect of detached observation, however, the paralleling of images of the same surfaces or objects, but shot from a different angle, elicits an unanchored, tactile gaze – as does the combination of textures, colours and feel (the warm colouring of blood seeping through folds of cloth contrasting with the cold smooth surface of a can of juice), and the evocation of various sensory affects, from vision to hearing (the close-ups on eyes; the manipulation of her camera; the sound of breathing over obscured screens which produces an odd sense of eroticism) and from touch to taste (the young woman tastes her own flesh, drinks thirstily from a can, then from a glass of water).

In the kind of images that are presented in the diptych that forms this sequence, and the ambiguous combination of the voluptuous with the horrifying, there is a ritualistic dimension that inevitably calls to mind Bataille's writings on eroticism:

> What we call the human world is necessarily a world of work, that is, a world of reduction . . . Taken that man has defined himself through work and consciousness, he not only had to moderate, but deny and, sometimes, curse his own sexual excess. In a way, this denial diverted man, if not away from the consciousness of objects, at least from the consciousness of himself. It engaged him simultaneously in the knowledge of the world and in the ignorance of himself.
>
> Now the ordinary man knows that his consciousness should open up to that which revolted him most deeply: that which revolts us violently, is in us. (Bataille 1957: 179, 218)

Esther commits the ultimate transgression – she mutilates, disfigures and thus renders dysfunctional a body that had been shaped to fit, represent and efficiently contribute to the perpetuation of a specific socioeconomic system. Yet, by the same token, she performs a process of self-reappropriation, and through the grotesque horror of it, reaches for that archaic dimension of the sovereign that, as Bataille has argued, a society entirely given to reason cannot tolerate. The split screen sequence of self-mutilation concludes with parallel but mismatched images of each of Esther's eyes: an outlandish gaze looking back at the camera, neither the affirmation of an objective perception nor quite an expression of subjectivity but, rather, as Tesson suggested earlier, the materialisation of the film's own gaze ('a film that looks at you'; Tesson 2001: 74).

Like de Van's disturbing foray into the world of corporate embodiment, Olivier Assayas' *Demonlover* charts the ineluctable fall of a character whose uncertain recovery of an 'un-programmed' sense of self may occur at the price of a descent into hell. But whereas *Dans ma peau* derives some of its alarming capacity to perturb from its mix of ordinary settings and extreme, viscerally affecting proceedings, Assayas' vision takes us beyond the familiar boundaries of the local and national and unfolds in the dislocated time and space of global business and the internet world.[25]

Demonlover is, in Jonathan Romney's words, a film made in the 'catastrophic mode', the exploration of a post-capitalistic '*société du spectacle*' grown out of a generalised contamination and formatting of reality that leaves no apparent means of escape. In effect, the deeply pessimistic assessment of our increasingly image-dominated world proposed by the Situationist and controversial media critic Guy Debord partly inspired the making of *Demonlover*.[26] The *malaise* that haunts the images of many

[25] By the same token, Assayas engages with a formal and thematic approach to filmmaking that extends beyond the customary province of French national cinema towards wider domains. Commenting on the versatility of a director who directed *Demonlover* after completing *Les Destinées sentimentales* (2000) – an ambitious literary adaptation composed and shot in the characteristic 'heritage cinema' costume-drama style – Serge Kaganski remarks that, in comparison with the 'so very French' tradition of psychological and historical cinema,

> *Demonlover* is a film conjugated in the present, international and, perhaps, even extra-terrestrial in scope ... To exaggerate a little, *Les Destinées* would be Flaubert, and *Demonlover*, Baudrillard: the former a product of an ultra-classical culture folded back on its temporal and geographical territory, the latter an object belonging to contemporary, borderless, globalised modernity. (Kaganski 2003: 22)

For Nicolas Azalbert, both films deal with the issue of individuals caught in the movement of things and (historical, social and economic) systems. The contrast is thus less of a rupture, more of a progression:

> The international traffic of goods and persons, the power of economic logic over individuals, and the acceleration of time to the point where everyone is left behind . . .: all of these things have continued and grown in the time that separates these two films. From the industrial revolution (*Les Destinées*) to the virtual revolution (*Demonlover*), it is not so much the modernisation of the conditions of production that interests Assayas, than the transformation of the modes of perception that it creates, and its repercussions on the evolution of our consciousness. (Azalbert 2002b: 878)

[26] Assayas was instrumental in the restoration and recent re-release of Debord's films, initially withdrawn from the public domain by Debord himself, but made accessible again at the beginning of the new century by his widow.

of the filmmakers who seek, in an aesthetic of sensation, a renewal of cinematographic practice is embedded in the same acknowledgement that founds Debord's critique: that there is a process of dissociation at work that leads, ultimately, to the separation of contemporary systems of representation and production from any form of 'reality' (as unpredictable, sensual and critical perception and experience of the world), in favour of an all-encompassing and preformatted ensemble of models and self-justified discourses. The series of thought-provoking aphorisms that are part of Debord's famous 1967 essay resonate with the troubling visions proposed in the films discussed in the previous pages, and that Assayas seems to bring to an even greater level of dystopian evocation:

> 1- In societies where modern conditions of production prevail, all of life presents itself as an immense accumulation of *spectacles*. Everything that was directly lived has moved away into a representation

> 10- Considered in its own terms, the spectacle is *affirmation* of appearance and affirmation of all human life, namely social life, as mere appearance. But the critique which reaches the truth of the spectacle exposes it as the visible *negation* of life, as a negation of life which *has become visible*.

At the heart of Debord's unrelenting work of exposure and denunciation, however, lies the awareness of the difficulty in finding, precisely, a position from which to assess and effectively criticise a system that cannibalises and integrates everything, including the critical and subversive discourses and modes of expression that could threaten it.

> 6- The spectacle grasped in its totality is both the result and the project of the existing mode of production. It is not a supplement to the real world, an additional decoration. It is the heart of the unrealism of the real society. In all its specific forms, as information or propaganda, as advertisement or direct entertainment consumption, the spectacle is the present model of socially dominant life. It is the omnipresent affirmation of the choice *already made* in production and its corollary consumption. The spectacle's form and content are identically the total justification of the existing system's conditions and goals. (Debord 1967 http://library.nothingness.org/)

This is also the conundrum that Assayas faces in his exploration, through cinema, of the power of the virtual;[27] indeed, the question of whether it

---

[27] The confusion arguably exists in the choice of the film title itself. *Demonlover* is both the title of the film and the name of the conglomerate that proposes to distribute the products patented by the company which employs the central character. Further analogies between the business world of internet entertainment represented here and today's cinema are suggested throughout the film.

remains possible to exercise a critical vision, or to maintain a dissident position, emerges not only in the diegetic unfolding but through the very form of the film.[28]

Often described as a 'cyber-thriller', *Demonlover* unfolds a multi-layered and elliptical tale of industrial espionage and ruthless warfare in the global world of digital media. Enhanced by the elegant *mise en scène* and the fluid camera movements and cool atmosphere created by Denis Lenoir's cinematography, the action moves from the interchangeable architecture of French and Japanese corporate buildings, where transparent and reflexive surfaces dominate, to transitory spaces (airports, hotel lobbies and rooms, car parks, subways, lifts, planes and cars), where the film's international cast of actors perform as a group of characters as unpredictable as their motivations and geographical destinations. Its protagonists, Diane de Monx (Connie Nielsen), Élise Lipsky (Chloë Sevigny) and Hervé le Millinec (Charles Berling), are employed by a multinational company dealing with network development and web distribution that includes explicit material. Making her way up the career ladder through ruthless means, Diane finds herself trapped in an increasingly complex web of double-crossing and blackmail which eventually leads to her agreeing to 'perform' for the Hellfire club, an interactive torture web-site.

Whereas the act that the central character of *Dans ma peau* repeatedly performs in secret and in isolation is clearly transgressive, it is the recuperation of the forbidden towards profitable aims that is at the heart of *Demonlover*'s fictional world. Hence, although the director mentions Bataille and Sade as references for the film (Guilloux 2002), such filiation

---

[28] Assayas' film had a mixed critical reception. Beyond the expected perplexity created by a complex, elliptical narrative that arguably leaves the viewer 'struggling to reconcile the slick, condemnatory cyber-thriller . . . with the dreamily incoherent sub-Lynchean nightmare' (Stables 2004: 53), the most convincing criticisms, born out of the implications of the film's premise itself, echo Debord's warnings about the all-inclusive power of self-justification of the 'society of spectacle'. To Kate Stables, Assayas is caught at his own game and his film fails to establish to distance necessary for critical observation:

> There's a fat and fatal strand of ambivalence throughout *Demonlover* which undermines any serious attempts at criticising either online porn or big business. The film seems half in love with the amoral jet-set criminals and ultra-transgressive internet eye-candy that it sets out to condemn, as if post-modern capitalism were just too damn shiny and pretty not to slaver over. (Stables 2004: 53)

For Rosanna Maule, Assayas' critical appraisal of the world he envisages remains the ruling principle throughout, and is best grasped when the film is read like an 'allegory of Global Corporate Media' (Maule 2004). While I equally endorse the film as a powerful critical vision, I would argue that it derives its impact less from its allegorical nature than from its unsettling of cinema's conventional audio-visual economy.

is consciously made problematic by the film's contemporary setting; in the world depicted in *Demonlover*, transgression itself is but one facet of the trade strategies, one of the measures of the 'level' of potential success reached in a system of generalised spectacular entertainment. Sex, eroticism and pornography, violence and pleasure are combined as interwoven elements in a unified method of production and exploitation of desires.

Each step or 'level' in the film's progression is not merely described as the next element of a cyber-thriller narrative logic, but corresponds to a further realisation of the brutality of the economics and ideology that drives a market cut off from the reality of actual suffering that it nevertheless feeds off. As such, the central character's descent into hell is not simply an occasion to draw a vivid and seductive journey into a fascinating and illicit parallel reality; rather, the film's evocation of the depth of terror that lies beyond the smooth surface of global corporate business is inseparable from the brutal rediscovery of the reality of actual pain and the results of wholesale, undifferentiated circulation of images that are the real price of the tyranny of mass entertainment.

Like the alternative worlds of images and sounds it explores, Assayas' film is a formal hybrid that samples a wide variety of styles as well as acoustic and visual qualities, alternating 35mm footage with animation film, digital images of video games and web-site images (created especially for the film) and co-opting the sensory effects and narrative strategies of the media which it evokes. The highly stylised and functional spaces – the corporate world's any-spaces-whatever – where the characters meet or which they briefly occupy in their travels evoke the spatial and colour arrangement of the virtual worlds of digital media and video games: a dominance of geometrical lines and perspectives in frosty blue-grey hues dotted with blocks of warm colours. Moreover, the world of the diegetic 'reality' is constantly permeated by images produced by a variety of media, from the screens of computers and video surveillance systems to televised images that are initially inserted in the film's own frame like inlays in computer-generated imaging. In the opening sequence, neither the sleep of the business-class travellers nor the subdued atmosphere of their luxury plane cabin, bathed in cool hues and filled with the soft murmur of voices and discreet hum of the engine, is challenged by the presence of the images of violent clashes and destruction that are being broadcast in blazing colours on a festoon of television screens above the rows of seats. Hence, the turning point that the visit to the Japanese studios producing adult animation represents: once the images of the Tokyo *anime hentaï* cease to be merely an element of the diegetic and narrative unfolding – an object of interest and discussion amongst business partners – and they actually fill our screens, the film becomes increasingly 'contaminated' by the kind of sensory effects and visual aesthetics associated with this sort of digital media, and the characters appear gradually more like 'point-and-click' figures caught in a web of synthetic spaces. In the sequences that follow, extracts of televised porn movies alternate with the lurid colours and pulsating light of crowded nightclub sequences while, soon after, characters appear to circulate through the corridors of deserted hotels like the human figures of a video-game world. Later on, as Diane drives through brightly lit Parisian streets, the rain that pours down the windscreen creates shifting pixelation effects that drown the surroundings in an abstract play of colourful dots. And when she reaches her office building late at night, she is first shot from a high angle, like the tiny silhouette of a video animation character at the beginning of a game, before her image is captured by the surveillance cameras of the security system. Around her, the rows of windows that line the walls of the building's courtyard offer a curious, slightly distorted perspective, as in a modern-day *Caligari* setting. As the young woman plunges deeper into the world of the Hellfire club, the degraded quality of video images broadcast on web-sites eventually becomes the dominant mode: badly lit, yellowish visions of mayhem caught in the chaotic mode of the hand-held camera.

Through the recurrence of frames-within-frames and the layering of successive screens, the film image appears gradually drained of its vividness and immediacy. The end of the film thus offers a chilling twist to the evocation of virtual imaging and desensitisation. In the concluding sequences, the action moves briefly to a new location – an American upper-middle-class suburban house, where an adolescent boy uses his father's credit card to log on to the Hellfire interactive torture site. Diane's face is then glimpsed haplessly gazing at us from beyond a computer screen, awaiting her fate, while next to the workstation, the teenager has now turned his attention to his homework. Poignantly, these last shots of the young woman are those of twice-derived images, caught through a surveillance camera and replicated on a computer screen which is itself appearing merely as one item amongst the clutter of the teenager's room being portrayed on our own screens.

Like the images, the sound-track creates a sense of coexisting strata of reality. Composed with the musicians of *Sonic Youth* (long-standing collaborators of Assayas, who also used their music for *Irma Vep*), its layers of sounds are carefully mixed so as to build up a sense of acoustic volume. The most persistent reminder of the existence of cross-connected levels of realities – as in a porous layering of planes of intensities – the sound-track is often crossed by a discreet and threatening buzz or hum (as if a computer was constantly switched on somewhere in the background, and the whole story nothing but a series of computer-generated twists). It weaves together diegetic and non-diegetic noises, combining strident electronic sounds with an array of technological acoustic traces: mobile phones, the grating noise of faxes and internet connections, the clicking of computer keyboards, cash machine and interphone keypads . . . . At the same time, and throughout the film, while the sound-track creates meticulously textured acoustic surroundings to each situation and action, the mixing also foregrounds specific sounds that acquire an enhanced sensual charge: the noise of the paper being ripped or punctured over the hum of the engine in the plane as Diane prepares to drug her fellow traveller, the sound of panic-stricken breathing in the airport sequences; the noise of the broken glass under Diane's feet when she breaks into a competitor's hotel room . . . . Linking the sensual quality of the sound to the other formal aspects of the film, Howard Hampton thus concludes: 'In the movie, there are countless incidents like that, where you have the feeling Assayas might prefer to linger as long as Sonic Youth does on the sound-track, going nowhere but deeper into a look, or shape or texture' (Hampton 2003: 16).

Combined with the changes in visual rhythm that the editing emphasises, the variations in the sound-track contribute to a contrasted succession of visual and acoustic atmospheres. The inaugural cut, from the credit sequence to the film proper, for instance, initiates a deft series of swift mood changes. From the lush visuals and energetic tempo of the opening credits (blurred, stain-like silhouettes moving in a fast montage sequence of monochrome images set to pulsating electronic rock music) the film moves abruptly to the suspended, sleepy atmosphere of the plane cabin filled with the discreet hum of the engines. In the following sequences, the characters' relation to the space delimited by the shots seems uncertain. They cross paths and move through the frame, but remain caught in the web of cool reflecting surfaces and choreographed movements and gestures that make up the airport's atmosphere of anonymous functionality. Only the woman executive drugged by Diane falls out of pace, her confusion (blurred vision and a dizzying 360-degree circular shot) soon contrasted with the frenzied effectiveness of Hervé's automatic and methodical actions (reclaiming his luggage, getting money from a cash machine, buying a porn magazine) captured in quick bursts of noises, frantic camera movements and rapid cuts.

Sonic Youth's contribution offers little in the way of actual melodies, yet minimal arrangements of guitars and piano chords add an unexpected sense of nostalgia to the film's more contemplative moments. Hence, the indefinable poignancy of the scene of the departure of the Japanese interpreter who is seen leaving Hervé's hotel room at dawn, a lonely silhouette traversing a series of deserted, anonymous any-spaces-whatever (a corridor, a hotel lobby, a massive empty courtyard overlooking the city's huge expanse) that elliptical editing disconnects and renders more eerie.

As with Claire Denis' *L'Intrus* in particular, a film that, like Assayas' feature, moves through a series of transitory spaces, *Demonlover*, considered as a whole, ultimately appears constructed like an organic ensemble of 'blocks' of sensations rather than a chain of logically articulated narrative moments. The editing together of the sequences never explicitly attempts to locate an event. Rather, the montage tends to catch the characters already in action, without recourse to links or establishing shots. But whereas the architecture and pace of *L'Intrus* suggest the gradual disengagement of a fading organism, Assayas' film evokes a series of seizures and chemical reactions. As Gavin Smith underlines, the second part of *Demonlover*, after the actual 'black-out' that follows the murder sequence, includes an increasing number of fades in and fades out (Smith 2003: 66). The effect does not merely mimic television or internet zapping or the process of moving through the different levels of a game, but opens the film up as a series of disturbing and fragmented sensory experiences. That the vocabulary used by the critics commenting on *Demonlover* almost systematically borrows from the language of diseases and their propagation does not come as a surprise. In effect, the film's gradually more chaotic narrative structure appears to function like an increasingly confused nervous system, crossed by fluxes of 'impure' images (Cohen 2002: 45) that slowly proliferate, taking over the narrative and film form like a virus infecting a body. Considered in relation to the body of the film as a whole, the arbitrariness that also seems to rule over the characters (apparent concern spelling indifference, allegiance mixed up with disloyalty, and gestures of tenderness becoming a prelude to murder) does not purely reflect their status as mere point-and-click pawns in a secret war game. Speaking in terms that strongly evoke the notion of Deleuzean becoming, Jean-Michel Frodon argues that the characters themselves do not function like conventional autonomous and psychologically defined entities, but rather like so many components in a wider ensemble, reacting as if they were subjected to fluxes of technological or chemical stimuli:

> *Demonlover* is an unsettling film. It breaks what we could call the 'anthropological pact' that rules over all spectacle, in cinema in particular – a tacit pact that consists of pretending that what we are looking at are real people whose adventures unravel on screen. Here, characters are but like the rest of all the components of a totality, a work whose very formula reproduces that of a globalised world, remodelled by the virtual and its codes of representation. Its impressive artistic quality, like an architectural

structure made up of variations in speeds, rhythm and light more than actions and dialogue, is also one of the work's components. (Frodon 2002)

If the film, then, draws the spectator 'in', rather than promoting character identification and a detached, narrative-led gaze, its powerful sensory impact, however, does not invalidate its critical scope. In effect, it is precisely when the sensory field created by the visual and acoustic arrangements escapes the domain of mere mimicry (where the viewer goes from simply appreciating the film as a stylised and, possibly, titillating evocation of the worlds of virtual imaging) and connects with the concrete (experiencing a visceral sense of repellence or fear) that the existential nucleus of the film surfaces:

> Because what is really at stake in the film is not a reflection about the place of images in the world from a societal point of view (censorship) but to reflect on the place of the other from a philosophical point of view (resemblance). To find oneself in the very place and situation that one refused to see, to bring representation back to that which can be directly experienced. (Azalbert 2002b: 78)[29]

As a powerful sensory composition that questions the impact of perception on our consciences, *Demonlover* becomes an experience of cinema as a 'body that thinks' – in this case, a body progressively 'contaminated' by the visual material it explores, brought close to hallucination by a saturation of sensory affects, and nevertheless traversed by a thought-provoking sense of disquiet and repellence.

Needles piercing through the protective film of a container of mineral water or the skin at the fold of the arm (to inject an invisible substance that will visibly distort perception); sounds piercing through the textured acoustic medley of the background; knives and cutters puncturing and slicing through flesh; a gaze directed into the camera, as if piercing through screens and reconnecting disconnected levels of realities – in Assayas' film,

---

[29] Hence, *Demonlover* does not merely open a space for the confrontation of different modes of image production. It also foregrounds the function of the 'cliché' as the screen that hides the image and anaesthetises our perception, thus calling to mind Deleuze's exploration of the conflict between these two regimes of the visible. For Deleuze, modern civilisation is less a civilisation of the image than of the cliché:

> Civilisation of the image? In fact, it is a civilisation of the cliché where all the powers have an interest in hiding images from us, not necessarily in hiding the same thing from us, but in hiding something in the image. On the other hand, at the same time, the image constantly attempts to *pierce* through the cliché, to get out of the cliché. (Deleuze 1989: 21; italics mine. I have translated '*percer*' used by Deleuze as 'pierce' rather than 'break through', as in the 1989 English translation)

as in de Van's, the act of perforating, piercing through, slicing open has a direct sensory impact that extends its metaphorical significance into a re-endorsement of embodied experience and knowledge. Theirs is a film-making that, in Hal Foster's world, 'probes the wound', bringing back into the progressively more coded, abstracting economy of the gaze, imposed by the growing reign of the virtual and globalised, the unruly, destabilising effect of cinema as a cinema of sensation.

Where de Van and Assayas' films account for the ambivalent mix of fascination and angst that the metamorphosis of modern man into 'homo professionalis' or 'homo technology' effects, in Gordon and Parreno's unusual film-portrait, the relationship between subjective body, media and technology opens on to an inspirational space of multiple becomings.

Becoming Film: *Zidane, A 21st Century Portrait*

I am eye. I have created a man more perfect than Adam; I created thousands of different people.

I am eye. I am a mechanical eye.

I, a machine, am showing you a world, the likes of which only I can see.

I free myself from today and forever from human immobility, I am in constant movement, I approach and draw away from objects, I crawl under them, I move alongside the mouth of a running horse, I cut into a crowd at full speed . . . I fall and soar together with falling and rising bodies.

This is I, apparatus, manoeuvering in the chaos of movements, recording one movement after another in the most complex combinations.

. . . freed from the frame of time and space, I coordinate any and all points of the universe, wherever I may plot them.

My road is toward the creation of a fresh perception of the world. Thus, I decipher in a new way the world unknown to you. (Vertov [1922] (1978): 5)

These are Vertov's well-known celebratory lines on the moving image as technological and creative wonder. The Soviet avant-garde saw in cinema a new medium that had the potential simultaneously to revolutionise and expand our perception and critical awareness of the world around us. However, written when film was still in its infancy, Vertov's text bristles with an artist-cum-technophile's enthusiasm that may sound outlandish in an era where television and the internet have made us wary of moving-image media. The late twentieth century has been characterised by a growing suspicion of audio-visual and related technologies of imaging and communication – a distrust that is, as we have seen, echoed in many a documentary and fiction film. Technological risks, distortion, disinformation, mass propaganda, the endless recycling of data, voyeurism and media vampirism, fetishism and image exploitation, intellectual and affective anaesthesia have become important topics for filmmakers seeking to offer a reflexive vision of their world as perceived and represented by their chosen medium. And yet, as Rosi Braidotti remarks, even if we take into account the misuses of technological advancement and global communication, as well as the 'power differentials and patterns of exclusion that are constitutive of advanced societies', there is a certain hypocrisy in reinstating 'the rhetoric of humanism in constructing the machines as antithetical to human evolution'. Braidotti argues for an 'in-between position [that is] neither technophobic nor naively technophilic, but rather sober enough to address the complexities engendered by our historicity' (Braidotti 2002: 147).

Landing on our screens like a strange object, Gordon and Parreno's film works precisely at that juncture. Indeed, if we could add the touch of nostalgia that time has grafted on to Gordon and Parreno's project, then Vertov's words would be a remarkably pertinent description of it. Neither documentary nor conventionally filmed portrait, between the experimental and the popular, their film is an audio-visual poem, a work that embraces all that the technology of sound and image has to offer to date to produce a thought-provoking and deeply affecting evocation of the twenty-first century's world of images. In Cyril Neyrat's words, it is not so much the picture of a collective dream, than the 'daydream of the image' ('*rêverie de l'image*': in accordance with Artaud's concept of cinema, one would have to insist on an essential differentiation – the film is not the representation of a dream, but film dreaming).

Known for their cross-disciplinary artists' work, Douglas Gordon and Philippe Parreno locate the source of their project in their shared experience of growing up with football in a world whose perception was increasingly shaped by television.[30] In Neyrat's words, their film is thus not conceived 'against television (*contre la télévision*), but, rather, as if *leaning against it – tout contre*, as Godard would put it' (Neyrat 2006: 29). 'As close as possible. As much as possible. As long as possible': the first intertitles, based on Zidane's childhood account of watching football on TV, express a mix of nostalgia and fascination that accounts for the film's invocation of the power of audio-visual expression as well as its, at times, surprisingly melancholic tone.

The work's initial time-frame is that of a match; it is shot in the 90 minutes between the kick-off and final whistle-blow of a Spanish league

---

[30] Using the resources of our present-day technology, Gordon and Parreno start again from where Hellmuth Costard left off when he completed *Fussball wie noch nie*, his portrait of George Best in 1971. A montage of sequences captured by several cameras on 16mm film in the course of one match, the film also focused solely on the one player.

game between Villarreal and Real Madrid. Gordon and Parreno managed
to bring together a team of the best cameramen and women with seventeen
cameras installed around the field, combining High Definition with 35mm
scope format and including two prototype cameras with extremely powerful tele-lenses. The end result has little to do with the usual football broadcast. As Jean-Max Colard puts it, by focusing this multiple gaze solely on
one player,

> Douglas Gordon and Philippe Parreno operate what could be called a small
> Copernican revolution: it is not the players who revolve around the ball, televised
> from up-high by an omniscient camera that embraces the footosphere . . ., it is, on
> the contrary, the galaxy of the stadium and its spectacular machinery that revolve
> around one single player. (Colard 2006: 54)

At the same time, paradoxically, stardom is hardly the issue here; if Zidane
is one of the most famous and best world players at this point in time, the
film does not seek to emphasise or pierce through the mystery of a legend
(albeit, as we will see, in strictly cinematic terms, by evoking the epic world
of the Western). Indeed, by borrowing the form of the Vitruvian man, the
logo composed of the letters of the player's name at the beginning and end
of the film announces a much looser and wider field of exploration: football, and the cinematic body of the footballer as the evocation of the cos-
mography of a microcosm.

Gordon and Parreno thus construct a portrait that is, first and foremost,
an expansive physical and sensory experience – a film that opens a space
for multiple 'becomings' and 'performs as a body'; a moving sculpture of
audio-visual matter that beckons the viewer; 'a way of seeing, of living
football differently, as if from the inside' (Collard 2006: 54), and, by extension, a way of seeing and living cinema differently. And, indeed, for the
spectators who allow themselves to be drawn in, the experience is one of
wonderful, ravishing sensory overload, a perception-expanding event
where the outer field, though never *seen*, is always felt, sensed and recom-
posed through the changes in intensity that affect the audio-visual field.

Playing on scale and texture, combining a multiplicity of angles, framing
and visual and sound qualities, the film takes the audio-visual matter from
one extreme of the figural spectrum to the other – from the figurative to
the abstract, from wide-angle views of the playing field to such enlarged
pictures that the screen becomes a pixelated colour field. The opening
credit sequence starts with low-resolution images of the whole pitch,
filmed off a TV screen and accompanied by the sound of a Spanish com-
mentator's voice mingling with a few electric guitar chords. As the camera
draws progressively closer, the image turns into an abstract composition,

a tactile surface which recalls the colourful interwoven threads of fabric or the shimmering effect of a pointillist painting. The music slowly grows into the film's leading track: an atmospheric, melancholic tune composed and played by Mogwai. The move to High Definition vision effects a sudden change of visual regime, switching from one form of hapticity (a low resolution and grainy feel) to another (detailed, clear-cut visuals with a fine texture). The sound-track undergoes a similar commotion, the noise of the crowd abruptly bursting in with forceful immediacy. Yet, as Neyrat argues, this is not 'the passage from TV to cinema' but 'entering into the thick of the image, giving in to daydreaming'. From then on, the film will alternate from the one to the other visual regime, combining shots of broadcast images with footage captured directly on the pitch by the seventeen cameras, and giving increasing pre-eminence to the latter as time goes by. Midway through the film, at half-time, Gordon and Parreno insert a montage of newsreels: images with intertitles, taken from television news broadcasts to form a kaleidoscopic evocation of events taking place on the same day as the match (from pictures of floods in Montenegro to images of Elián González on Cuban TV, from the announcement of the sale of a *Star Wars* spaceship on e-bay to news of the recording of plasma waves by Voyager, and the description of a terrorist attack in Najaf, Iraq, that includes a glimpse of a passer-by sporting a Zidane T-shirt . . .). The film, thus, superimposes a variety of moods and temporal layers: the mournful evocation of the twentieth century through old-fashioned television broadcasts combining with the futuristic edge of global interconnections and High Definition imaging, as well as the precise framework of the match captured in 'real time' and the enthralling, fluctuating beat of the film as the present event.

Instead of constructing the conventional, narrative and drama-led account of a match, 'dominated by the score, the goal, the action', Gordon and Parreno use the multiple-angle audio-visual material like sculpting matter, literally shaping the film as a body of changing textures and intensities, 'full of oddities, of holes, of obscure regions' (Colard 2006: 54). Indeed, to focus on a single player is to turn the match into an unusual event, one that is full of lulls, moments of expectancy, broken by abrupt changes of rhythm.[31] As Colard stresses, the affective power of the film is generated less by the drama of the match as a sequence of events than by the drama of the film's material transformation. The film is built on a series of alternations – changes in direction within the shot, changes in scale and focus, in angles

---

[31] This sense of expectancy created by large periods of inaction is also true of Costard's 1971 film.

and point-of-view – brought together through virtuoso editing that matches diverse shots of the same action in rhythmic and tonal combinations. As in a musical composition, these alternations are interwoven with or played against the fluctuations of the sound-track. Most striking is the passage from formless or near-abstract compositions to clear-cut perception, from extreme close-up to wide-angle vision, from the inchoate roaring of the crowd to the sound of an isolated voice or that of Zidane's breathing or him calling for the ball. Operated by the tele-lens eye and sound-track, the disappearance and reappearance of the figure – seemingly dissolving under the concentrated beam of thousands of gazes, or fusing with the background, with the teeming, collective body of the crowd – generates a sense of elation rather than threat. It is the thrill of an endless potential for 'becoming' that is encapsulated in these fluctuations in focus and sound-mixing and that is echoed in Zidane's description of his perception of his environment when on the pitch, given in a brief series of intertitles: 'When you are deep into the match, you don't really hear the crowd. At the same time, you can almost choose what you want to hear.'

Gordon and Parreno make salient use of the tele-lens prototype. As well as arresting shifts of focus from player to crowd, the film includes oddly poignant inserts of visual and sound details: the repeated shots of the player's feet, the tips of his shoes brushing against the ground; a hand suspended in mid-air; the sound of a sigh. . . . The device gives an uncanny sense of intimacy to certain shots, obliterating the sense of depth to the point where we feel the camera gaze literally touch the body of the player. Strikingly, in the extreme close-up on the face, the recording of minute facial moves and pouring sweat, and, in the moments of action in particular, the way the tele-lens crushes the figure into the background, the film recalls the world of the western,[32] and, in particular, the heightened effects favoured by Sergio Leone; in the brutal accelerations of speed, the tumult of bodies jostling, the sound of blows, one finds the sudden echo of cavalcades and shoot-outs, of packs of horses and hooves hammering the ground.

The evocation of the pack is thus one amongst a multitude of potential 'becomings' that the film suggests, one amongst many possible exchanges that affect and connect the various bodies/components that meet across

[32] As do certain facets of Zidane's own persona; his charismatic presence as well as the mix of gentleness and quick temper that account for his famously unpredictable reactions sometimes recall that of the ambivalent heroic figures of late Westerns. Gordon and Parreno's film concludes with Zidane receiving a red card after an altercation with another player and being sent off the pitch: an odd presage (almost a pre-play) to the event that marred the final match of the World Cup a few months later.

the film's field of intensities: film-spectator/player/team/football-spectator/crowd. In spite of, or thanks to, its play on scale and textures and its montage format, Gordon and Parreno's film does not effect a fragmentation of the body, but constructs distinctive new assemblages that combine the body as flesh (individual and collective, on screen and off screen) and as abstract entity (viewer, player, team and crowd as cultural, social, historical constructs). Ultimately, *Portrait* thus performs as what Deleuze and Guattari, borrowing the expression from Artaud, call a 'body-without-organs': 'What we need to consider is not fundamentally organs without bodies, or the fragmented body, it is the 'body-without-organs', animated by various intensive elements' (Deleuze and Guattari 1987: 171). Like the concept of becoming, in Deleuze and Guattari's alternative philosophy, the body-without-organs is an attempt to rethink the relation between body and mind, between subjective body and objective world:

> Bodies are no longer perceived as just corporeal, flesh-and-blood bodies, but the concept takes on a more complex and assemblaged notion . . . Deleuze and Guattari describe the body as a set of various speeds and intensities. It is conceived in relation to other bodies, particles of other bodies or entities. . . . the body and mind are 'modifications' of the same substance. Thus all of life, in a sense, becomes 'body' in material and molecular connection. Bodies, then, are not stable units, but become elements in assemblage, fluid and mutable, constituting life through 'becoming'. (Kennedy 2000: 98–9)

If Gordon and Parreno's film can prove such an affecting experience, it is because, through its celebration of film's corporeal dimension, it opens a space where dual thinking (inside/outside, subjective body/objective world, abstract meaning/concrete experience) ceases to make sense. For the duration of the film at least, the spectator can be in the past and in the present, play the field as a legend or as a team, become-camera or become-crowd, or, simply, let him/herself be immersed in the film's intense sensory field.

Dominating or accompanying the sound-waves emitted by the audience, the sonorous traces of a 'becoming-crowd', the pounding of drums, resonate through the field like an irregular, collective heart-beat. Could this be the antithesis to Jean-Luc Nancy's 'intruder', to the actual experience and metaphorical tale of the foreign heart transplanted into the body? In any event, what this connection certainly brings to mind is the great paradox that underpins Gordon and Parreno's *21st-Century Portrait*: in a contemporary France suffused with xenophobic fears, the most famous and admired man is a footballer of Algerian-Kabyle origins called Zinédine Zidane.

Epilogue

'Give me a body then': this is the formula of philosophical reversal. The body is no longer the obstacle that separates thought from itself, that which has to be overcome to reach thinking . . . It is through the body (and no longer through the intermediary of the body) that cinema forms its alliance with the spirit, with thought. (Deleuze 1989: 189)

Lady Chatterley passes the gate and her silhouette is literally absorbed into the richly patterned surroundings of the forest. As she crosses the wooded expanse that separates her husband's house from her lover's lodge, the film chronicles, with the meticulousness and unpredictability of a devoted but disorderly botanist, the bristling, teeming life of the nature that beckons her. *Lady Chatterley*, Pascale Ferran's latest opus, is a sensory feast, a work in which cinema's sensual, haptic and synaesthetic powers of evocation are explored to the full so as to invoke 'Desire's variable plane of immanence, as Deleuze theorised it' (Burdeau 2006: 8–9).[1] Yet her film is also a 'costume drama' and a literary adaptation. Does this mean that Ferran's project boils down to the naïve and nostalgic account of a relationship between man and nature that is only possible if imagined in the past tense? Not quite. The story of Lady Chatterley's sensual awakening unfolds against a backdrop of war destruction as well as class and gender divides that have maimed and reduced minds and bodies. As a counterpoint to these visible and invisible mutilations, the film develops, as Jean-Christophe Ferrari puts it, like an 'invention of tenderness' (Ferrari 2006: 43; see also Burdeau 2006: 8): not merely in the way the lovers touch each other, but in the mode of address adopted by the attentive gaze of the camera in its relation to the pro-filmic. In Parkin's cabin, Lady Chatterley slips on one of the forester's gloves; it is far too big for her hand, its texture is rough, yet we can 'feel' that its smooth internal surface still retains the warmth of the lover's hand. Neither identification nor projection, in

---

[1] Burdeau describes Ferran's film as the invocation of one of Deleuze's favoured formula: 'To love without defining'. (The expression used in the formula – 'aimer sans *faire le point*' – is also a cinematic expression meaning 'not to focus'.) Deleuze was a keen reader of Lawrence, and Ferran asked the philosopher's wife and son to translate Lawrence's original dialogues.

Ferran's film, the relation between the lovers is like touch, based on the reversibility of experience. Accordingly, through its own operations, the film 'thinks' the relationship of subjective body to objective world in the style of a caress (Ferrari 2006: 42). Framing, sound, camera movement and duration – here, the filmmaking encompasses what Sartre defines as 'the ensemble of the ceremonies that incarnate the other' (Sartre 1943: 430). This is about desire, and consumed physical desire, and yet neither the relationship of the lovers nor that of the camera and filmmaker to the subjects and objects that make up the filmic matter is one of appropriation or exploitation (hence, as unlikely as it may seem, the connection, or complementary relationship, that one can establish between two works as apparently antithetic as *Lady Chatterley* and *Baise-moi*).

To immerse oneself in the universe created by a filmmaker who chooses to travel the 'third path' is to experience specific spectatorial pleasures. There is the engagement with the sensory jolts and delights afforded by the materiality and temporality of the film event itself. There is also pleasure in becoming attuned to the film's operations, to opening oneself to this form of thinking in movement.

From abjection to caress, and transgression to 'becoming', from *La Vie nouvelle* to *Zidane, A 21st-Century Portrait* and from *Leçons de ténèbres* to *Lady Chatterley*, what cinema, as the medium of the senses, 'thinks' through so vividly is the changing relation of the subject to the world. The haptic audio-visual mode that characterises the cinema of sensation undermines conventional patterns of optical appropriation; it challenges the 'consumer' gaze to suggest a more reversible – threatening or empathetic – mode of understanding of the 'object' of the gaze. The questioning of identity and otherness thus becomes imprinted in the make-up and 'in the flesh' of the filmic body itself. Destabilising spectatorial position and radically challenging familiar notions of 'inside' and 'outside', it then offers an intuition of how we can break free from some of the deadlocks generated by established – binary – modes of thinking.

Ferran's is the latest amongst a series of French films where cinema's corporeality is explored anew – a sign that there is still space, thanks to the unusual range and diversity of the French production, for cinematic practices to reinvent themselves, and for cinema to remain one of the ways by which a culture addresses and thinks through the consequences of its historicity. As a filmmaking practice, the cinema of sensation acquires a particular significance here because it specifically re-endorses film's often undervalued yet most essential of privileges: the ability to reach a spectator's mind through the intelligence of the affective.

Bibliography

Alnoy, Siegrid (2004), DVD audio commentary, Paris: Gaumont.

Arata, Stephen (1990), 'The Occidental Tourist: Dracula and the Anxiety of Reverse Colonisation', *Victorian Studies* 33, pp. 621–45.

Armstrong, Philip (2000), *Shakespeare's Visual Regime: Tragedy, Psychoanalysis and the Gaze*, London: Palgrave.

Arnaud, Philippe (1995), 'Les vampires: l'être radiographié, le corps dans tous ses états', in Jacques Aumont (ed.), *L'Invention de la figure humaine – Le Cinéma: l'humain et l'inhumain*, Paris: Cinémathèque française, pp. 305–19.

Artaud, Antonin [1928] (1972), 'The Shell and the Clergyman', trans. Alastair Hamilton, in *Collected Works*, London: Caldon & Boyars, pp. 19–25.

Artaud, Antonin [1933] (1972), 'The Precocious Old Age of the Cinema', trans. Alastair Hamilton, in *Collected Works*, London: Caldon & Boyars, pp. 76–9.

Astic, Guy (2004), *Le Purgatoire des sens: 'Lost Highway' de David Lynch*, Paris: Rouge Profond.

Audé, Françoise (1999), 'Vive la mort?', *Positif* 456, pp. 8–9.

Aumont, Jacques (1995), 'Avant-propos', in Jacques Aumont (ed.), *L'Invention de la figure humaine – Le Cinéma: l'humain et l'inhumain*, Paris: Cinémathèque française, pp. 7–8.

Aumont, Jacques (2005), *Matière d'images*, Paris: Images Modernes.

Austin, Guy (1996), *Contemporary French Cinema: an Introduction*, Manchester: Manchester University Press.

Azalbert, Nicolas (2002a), 'Le Corps défendant – *Dans ma peau* de Marina de Van', *Cahiers du cinéma* 574, pp. 82–3.

Azalbert, Nicolas (2002b), 'Connected People – *Demonlover* d'Olivier Assayas', *Cahiers du cinéma* 573, pp. 78–9.

Bahcelioglu, Aïcha (2005), 'Expériences de la catastrophe: l'humanité tremblée', in Nicole Brenez (ed.), *La Vie nouvelle: nouvelle vision*, Paris: Léo Scheer.

Balázs, Béla [1923] (1972), *Theory of the Film*, trans. Edith Bone, New York: Arno.

Balázs, Béla [1948] (1979), *Le Cinéma, nature et évolution d'un art nouveau*, Paris: Payot.

Bassan, Raphaël (1989), 'Trois néobaroques français', *La Revue du cinéma* 449, pp. 45–53.

Bataille, Georges (1929), 'Informe', *Documents* 7, p. 382.

Bataille, Georges (1957), *L'Érotisme*, Paris: Éditions de Minuit.

Bataille, Georges (1961), *Les Larmes d'Éros*, Paris: Pauvert.

Bataille, Georges [1949] (1988–1991), *The Accursed Share: An Essay on General Economy*, trans. Robert Hurley, New York: Zone.

Baudelaire, Charles [1866] (1976), *Œuvres Complètes*, Paris: Gallimard.

Baudrillard, Jean (1993), *The Transparency of Evil: Essays on Extreme Phenomena*, trans. James Benedict, London: Verso.

Bazin, André (1967), *What Is Cinema?*, Berkeley: University of California Press.

Bégaudeau, François (2004), 'Trop fort. À Propos d'*Adieu*', *Cahiers du cinéma* 596, pp. 76–7.

Béghin, Cyril, Stéphane Delorme, Mathias Lavin (2001), 'Interview with Philippe Grandrieux', *Balthazar*, 5 September, www.cyrilbg.club.fr/grandrieux.html, accessed March 2006.

Bellour, Raymond (2005), 'Bords marginaux', in Nicole Brenez (ed.), *La Vie nouvelle: nouvelle vision*, Paris: Léo Scheer, pp. 16–17.

Benjamin, Walter [1969] (1986), 'The Work of Art in the Age of Mechanical Reproduction', trans. Harry Zoh, in Hannah Arendt (ed.), *Illuminations*, New York: Shocken.

Bernheim, Emmanuelle (2002), 'Dossier de presse du film *Vendredi soir*', Paris: Bac.

Beugnet, Martine (2000), 'Le Souci de l'Autre – Nouveau Réalisme et critique sociale dans le cinéma français contemporain', *IRIS* 29, pp. 52–68.

Beugnet, Martine (2001), 'Filming Jealousy: Akerman's *La Captive*', *Studies in French Cinema* 2/3, pp. 156–64.

Beugnet, Martine (2004a), 'Poétique de la marge: *Les Glaneurs et la glaneuse* d'Agnès Varda', in *Champs visuels – Cinémas contemporains: état des lieux*, Paris: L'Harmattan.

Beugnet, Martine (2004b), *Claire Denis*, Manchester: Manchester University Press.

Beugnet, Martine (2005a), 'Die Sinnliche Leinwand: *L'Intrus*', in M. Omasta, I. Reicher (eds), *Claire Denis*, Vienna: FilmmuseumSynemaPublikation, pp. 65–79.

Beugnet, Martine (2005b), 'Cinema of Evil: Philippe Grandrieux', *Sombre* and *La Vie nouvelle*', *Studies in French Cinema* 5/3, pp. 175–84.

Beugnet, Martine (2006), 'Close-up Vision: Re-mapping the Body in the Work of Contemporary French Women Filmmakers', *Nottingham French Studies*, special issue edited by Gill Rye and Carrie Tarr, 45:3.

Beugnet, Martine (2007a), 'Figures of Vampirism: French Cinema in the Era of Global Transylvania', *Modern and Contemporary France* 15:1, pp. 77–88.

Beugnet, Martine (2007b), 'French Experimental Cinema: the Figural and the Formless – Nicolas Rey's *Terminus for You* (1996) and Pip Chodorov's *Charlemagne 2: Piltzer* (2002), in Graf, Alexander (ed.), *Avant-Garde Film*, Amsterdam: Rodopi.

Beugnet, Martine, Marion Schmid (2005), *Proust at the Movies*, Aldershot: Ashgate.

Blouin, Patrice, Jean-Sébastien Chauvin, Jean-Marc Lalanne (2002), 'Le Sexe, 7 façons de s'en servir', *Cahiers du cinéma* 574, pp. 12–16.

Bonitzer, Pascal [1978] (2001), 'Décadrages', first published in *Cahiers du cinéma* 284, reprinted in *Théories du cinéma*, Paris: Cahiers du cinéma, pp. 123–33.

Bonitzer, Pascal [1981] (1999), *Le Champ aveugle: Essais sur le réalisme au cinéma*, Paris: Cahiers du cinéma.

Bonitzer, Pascal [1982] (1999), *Le Champ aveugle*, Paris: Cahiers du cinéma.

Bouquet, Stéphane [1998] (2001), 'De Sorte que tout communique', first published in *Cahiers du cinéma* 527, reprinted in *Théories du cinéma*, Paris: Cahiers du cinéma, pp. 200–12.

Braidotti, Rosi (2005), *Metamorphoses: Towards a Materialist Theory of Becoming*, Cambridge: Polity.

Brenez, Nicole (1998), *De la figure en général et du corps en particulier – L'Invention figurative au cinéma*, Paris: De Boeck & Larcier.

Brenez, Nicole (2001), 'Le Grand Style of the Epoch', www.latrobe.edu.au/screeningthepast/classics/cl0703/nbcl15.html, trans. Aïcha Bahcelioglu with Adrian Martin. Text originally appeared in *Trafic* 39 (Autumn 2001).

Brenez, Nicole (2003), 'The Body's Night: an Interview with Philippe Grandrieux', *Rouge* 1, A. Martin (ed.), www.rouge.com.au/1/grandrieux.html, accessed March 2004.

Brenez, Nicole (ed.) (2005), *La Vie Nouvelle: nouvelle vision*, Paris: Léo Sheer.

Burdeau, Emmanuel (2004), 'En route: *Adieu*, d'Arnaud des Pallières', *Cahiers du cinéma* 593, pp. 14–16.

Burdeau, Emmanuel (2005), 'La Femme et le tympan', *Cahiers du cinéma* 602, pp. 40–1.

Burdeau, Emmanuel (2006), 'Tendresse: *Lady Chatterley* de Pascale Ferran', *Cahiers du cinéma* 617, pp. 8–10.

Cassavetti, Hugo (2005), 'L'Enfer au coin du trottoir', *Télérama* 2889, 25 May, pp. 89–90.

Cavell, Stanley (2005), 'What Becomes of Thinking on Film?', in Wartenberg, Thomas E., Curran, Angela (eds), *The Philosophy of Film: Introductory Text and Readings*, Oxford: Blackwell, pp. 167–210.

Chauvin, Jean-Sébastien (2001), 'Au delà des genres', *Cahiers du cinéma* 559, pp. 77–8.

Cohen, Clélia (2002), 'Fantasme interrompu', *Cahiers du cinéma* 569, p. 45.

Colard, Jean-Max (2006), '*Zidane, Un Portrait du XXIème siècle* de Douglas Gordon et Philippe Parreno', *Les Inrockuptibles* 547, p. 54.

Coumoul, Sylvain (2006), 'Craquelures', *Cahiers du cinéma* 610, p. 22.

Creed, Barbara (1986), 'Horror and the Monstrous-Feminine: an Imaginary Abjection', *Screen* 27:1, pp. 44–70.

Cytowic, Richard E. (1993), *The Man Who Tasted Shapes: A Bizarre Medical Mystery Offers Revolutionary Insights into Emotions, Reasoning and Consciousness*, New York: Warner.

Daly, Fergus, Garin Dowd (1999), *Leos Carax*, Manchester: Manchester University Press.

Darras, Matthieu (2006), 'Flandres. Guerre perpétuelle, bonheur éphémère', *Positif* 547, pp. 88–90.

De Baecque, Antoine (1999), 'La Peur du loup', *Cahiers du cinéma* 532, pp. 37–9.

De Baecque, Antoine, Thierry Jousse (1999), 'Le Monde à l'envers: entretien avec Philippe Grandrieux', *Cahiers du cinéma* 532, pp. 39–41.

De Bruyn, Olivier (2002), 'Corps à corps – *Dans ma peau*', *Positif* 502, pp. 26–7.

Deleuze, Gilles (1986 and 1989), *Cinema 1: The Movement-Image* and *Cinema 2: The Time-Image*, trans. H. Tomlinson and B. Habberjam, Minneapolis: University of Minnesota Press.

Deleuze, Gilles (1988), *Le Pli: Leibnitz et le baroque*, Paris: Éditions de Minuit.

Deleuze, Gilles (2001), 'L'Image de la pensée' and 'Cinéma et pensée', *La Voix de Gilles Deleuze*, series of lectures from 1981, recorded and transcribed by l'Association siècle Deleuzien, www.univ-paris8.fr/deleuze/article.php3?id_article=4.

Deleuze, Gilles [1981] (2002), *Francis Bacon, logique de la sensation*, Paris: Seuil.

Deleuze, Gilles, Félix Guattari (1984), *Anti-Oedipus: Capitalism and Schizophrenia*, trans. Robert Hurley, Mark Seem, Helen R. Lane, London: Athlone.

Deleuze, Gilles, Félix Guattari (1987), *A Thousand Plateaus: Capitalism and Schizophrenia*, trans. Brian Massumi, London: Athlone.

Deleuze Gilles, Claire Parnet [1987] (1996), *Dialogues*, Paris: Champs, Flammarion.

Del Río, Elena (1996), 'The Body as Foundation of the Screen: Allegories of Technology in Atom Egoyan's *Speaking Parts*', *Camera Obscura* 37/38, pp. 94–115.

Denis, Claire (2002), 'Dossier de presse du film *Vendredi soir*', Paris: Bac.

Denis, Claire (2004), Interview, *Pastemagazine*, http://pastemagazine.com/action/article?article_id=1325, accessed January 2005.

Docherty, Thomas (1996), *Alterities: Criticism, History, Representation*, Oxford: Clarendon.

Duvignaud, Jean (1970), *Anomie et mutation sociale*, Paris: Anthropos.

Eisenstein, Sergei (1943), *The Film Sense*, London: Faber & Faber.

Eisenstein, Sergeï [1940] (1974), *Au delà des étoiles*, Paris: Union générale d'éditions 10/18.

Fabre, Jérôme (1999), Review of *Sombre*, *Jeune cinéma* 254, March–April, pp. 46–7.

Ferrari, Jean-Christophe (2006), '*Lady Chatterley:* Ma main sur ton sein [l'invention de la tendresse]', *Positif* 549, pp. 42–3.

Foster, Hal (1996), *The Return of the Real: The Avant-Garde and the End of the Century*, Cambridge, MA: MIT Press.

Frodon, Jean-Michel (2002), 'Variations de rythme', *Le Monde*, 21 May.

Frodon, Jean-Michel (2005), 'En mouvement', *Cahiers du cinéma* 606, p. 5.

Gallagher, Tag (2004), 'Ford et Murnau', *Positif* 523, pp. 90–4.

Game, Jérôme (2001), 'Cinematic Bodies: The Blind Spot in Contemporary French Theory on Corporeal Cinema', *Studies in French Cinema*, 1:1, pp. 47–53.

Garbaz, Franck (1997), 'Mère, pourquoi nous as-tu abandonnés?', *Positif* 432, pp. 38–9.

Gelder, Kenneth (1994), *Reading the Vampire*, London: Routledge.

Grand, Gilles (2004), '*Adieu*: le son ou l'art du faux', *Cahiers du cinéma* 596, pp. 79–80.

Grandrieux, Philippe (1999a), 'Les Morsures de l'aube', *Les Inrockuptibles*, 27 January, p. 60.

Grandrieux, Philippe (1999b), 'Entretien avec Philippe Grandrieux' (Nicolas Renaud, Steve Rioux, Nicolas L. Rutigliano), 14 October, www.horschamp. qc.ca/Emulsions/grandrieux.html, accessed November 2006.

Grandrieux, Philippe (1999c), 'Sombre', *Cahiers du cinéma* 532, pp. 39–41.

Grandrieux, Philippe (2000), Interview, Cahiers du cinéma, Hors série 'Le Siécle du cinéma'.

Grandrieux, Philippe (2001), 'Philippe Grandrieux: Entretien avec Balthazar', *Balthazar* 4, http://perso.club-internet.fr/cyrilbg/grandrieux.html, accessed March 2004.

Grandrieux, Philippe (2002), 'Le Chaos organisé de "*La Vie nouvelle*"', *Cahiers du cinéma* 570, pp. 34–5.

Grandrieux, Philippe (2003), 'Un Cinéma visionnaire', *Le Technicien du film* 530, pp. 24–8.

Guichard, Louis (2006), 'Entretien avec Bruno Dumont', *Télérama* 2955, pp. 26–8.

Guilloux, Michel (1997), 'De l'Amour est passé', *L'Humanité*, 29 January, p. 12.

Guilloux, Michel (2002), 'Un cauchemar éveillé du monde actuel', *L'Humanité*, 6 November, p. 12.

Guterman, Lila (2001), 'Do You Smell What I Hear?, Neuroscientists Discover Crosstalk Among the Senses', *Chronicle of Higher Educaiton* A17, and at http://chronicle.com.

Hampton, Howard (2003), '*Demonlover*', *Sound and Vision* 39:5, p. 16.

Hayward, Susan (1991), *French National Cinema*, New York: Routledge.

Hayward, Susan (2001), 'Claire Denis' films and the Post-Colonial Body: *Beau Travail*', *Studies in French Cinema* 1/3, pp. 159–65.

Hayward, Susan, Ginette Vincendeau (eds) (1990 first edition), *French Film: Texts and Contexts*, London: Routledge.

Henric, Jacques, Catherine Millet (2006), 'Bruno Dumont: Droit dans le réel', *Art Press*, pp. 28–35.

Hurst, Heike (1999), *Fondu au noir* (*Radio libertaire*) 'Interview with Philippe Grandrieux', www.federation-anarchiste.org, accessed March 2004.

Johnston, Claire (1973), *Notes on Women's Cinema*, London: Society for Education in Film and Cinema.

Jones, Kent (2000), '*L'Humanité*', *Film Comment* 36:6, p. 73.

Jousse, Thierry (1999), 'Les Mystères de l'organisme', *Cahiers du cinéma* 534, pp. 39–41.

Jousse, Thierry (2006), *Wong Kar-Wai*, Paris: Cahiers du cinéma, Éditions de l'Étoile.

Joyard, Olivier (2002), 'Sexe: La Prochaine Frontière du cinéma', *Cahiers du cinéma* 574, pp. 10–12.

Kaganski, Serge (1999), 'Sur la ligne sombre', *Les Inrockuptibles* 183, p. 58.

Kaganski, Serge (2002), 'Toute une nuit', *Les Inrockuptibles* 356, p. 36.

Kaganski, Serge (2003), 'Corporate vampires, bloody catfights, global cyber spy games – welcome to Oliver Assayas's desert of the real', *Film Comment* 39:5, pp. 22–5.

Kawin, Bruce (1978), *Mindscreen: Bergman, Godard, and First-Person Film*, Princeton: Princeton University Press.

Kennedy, Barbara (2000), *Deleuze and Cinema: The Aesthetics of Sensation*, Edinburgh: Edinburgh University Press.

Krauss, Rosalind (1985), *The Originality of the Avant-Garde and Other Modernist Myths*, Cambridge, MA: MIT Press.

Krauss, Rosalind E., Yves-Alain Bois (1997), *Formless: A User's Guide*, Cambridge: Zone.

Kristeva, Julia (1982), *Powers of Horror*, trans. Leon S. Roudiz, New York: Columbia University Press.

Kristeva, Julia (1994), *Strangers to Ourselves*, trans. Leon S. Roudiez, New York: Columbia University Press.

Lacan, Jacques (1978), *The Four Fundamental Concepts of Psychoanalysis*, trans. A. Sheridan, New York: W.W. Norton.

Lalanne, Jean-Marc (2001), '*Trouble Every Day*', *Libération*, 11 July, p. 24.

Lapsley, Rob, Michael Westlake (1992), 'From *Casablanca* to *Pretty Woman*: the Politics of Romance', *Screen* 33(1), pp. 27–49.

Lardeau, Yann (2001), 'Le Sexe froid', in *Théories du cinéma*, Paris: Cahiers du cinéma, pp. 135–55.

Le Cain, Maximilian (2002), 'Fresh Blood: *Baise-moi*', *Senses of Cinema* 22, Sept-Oct, www.sensesofcinema.com/contents/02/22/baise-moi_max.html

Le Forestier, L. (2004), 'Jean Epstein', www.bifi.fr/cgi/cinesource/Epstein, accessed March 2004.

Legendre, Pierre (1998), *La 901ᵉ conclusion, étude sur le théâtre de la raison*, Paris: Fayard.

Lifshitz, Sébastien (2003), 'Dossier de presse for *Wild Side*', www.advitamdistribution.com.

Macey, D. (2000), *Dictionary of Critical Theory*, London: Penguin.

Maddock, H. Trevor, Ivan Krisjansen (2003), 'Surrealist Poetics and the Cinema of Evil: the Significance of the Expression of Sovereignty in Catherine Breillat's *À ma sœur*', *Studies in French Cinema* 3:3, pp. 161–71.

Marks, Laura U. (2000), *The Skin of the Film: Intercultural Cinema, Embodiment, and the Senses*, Durham: Duke University Press.

Marks, Laura U. (2002), *Touch: Sensuous Theory and Multisensory Media*, Minneapolis: University of Minnesota Press.

Martin, Adrian (1999), 'Holy Terror: Philippe Grandrieux's *Sombre*', *Senses of Cinema*, www.sensesofcinema.com/contents/00/1/, accessed March 2006.

Martin, Adrian (2000), 'Delirious Enchantment', *Senses of Cinema*, www.sensesofcinema.com/contents/00/5/delirious.html, accessed July 2005.

Maule, Rosanna (2004), '*Demonlover* as Allegory of Global Corporate Media', paper presented to the Studies in French Cinema conference, London.

McKibbin, Tony (1999), 'Abject Cinema', *Film West* 37, July, pp. 32–6.

Merleau-Ponty, Maurice [1948] (1964), *Sense and Non-Sense*, trans. Herbert Dreyfus, Patricia Allen Drey fuss, Evanston: North Western University Press.

Merleau-Ponty, Maurice [1948] (2004), *The World of Perception* (*Causeries*, 1948), London: Routledge.

Merleau-Ponty, Maurice [1962] (2002), *Phenomenology of Perception*, trans. Colin Smith, London: Routledge.

Merleau-Ponty, Maurice [1964] (1968), *The Visible and the Invisible*, trans. Alphonso Lingis, Evanston: Northwestern University Press.

Millroy, Jana (2005), 'Gestures of Absence: Eros of Writing', *Janus Head* 8/2, pp. 545–52.

Moretti, Franco (1988), 'Dialectics of Fear', in *Signs Taken for Wonders: Essays in the Sociology of Literary Form*, London: Verso.

Morice, Jacques (2001), '*Trouble Every Day*', *Télérama*, 11 July, p. 36.

Morrey, Douglas (2004), 'Textures of Terror: Claire Denis's *Trouble Every Day*', *Belphégor* vol. III:2. http://etc.dal.ca/belphegor/vol3_no2/articles/03_02_Morrey_textur_en_cont.html

Moutout, Jean-Marc (2004), Interview with Heike Hurst, *Jeune cinéma* 287, January–February, pp. 11–14.

Muchembled, Robert (2003), *History of the Devil*, Cambridge: Polity.

Muray, Philippe (2000), 'Et voilà pourquoi votre film est muet', *Le Débat* 110, pp. 122–35.

Naficy, Hamid (1993), *The Making of Exile Cultures: Iranian Television in Los Angeles*, Minneapolis: University of Minnesota Press.

Nancy, Jean-Luc (2000), *L'Intrus*, Paris: Galilée.

Neyrat, Cyril (2006), 'Rêverie d'un solitaire', *Cahiers du cinéma* 613, pp. 29–30.

Niney, François (2002), 'L'éloignement des voix répare en quelque sorte la trop grande proximité des plans', *Théorème 6*, Paris: Université de la Sorbonne nouvelle, pp. 101–6.

Noguez, Dominique [1979] (1999), *Éloge du cinéma expérimental*, Paris: Paris Expérimental.

O'Shaughnessy, Martin (2005), 'Eloquent Fragments, French Fiction Film and Globalisation', *French Politics, Culture and Society*, 23:3, pp. 75–88.

Pächt, Otto (1977), *Questions de méthode en histoire de l'art*, trans. Jean Lacoste, Paris: Macula.

Penley, Constance (1988), *The Future of an Illusion: Film, Feminism and Psychoanalysis*, London: BFI.

Péron, Didier (2002), 'Dans de beaux draps: *Vendredi soir* de Claire Denis', *Libération*, 11 September, p. 18.

Powell, Anna (2005), *Deleuze and Horror Film*, Edinburgh: Edinburgh University Press.

Powrie, Phil (2007, forthcoming), 'French noir to hyper-noir', in *European Film Noir*, A. Spicen (ed.), Manchester: Manchester University Press.

Prédal, René (2002), *Le Jeune Cinéma français*, Paris: Nathan.

Quandt, James (2004), 'Flesh and Blood: Sex and Violence in Recent French Cinema', *Artforum*, February, www.artforum.com, accessed July 2005.

Ray, Robert B. (1985), *A Certain Tendency of the Hollywood Cinema, 1930–1980*, Princeton: Princeton University Press.

Reader, Keith (2006), *The Abject Object: Avatars of the Phallus in Contemporary French Theory, Literature and Film*, Amsterdam: Rodopi.

Renaud, Nicolas (2005), 'Disparition du Kodachrome: La Fin d'une image hors du temps', www.horschamp.qc.ca/article.php3?id_article=188, July.

Renaud, Nicolas, Steve Rioux, Nicolas L. Rutigliano (1999), 'Au commencement était la nuit – Interview with Philippe Grandrieux', *Hors Champ*, 14 October, www.horschamp.qc.ca/Emulsions/grandrieux.html, accessed March 2004.

Reynaud, Berenice (2002), '*Baise-moi*: A Personal Angry-Yet-Feminist Reaction', *Senses of Cinema* 22, Sept.–Oct.

Riegl, Alöis [1902] (1995), 'Excerpts from "The Dutch Group Portrait"', trans. Benjamin Binstock, *October* 74, Autumn, pp. 3–35.

Riegl, Alöis [1902] (1999), The Group Portraiture of Holland, trans. Evelyn M. Kain and David Britt, Los Angeles: Getty Research Institute.

Rosello, Mireille (2001), 'Portrait of the Artist as an Old Lady', in *Studies in French Cinema* 1:1, pp. 29–36.

Rosenbaum, Jonathan (1999), ' Problèmes d'accès', *Trafic* 30, pp. 54–71.

Ross, Kristin (1999), *Fast Cars, Clean Bodies: Decolonization and the Reordering of French Culture*, Cambridge, MA: MIT Press.

Rouyer, Philippe (1997), *Le Cinéma gore: une esthétique du sang*, Paris: Éditions du Cerf.

Rouyer, Philippe (2002), 'Le Corps-objet – Entretien avec Marina de Van', *Positif* 502, December, pp. 28–31.

Rouyer, Philippe (2003), '*Twentynine Palms*: Wild at Heart', *Positif* 511, pp. 15–16.

Rouyer, Philippe, Claire Vassé (2005), 'Entretien avec Bruno Dumont', *Positif* 511, pp. 17–20.

Rouyer, Philippe, Yann Tobin (2006), 'Entretien avec Bruno Dumont', *Positif* 547, pp. 90–4.

Sartre, Jean-Paul (1943), *L'Être et le néant, Essai d'ontologie phénoménologique*, Paris: Tel-Gallimard.

Sartre, Jean-Paul (1964), *Nausea*, trans. Lloyd Alexander, New York: New Directions.

Shaviro, Steven (2004, fourth edition), *The Cinematic Body*, Minneapolis: University of Minnesota Press.

Silverman, Max (1999), *Facing Postmodernity: Contemporary French Thought on Culture and Society*, London: Routledge.

Silverman, Max (2006), 'Horror and the Everyday in Post-Holocaust France: *Nuit et Brouillard* and Concentrationary Art', *French Cultural Studies* 17:1, pp. 5–17.

Smith, Alison (1998), *Agnès Varda*, Manchester: Manchester University Press.

Smith, Gavin (2003), '21st Century Blues', *Film Comment* 38:4, May, pp. 66–8.

Sobchack, Vivian (1992), *The Address of the Eye: A Phenomenology of Film Experience*, Princeton: Princeton University Press.

Sobchack, Vivian (2000), 'What My Fingers Knew: The Cinesthetic Subject, or Vision in the Flesh', *Senses of Cinema*, www.sensesofcinema.com/contents/00/5/fingers.html, accessed July 2006.

Sobchack, Vivian (2004), *Carnal Thought: Embodiment and Moving Image Culture*, Los Angeles: University of California Press.

Souiller, Didier (1988), *La Littérature baroque en Europe*, Paris: Presses Universitaires de France.

Stables, Kate (2004), '*Demonlover*', *Sight and Sound* 14:5, May, p. 53.

Tesson, Charles (2001), 'Vrais semblants', *Cahiers du cinéma* 562, pp. 72–4.

Thompson, David (2004), 'Stop Making Sense', *Sight and Sound* 14/5, pp. 28–31.

Turnock, Julie (2001), 'A Cataclysm of Carnage, Nausea, and Death: *Saving Private Ryan* and Bodily Engagement', in *Affective Encounters: Rethinking Embodiment in Feminist Media Studies*, Turku: University of Turku, n49, pp. 264–9.

Vertov, Dziga [1922] (1978), 'Selected Writings', in A. Sitney (ed.), *The Avant-garde Film*, New York: New York University Press, pp. 1–14.

Vincendeau, Ginette (2002), '*Baise-moi*', *Sight and Sound* 12:5, p. 38.

Wall, Geoffrey (1984), 'Different from Writing: *Dracula* in 1897', *Literature and History* 10/1, pp. 15–23.

Williams, Linda (1991), 'Film Bodies: Gender, Genre and Excess', *Film Quarterly* 44, pp. 2–13.

Williams, Linda (1999), *Hard Core: Power, Pleasure, and the "Frenzy of the Visible"*, Berkeley: University of California Press.

Wilson, Emma (2001), 'Deforming Femininity: Catherine Breillat's *Romance*', in Lucy Mazdon (ed.), *France on Film*, London: Wallflower, pp. 145–57.

Wölfflin, Heinrich [1915] (1996), *Principes fondamentaux de l'histoire de l'art*, Paris: Gallimard, p. 43.

Worringer, Wilhem (1967), *Abstraction and Empathy*, trans. M. Bullock, London and New York: International University Press.

Selected Filmography

(See Index for other films mentioned.)
Adieu, Arnaud des Pallières, 2003
À ma sœur, Catherine Breillat, 2000
Baise-moi, Virginie Despentes and Coralie Trinh Thi, 2000
Beau Travail, Claire Denis, 1999
La Blessure, Nicolas Klotz, 2004
La Captive, Chantal Akerman, 2000
Dans ma peau, Marina de Van, 2002
Demonlover, Olivier Assayas, 2002
Elle est des nôtres, Siegrid Alnoy, 2003
L'Emploi du temps, Laurent Cantet, 2001
Flandres, Bruno Dumont, 2006
Les Glaneurs et la glaneuse, Agnès Varda, 2000
L'Humanité, Bruno Dumont, 1999
L'Intrus, Claire Denis, 2005
Les Invisibles, Thierry Jousse, 2005
Lady Chatterley, Pascale Ferran, 2006
Leçons de ténèbres, Vincent Dieutre, 1999
Nénette et Boni, Claire Denis, 1997
Pola X, Leos Carax, 1999
Romance, Catherine Breillat, 1998
Sombre, Philippe Grandrieux, 1999
Tiresia, Bertrand Bonello, 2003
Trouble Every Day, Claire Denis, 2001
Twentynine Palms, Bruno Dumont, 2003
Vendredi soir, Claire Denis, 2002
La Vie nouvelle, Philippe Grandrieux, 2002
Wild Side, Sébastien Lifshitz, 2004
Zidane, un portrait du XXIème siècle, Douglas Gordon, Philippe Parreno, 2006

Index